Psychology of
Physical Illness

Psychology of
Physical Illness

PSYCHIATRY APPLIED TO MEDICINE, SURGERY AND THE SPECIALTIES

Edited by

Leopold Bellak, M.D.

Clinical Assistant Professor of Psychiatry,
New York Medical College, Flower and
Fifth Avenue Hospitals, New York City

GRUNE & STRATTON

NEW YORK •   1952

Printed in U.S.A. by Waverly Press, Inc., Baltimore, Md.

Bound by Moore & Co., Baltimore, Md.

in pyroxylin impregnated, water-repellent cloth

Contents

RC
49
B43
1952

v

Orandum est ut sit mens sana in corpore sano

IUVENAL

CHAPTER 1

Introduction

LEOPOLD BELLAK, M.D.

Dr. Bellak studied medicine at the University of Vienna Medical School and at New York Medical College. He had an internship and psychiatric residence at St. Elizabeths Hospital in Washington, D. C., and engaged in graduate studies in psychology at Harvard University (where he received an M.A.) and the Harvard Psychological Clinic where he was appointed Austin Fellow and Rantouil Fellow. He graduated from the New York Psychoanalytic Institute.

Dr. Bellak is Assistant Clinical Professor of Psychiatry at New York Medical College and Associate Psychiatrist at Flower and Fifth Avenue Hospitals, New York. He was formerly Lecturer in Psychology at New York University and is, at present, Lecturer in Psychology at the New School for Social Research and Visiting Professor of Psychology, Graduate School, College of the City of New York. He has been a Psychiatric Consultant to the Altro Health and Rehabilitation Services where his work is with tuberculous and cardiac patients.

Dr. Bellak is a Fellow of the American Psychiatric Association, Associate Member of the New York Psychoanalytic Society, Fellow of the American Association for the Advancement of Science, Member of the New York Academy of Sciences, Fellow of the Society for Projective Techniques.

The Meaning of Illness

IN RECENT YEARS much has been made of psychosomatic medicine—and justly so. All of our contemporary science has moved toward a more wholistic approach; medicine has come to view the person as one, and not to separate the body's response to trauma, infection and general stress from the reaction to impact of psychogenic stimuli. Via the autonomic nervous system and cortical-subcortical stimuli, psychogenic illness can be seen as cerebrogenic disorder. This is not said in an attempt to make psychogenic illness more palatable, but to illustrate how strange it would be to insist that part of the organism be excluded in a consideration of illness.

Psychosomatic medicine is generally conceived of as that aspect of medicine concerned with the psychogenesis of somatic disorders. Strange as it may seem, a general recognition of the causation of psychological problems by somatic illness (and, in turn, the former's effect on the soma) has generally come even later than psychosomatic medicine (with the exception of the fact that Ferenczi wrote early of pathoneurosis—neurosis reactive to organic illness—which dynamically affected previously weak points in the emotional development[5]).

1

If "psychosomatic" is used to connote only one direction of pathogenesis, a new term is needed to incorporate the totality of processes. In distinction to the cellular conception or the humoral preference of past medical eras, and instead of separating psyche and soma as in the recent past, we might speak of "wholistic medicine." "Comprehensive medicine" has also been suggested and "Organismic medicine" might also express the interest in the human being as one integrated, inseparable whole. It is to be hoped that none of these qualifying terms will be necessary for long and that the word "medicine" alone will connote the broad meaning.

My own interest in the psychiatric aspects of somatic illness was especially aroused by my work as psychiatrist with tuberculous and cardiac patients.[1, 3] I was impressed by the fact that not infrequently, anxiety and depression in a patient were directly related to the patient's concept of his illness. When a patient is given a diagnosis he has to absorb the information in terms of the knowledge he has of it, and in terms of the knowledge the doctor gives him. Thus, the meaning of a diagnosis given him will certainly vary from patient to patient. In the lay person, the meaning of the illness will be determined—first of all—by other cases of what he considers the same disease, whether really relevant or not. The doctor's first job is to investigate the superficial meaning of the illness for the patient, in common sense terms, and to tell him that the circumstances of his neighbor's or relative's illness were not the same as his own.

The importance of the subjective meaning of illness is stressed by Pinner in the preface to a most instructive book, *When Doctors are Patients*.[6] In this collection of papers by doctors about their own illness little doubt is left of the importance of the modification of an illness by a given personality and the modification of the personality by the disease.

The problem of the meaning of the disease for the patient becomes more involved if his notions derive from *less conscious sources*. Let us say that this person had a close relative who, during our patient's childhood, suffered from the disease we now diagnose in our patient. When a child, the patient may have formed all kinds of dramatic notions typical of children's misconceptions and anxieties and apply all that terror to his own case. If the case the patient knew earlier was that of an invalid, he may now see himself in that light. There are cases, e.g., in which the mother had heart disease and in which the son may now feel that he is really a "sick woman" as mother was—whereupon his panic would stem from that. All kinds of childhood notions may become mixed up with this and cause more or less trouble depending upon the personality with which we deal.

To some people an ulcer represents a "hole" in the body and it is this idea which upsets them. Much of the emotional charge about this "hole" may be derived from infantile notions of the differences between boys and girls—and the feeling that girls are different sexually because they have been somehow damaged. The concept of the ulcer as a hole then revives such early fears and derives much of its irrational horror from this source.

By the same token, malignancies may be conceptualized by the patient as "a hole being eaten into him." On the other hand, some patients vizualize the malignancies as a growth. Even limited psychiatric investigation sometimes reveals that this growth inside the body is equated with another type of growth—a pregnancy. Since a little child cannot know about the facts of life, and since unconsciously the ideas and fears of childhood live on to distort our grown-up rational understanding, such notions often add an additional horror to the realistic dangers of a malignancy. It is the task of the psychiatrically versed doctor to understand such fears in some of the random remarks patients make, and to help them deal with this unreasonable excess of anxiety in order to better cope with the realistic enough concern every illness merits.

The organic picture which the patient has in his mind, of his body, was called the *body-image* by Schilder.[7] In illness, this image changes. When ill of heart disease or some other organ, the patient develops a special image of that organ; one might call it an organ-image. Soon the patient may think of this part of the body the way a New Yorker thinks of the United States in those well-known comic maps: it looms so much in the foreground as to practically obliterate the remainder of the country. His attitude toward the sick organ may so change that it, itself, becomes *anthropomorphized*: he thinks of it as something independent, something that needs special care. The patient's attitude towards his organ (and thus, towards himself) may become that of an over-anxious mother towards a child— always worrying, always over-protecting. This over-solicitude may well reflect the patient's wish to be fussed over again, like a child.

This hypochondriacal over-investment can sometimes be therapeutically interfered with by discussing the reality aspects of the illness and by explaining the anatomical situation. I have found it useful, e.g., to compare a coronary infarction with a broken arm. I go into details of healing by collateral circulation and stress that the infarct may become organized and new channels may take over. I do not propose to paint an over-rosy picture, pointing out that even if an arm were broken, it may often need some careful handling years after, particularly under stress.

FORMS OF REACTIONS TO DISEASE

The psychological effect of an illness upon a patient will be a function of the previously existing personality of this patient. All other things being equal, the more neurotic the person was before, the more pathologic will be the reaction to disease.

Schematically, one might speak of the following reactions:

(a) a "normal" reaction: this implies some anxiety, some depression, which very soon decreases to a concern approximately commensurate with the organic illness.

(b) an avoidance reaction: manifestly unperturbed, denial of illness with overactivity, false gaiety; probably will soon turn into a depression, anxiety or self-harm by non-obediance of medical instructions.

(c) reactive depression: prolonged depression, hypochondriasis in a person manifestly relatively well-adjusted prior to organic difficulty. This is usually self-limited.

(d) channeling of all previously existing anxiety of a rather disturbed person into the new groove of concern; this may sometimes cause the patient to give up more diffuse manifestations of disturbance and cause them to appear more tractable.

(e) psychological invalidism: this exists when a patient who principally is physically well enough to function occupationally and socially, has fears or symptoms or attitudes which make him an invalid.

All severe, temporarily incapacitating illnesses increase the need to be loved and to be cared for. Enforced inactivity, in turn, adds to the wish to return to a dependent, more or less childlike status. Such an unconscious desire may express itself in rationalizations, inappropriate symptoms and "demandingness." Fears of possible harm by lack of care, stand in the center of rationalizations.

To a large extent, attitudes or advice of doctors may precipitate excessive fears and invalidism. Also, the doctor must understand that the illness may often affect the social and emotional structure of the family setting—or specifically—the relationship of the patient to the family and associates and vice versa. The patient may feel angry that he should have had the misfortune to have the illness and, deep inside, may feel resentful towards the people who are unimpaired. At the same time, his own feelings for the family and others close to him become somewhat mixed; he may wonder about their attitudes towards his possible death and resentments may bestir him. The average person does not permit himself to become conscious of such thoughts and sentiments, but they nevertheless exist.

One result may be depression. Another may be a great deal of friction in the home. The patient may use his invalidisms as a weapon to terrorize the family. On the other hand, an aggressive family member may use medical restrictions as a whip. Such attitudes have been expressed in the quip of the wife referring to a patient on a diet: "The doctor said he can eat anything *I want!*"

THE FUNCTION OF TAKING THE MEDICAL HISTORY

The alert and informed doctor will use the taking of the medical history as an occasion for appraising not only the somatic aspects of the onset of symptoms, chief complaints, and the like, but also for a stock-taking of such emotional involvements as already mentioned.

At the time of history-taking, the patient and the doctor have maximal contact as human beings.* The patient has held his fears in check to this point and now he opens the floodgates. He faces the doctor and emotional tension prevails; he watches the doctor's face for signs of interest, alarm, deprecation or reassurance. We are concerned with the fact that in this same situation the doctor has a chance to observe the emotional behavior of the patient, his mood, his anxiety, his attempts to ward off concern or to exaggerate. If the doctor practices careful listening at all, he will often become aware of the patient's choice of words, words that will convey the affective meaning the patient's symptoms contain for him.

One patient recently came into an office and said: "It smells a little like an eye hospital I was once in. I was a little girl and had to go for a stye operation. The eye was all swollen and I was terribly afraid of being cut." These were the introductory words of the patient, apropos of nothing. Anyone who cares to listen can translate these words freely as meaning: "Coming here makes me as afraid of being hurt as I was when I was a little girl, when . . . ." The attentive doctor knows then, that this patient is especially afraid of being traumatized.

Another patient may speak of some laxative tablets as "those little bombs," thus telling us—under the guise of humor—that the abdominal cramps arouse in him the anxiety of being torn apart (as he felt when he used to be given enemas, perhaps).

Still another patient may describe the locking of a knee, due to joint mice, "as if I were paralyzed with polio," thus telling us that she worries a great deal about being very seriously immobilized.

Such examples could be multiplied by the thousands. Once doctors have properly learned fundamental psychodynamics in medical school, this kind of listening will be easy for them. Meanwhile, most of them will have to train themselves to a task which becomes automatic with practice.

A more systematic task of taking a useful history consists not only of eliciting the character and development of the physical symptoms, but also of *investigating the general life situation of the patient at the time these*

* See also Chapter 15, The Personality of the Physician as a factor and Chapter 14, Dentistry.

symptoms arose. When the barest outline of the complaints has been noted, the patient might be tactfully asked about what work he is engaged in, how he is living, and what significant or insignificant events in his life may have occurred at the time his physical complaints began. Such a procedure is not meant to take the place of proper physical examination, but to supplement it! Many a case of puzzling nature may resolve itself as clearly related to, or exacerbated by emotional events. The intractable nausea and vomiting may be related to the death of a favorite aunt from a gastric malignancy; and the urinary frequency uncorroborated by laboratory or clinical findings, may have begun when the sister became pregnant.

A factor that is too much neglected for the attainment of good rapport and understanding with the patient, is the basic necessity of maintaining conditions of *physical privacy.* The patient whose neighbor is sitting in the waiting room and who has heard the previous patient pour out his troubles to the physician, will be little inclined to offer confidences or even to feel at ease. A soundproof office is a basic prerequisite. An arrangement for history-taking, where a minimum of disturbance is caused by phone calls and other office personnel, is most helpful. It is the personal feeling of rapport, of being listened to and taken seriously, that often determines the amount of confidence a patient has in his doctor, and with it, the degree of his cooperation in attaining mutually satisfactory results.

To summarize: We do not mean to replace the sound practice of medicine surgery and the specialties by psychiatry. *An overpopularization of psychiatry can only do harm.* It would be worse to ignore somatic problems for the sake of psychiatric ones. Horse sense must always come first.

We do not propose that the doctor wonder what terrible psychopathology is brewing in every new patient. We do expect that the doctor be as alert to manifestations of psychiatric problems as he is to any manifestation of other illness. With the relatively *well adjusted* patient there need be only a minimum of psychological consideration—such as is dictated by tact, humanness, the precepts of medicine in general, and the principles of communicating with people in emotionally charged situations.

With the extremely *disturbed patient*, psychiatric consultation and treatment should be arranged. However, our discussion centers about that majority of people between these two extremes: the person who, when affected by an illness, will distort the specific features of the illness by all kinds of rather common misconceptions and a few personal irrationalities. He will thus add a great additional emotional burden to the realities and inconveniences of the illness. It is this person who can be greatly helped.

It will be most useful if the doctor can explore the meaning of the illness for the patient. He can then clarify the matter in simple terms and decrease the anxiety which always accompanies something one does not understand. The physiology and anatomy of the body remains a big, and often, dark and forbidden secret to many people. This attitude often stems from ideas they have grown up with—particularly those concerning the sexual parts and functions of the body. A little straight-forward education may go a long way. The functions and relationships of some organs, such as the pancreas, remain a mystery to the majority of people.

Explaining the rationale of the disease process and healing, may help the patient to bear it; again, it removes the dark, threatening bogeyman factor and better enables the patient to deal with his trouble. Of course, people differ; the ones with avoidance reactions may give the impression that they are so unconcerned that they seem better left alone. Chances are that this is merely on the surface and that they will be more cooperative patients if this attitude is decreased by telling them that they do not have to be so frightened as to pretend that there is nothing wrong at all. If they have to deny their concern so much they will probably not carry out the therapeutic measures, thus seriously handicapping treatment.

If some patient is hypochondriacal and has already misread and misinterpreted all the books he could lay a hand on, information may be given to him with a primary emphasis upon correcting the learned misinformation.

Some people with a good deal of psychological illness to start with may be happy to pin all their complaints and worries onto their current illness. They are candidates for long, drawnout invalidism, unresponsive to the doctor's best prescriptions. Understanding this tendency and behaving accordingly, may at least limit this process—if not obviate it.

The doctor should refrain from causing undue alarm and avoid producing psychological invalidisms as much as he avoids somatic damage. If a person cannot function, it makes no difference whether he doesn't function somatically or psychologically. Recent surveys of patients diagnosed as suffering from cardiac illness have shown impressive statistics of people unnecessarily crippled by their doctor's verdict. This may evolve either by misunderstandings or by the fact that some doctors project their own fears into their patients' illness, etc. The chapter on the physician's personality as a factor in the patient's progress will deal with this problem in detail.

"ADJUNCT PSYCHOTHERAPY"

If a really obviously excessive neurotic reaction occurs in connection with a somatic illness, calling in a psychiatrist may be indicated. Psychiatrists will have to learn to give *adjunct psychotherapy;* by this is meant some limited, brief psychotherapy specifically centered upon helping a patient with a circumscribed somatic problem. For instance, a dermatologist should be able to send a patient to a psychiatrist to work out some of the emotional problems around a dermatosis while the actual somatic care before, during and after psychotherapy, remains with the dermatologist.

The best psychiatrists and psychoanalysts have been the most ambitious ones—probably—and have frowned upon doing anything other than extensive treatment—psychoanalysis proper—with the hope of producing basic changes and fundamentally healing their people. The need of reality commands, however, the application of the entire range of knowledge and skill derived from Freud to relatively circumscribed areas of psychotherapy for the large majority of all sufferers.

I believe that "symptom removal"—dynamically done—has a perfectly good place, particularly as an *adjunct to somatic treatment.*

In time, it is hoped that psychotherapy will increasingly become an applied science; psychoanalysis proper is always a research activity aside from a therapeutic procedure. The classical psychoanalyst is in part a pure scientist whom we thank for most of what is useful in psychodynamics today, and he will probably contribute the fundamental new insights of the future. The psychotherapist will have to work, as have other doctors, under imperfect conditions with imperfect technics based on general psychoanalytic knowledge, battling with the limitations of the environment. Bibring[4] has pointed out procedures for social work which may be helpful for medical problems too.

Nevertheless, adjunct psychotherapy, like clinical medicine, has a definite place and still needs to refine its procedures. Just as much as there are certain rough and ready guidelines in the somatic management of an ulcer or a cardiac emergency, so is it necessary to work out specific guidelines for the psychotherapy of such specific conditions. Such procedures must be predicated upon generalizations which, of necessity, cannot integrate all subtleties but will have the advantage of being routinized and teachable to possibly only moderately skilled personnel.

For instance, I believe that a future textbook of adjunct psychotherapy should list various somatic and psychosomatic conditions, give the principal emotional factors involved and prescribe the principal therapeutic steps. A chapter heading might be: Anal Pruritus. Under this heading there should then be a brief discussion of the anal stage of emotional development, factors which predispose to special emotional investment in this area (coercive cleanliness training, enemas, passive relationship to a domineering adult with the engendering of wishes for stimulation in this area, lack of complete genital development, great lack of affection, and with it a wish for any kind soothing contact, etc.). Then there should be a discussion of the therapeutic procedure: a relationship in which the patient feels that the doctor is interested and protective (anaclitic relationship). The onset of the itching should be related to specific events at the given time, and the need for affection should be discussed apropos of the scratching—the patient's aggressions need careful airing, and if and when advisable, the passive wishes should be discussed.

This is merely presented in outline form, possibly not even presenting correct and essential facts and certainly not sufficiently. This is not the place for details of therapy. I have tried such a specific formulation for the treatment of acute depressions.[2] All I mean to stress is that we need a similar approach to the multitude of specific disorders, and the more we learn about etiology and pathogenesis, the more specific our treatment plans for limited goals can become as an adjunct to everyday medical practice.

Non-psychiatric physicians, on the other hand, will have to learn to handle a certain amount of psychiatry themselves, and to cooperate comfortably with a psychiatrist when the disturbance is of necessity out their reach, as they do when they consult with other medical specialists.

Future Medical Education

At present, psychiatry is being taught in medical schools primarily as a field entirely unrelated to the rest of medicine. Frequently, the student still hears something about psychosis and neurosis in a way which leaves him largely frightened and contemptuous of these "queer" people. He learns little of psychodynamics, and next to nothing about the psychological problems which will confront him every moment of his practice.

As we mentioned, psychodynamics needs to be taught as *a basic science*, as is physiology—and psychiatry needs to be taught as a basic clinical field, as is general medicine. We have come to a point of development where a surgeon cannot be a good surgeon unless he also is a good medical man and knows about preoperative and postoperative care. We have learned to see man as a whole—not as a departmentalized machine; the worst diehards cannot deny the importance of emotions via the autonomic nervous system. Like physiology and general medical principles, psychodynamics and some form of psychiatric knowledge enters into every patient's problem if for no other reason than because the relationship between doctor and patient is an emotionally charged one.

Aside from a general psychodynamic foundation as part of medical education, it must be remembered that every speciality of medicine and surgery has its special psychological problems. The chapters in this book are arranged with this idea in mind.

These suggestions imply a number of consequences for the medical curriculum. In the first place, instead of the sterile course in experimental psychology which all too frequently caused the later medical student to think of the whole field as hopelessly abstruse, the pre-medical curriculum will need to include (1) some dynamic courses on the psychology of personality; (2) general psychodynamics will have to find a significant space in the already crowded pre-clinical years; (3) special psychodynamic problems of a given area will have to be taught—at least a few hours worth—with every medical-surgical specialty. When obstetrics is taught, psychiatry lectures ought to be integrated with it so that the student is as much exposed to the psychodynamic implications of a vaginal examination or excessive morning sickness as he is to the toxemias of pregnancy. When surgery is taught, the student should be instructed simultaneously in the psychological problems attending it—as regular a part of surgery as the physiologic implications of tissue trauma. With orthopedics ought to go a discussion of the problems of the body-image and with neurology, the dread of loss of control, etc. This type of instruction will help the student to see the patient as a whole and will make him infinitely more fit to deal with daily practice.

A psychiatry course proper will have to discuss the major neuroses and psychoses as well as some simple aspects of psychotherapy.

This is a large-sized request. It will be difficult to fulfill from the standpoint of time in the schedule and from the standpoint of finding properly schooled psychiatrists. Many a good start may end with a miserable fiasco because the psychiatrists available often leave much to be desired. But, in the end, this is the way development will have to move.

MEDICAL PRACTICE

This foundation in psychodynamics may come to the rescue of a manifestly unrelated problem area—namely, that of the ever-increasingly difficult one of the general practitioner (from the doctor's own point of view) and the problem of the increasing unavailability of the "family doctor" (from the patient's point of view). Both laments are well known enough to need but the most scanty reference. Increasing specialization has made the lot of at least the city dwelling general practitioner a difficult one and patients have felt more and more like customers in a department store in the efficiency geared offices.

This unhappy situation may be saved for both sides if the general practitioner becomes a psychiatrically sophisticated family doctor; a kind of "family psychiatrist." Instead of well-meant—but often strictly subjective—advice, the general practitioner may be able to help all the members of his patient's family. This would fill a strongly felt need. In the first place, there are not—and probably never will be—enough psychiatrists available to fill the needs of the general population. In the second place, the large majority of psychiatric problems are not of major proportions and need not (or should not) receive major psychotherapy. In the third place, the family doctor is in a particularly good strategic position for prevention and care of psychological problems; he knows the socio-economic, cultural setting of his patient, knows the other family members, and carries a great deal of prestige and emotional investment. And finally, he is the one who will first be presented with any emotional problems that arise—often in the guise of a physical complaint—as the subsequent chapters point out.

Our suggestion is not to be taken as one encouraging psychiatric quackery. Contrary to what some authors have proposed, common sense psychiatry compares to the common sense medicine of our grandmothers: sometimes it is uncannily wise and sometimes it is irrational or even ignorantly dangerous.

If the medical student receives the training briefly outlined, the doctor should at least acquire what one might call a psychotherapeutic attitude; able to listen objectively, not be harmful by sadistic or over-active interference, and, at least sometimes to be able to give an amount of insight which may be helpful. One might think of this area as *"minor psychiatry"* the way one thinks of "minor surgery." Every doctor, and particularly the general practitioner, should know enough of the general principles and the basic skills to handle minor situations. He must know enough to recognize when a problem is of such major proportions as to require more specialized help. In this context, particularly, it seems feasible that a general practitioner might consult with an experienced psychiatrist or psychoanalyst and possibly carry some of his patients psychotherapeutically under some consultation—supervision—much like young psychoanalysts carry their patients under such experienced tutelage, and similar to the way in which a general practitioner may carry out cardiac or orthopedic care under advice from the specialist.

The public may become accustomed to paying the general practitioner for such psychotherapeutic services. Economic factors must not be overlooked. The general practitioner has to make a living in part predicated upon what business men call "a large turnover," at a small profit per each patient. No amount of moralizing will make doctors see patients for an hour's psychotherapy at a fee calculated to compensate him for a time investment of fifteen minutes. The doctor has his own personal and financial needs and if he is to play the role of a martyr, impatience and unconscious resentment counteract any good he may be doing. Our high standard of living and the resultant high pressure on earning is to a considerable extent responsible for the prevalent complaint that the patient does not have the old type of family doctor any more with whom one can sit and talk. If the doctor will be able to charge for the time invested when he has to invest more on some occasions—possibly by establishing a fee schedule primarily predicated upon time spent with a patient—then the general practitioner can afford his role as family doctor again, with all the emotional and psychotherapeutic connations necessary.

It must be doubted—as some might fear—that every doctor will thereupon want to be a full time psychotherapist. There are a number of realistic limitations. For one thing, the pleasures of psychotherapy are not so great as to do away with the sound satisfaction inherent in prompter physical-chemical help one may give to a physically ill person. For another thing, the financial remuneration on the basis of a fee for a psychotherapeutic session does not compare favorably with the returns on some briefer doctor-patient contacts of the ordinary consultation for physical illness.

Medical practice in hospitals has to blaze the trail for the integration of psychiatry with other specialties. A number of enlightened institutions have already organized programs whereby a psychiatrist belongs to the routine diagnostic staff and possibly also to the therapeutic team. Surgical, obstetrical and all other patients should be investigated for their psychiatric status as much as for their hematologic problems and as much prepared psychiatrically for medical-surgical difficulties as they are hematologically prepared. For this purpose, psychiatrists will have to serve in every part of a modern hospital.

*   *

*

We offer this book with the hope that we may contribute to a better medical practice—one which is more enjoyable for the doctor and more beneficial to the patient.

The chapters of this book are so organized as to primarily present the psychological implications of the medical-surgical disorders of each field. Secondarily, the psychogenic aspects of somatic complaints are discussed for convenience of organization and because psychosomatic and somato-psychic problems often interact.

Each chapter is written by authors with experience in both the medical-surgical specialty and psychiatry. By this means we hope to present not irrelevant theory, but practical useful data by men with real experience. An attempt has been made to integrate the various contributions in such a way as to avoid repetition. A special effort has been made to have the chapters attain approximately an equal level of sophistication and similarity of style. For this purpose, each contributor was acquainted with the chapters of the other contributors, individually as well as in conferences, aside from the fact that the editor suggested definite organization of material and viewpoints.

It would have been nearly impossible to make this book an exhaustive study of emotional aspects of somatic illness. The subject matter is so large that most papers could only be concentrated upon the main problems, and often only specific examples and illustrations could be made on the main problem areas rather than treatment of the many separate issues. Some of the specialties could not be considered at all. Proctology is one field, and ophthalmology is another. I was unable to find physicians who were competent in these fields who were at the same time competent in psychiatry. In the spirit of the book, I did not want to have papers written by people with only distant relations to the specialty, however good psychiatrists they might be. I can only hope that there are experts in these areas whom I have not found and who will come forward with their own contributions. I hope, in fact, that each of the present authors will sooner or later enlarge his chapter into a monograph that really does the subject matter justice.

A slight amount of repetitiveness concerning some basic principles, such as the meaning of illness, distortion of body image, and defensive ways of dealing with the traumatic impact, were intentionally permitted to remain. In the event someone reads only one specific chapter relevant to his specialty, he should at least be made minimally aware of the general implications. No doubt, however, for maximal benefit—all the chapters ought to be read by each specialist since each affliction of man is related to many others.

This book is meant to serve a need for integrated medicine. May it become a general practice so soon that this volume is speedily outmoded.

Acknowledgments

I wish to express my thanks here to all the contributors for the scientific and unselfish spirit with which they undertook their tasks. They accepted each other's and my suggestions with amazingly good grace. If this book falls short of perfection, it is surely not their fault.

I owe a special expression of gratitude and appreciation to Dr. Victor Rosen: aside from his own splendid contribution, he took particular pains with a searching analysis of the other papers. He helped me find authors, offered many useful suggestions and generally gave a great deal of his time and effort. Dr. Elias Schneider, of the College of Physicians and Surgeons, Columbia University, willingly gave assistance, particularly in regard to the chapter on Dermatology. I am also grateful to Dr. Max Schur, for many years an outstanding internist and practicing psychoanalyst—who gave counsel and read several papers critically. My wife, Sonya Sorel Bellak, again has been of great help and comfort with the innumerable editorial chores.

BIBLIOGRAPHY

1. Bellak, L.: Psychiatric aspects of tuberculosis. Soc. Casework. *31:* 5, 1950.
2. ——: The emergency psychotherapy of depressions. *In:* Bychowski, G. and Despert, L.: Specialized Techniques in Psychotherapy. New York, Basic Books, Inc., 1952.
3. —— *In:* Hazelkorn, F. and Bellak, L.: A multiple service approach to cardiac patients. Soc. Casework. *31:* 7, 1950.
4. Bibring, G.: Psychiatric principles in casework. Soc. Casework, *30:* 230–235, 1949.
5. Ferenczi, S.: Disease or pathoneurosis. *In:* Further Contributions to the Theory and Technique of Psychoanalysis. London, Hogarth Press, 1926.
6. Pinner, M. and Miller, B. F.: When Doctors Are Patients. New York, W. W. Norton, 1952.
7. Schilder, P.: The Image and Appearance of the Human Body. Psychological Monographs. London, Kegan Paul, 1935.

CHAPTER 2

Psychiatric Considerations in General Practice

MILTON MALEV, M.D.

Dr. Malev received his M.D. from Yale University School of Medicine; interned at Fordham Hospital, New York, took residencies in Tuberculosis at Riverside Hospital in New York, in Cancer at New York City Cancer Institute, and Essex County for Contagious Diseases.

He was a general practitioner in the Bronx for a number of years; then he took a two year residency at the New York Psychiatric Institute and Hospital, followed by a course of training at the New York Psychoanalytic Institute from which he graduated. He is now an Associate Member of the New York Psychoanalytic Society.

The Role of the General Practitioner

IT IS OUR PURPOSE to discuss here the special problems encountered by the doctor who practices "neighborhood" medicine. Another chapter in this book ("The Personality of the Physician as a Factor") discusses the interrelationship of the various personality elements of the doctor and his patient.

Central to any such discussion as this is an understanding of all that the patients expects of his doctor. Patients expect, and rightly, very much of their doctor, but it is astonishing how little aware they are of what they really are demanding, and are entitled to, and almost invariably get. One study[1] among patients, asking "What They Expect of Their Doctor" yielded the following most popular answers: (1) to be ready and prepared to help at any given moment; (2) to "know very much;" (3) to be always well informed about the newest scientific developments; (4) to be "devoted, cheerful, generous, altruistic, patient, gay, optimistic; and, (5) to be physically indefatiguable. Superhuman as these demands are, patients actually get much more, if the patient-doctor relationship is not impaired, and their true expectations are quite tangential to those listed above. One eminent psychoanalyst[2] writes as follows:

"Adherence to scientific principles enlists a few millions of intelligent individuals today, but the great bulk of the people of the world still knows nothing of them. . . . The world is glad to use the gadgets of science but its methods, principles and its workers are still regarded by the mass of population with a mixture of amused tolerance and hostile suspicion. From the standpoint of the patient, it has been and still

15

is quite immaterial whether a physician employs amulets, arsenic, or abracadabra; these are the physician's business, not his. Basic expectation: from physicians have not changed since the earliest days of human society; they are the same whether the physician be a medicine man, a quack, or the most highly skilled scientist. . . .

"What does the patient expect from the doctor? In what way does he expect the doctor to render him the aid, the relief, the reconstruction he needs? To the patient the affliction for which he goes to the physician is something in himself which he wants changed, and the change is to be effected in three ways: (1) by having something given or added to him, e.g., some 'iron for his blood'; (2) by having something taken away from him, e.g., bleeding, catharsis, appendectomy; (3) by having something 'done to him', e.g., shoulder joint reduction, massage. Change during the centuries, is only the nature of the substances 'added' and 'taken away.' "

Herein lies the explanation for the functioning of the medical man and for his efficacy. So far as the patient knows, he comes for medicine (the newer the better); for advice (the more scientific the better); and for manipulation (the more skilled the better). He gets all of these things and the quality or forms of these services have altered and improved through the ages, as the falling death rate, the increased expectation of life, and the decreased morbidity from many diseases will testify. In the deeply unconscious sense, however, the patient has always demanded of the doctor, and still demands today, that what is "added" shall be not only "iron for the blood," but love, which to him unconsciously is life; what he wants "taken away" is not only his appendix but his sense of guilt; what he wants "done to him" is not merely reduction of his shoulder dislocation but to be "touched." The meaning of this "touching" is unconscious to him and depends on his own unconscious needs, may have one or more of a whole variety of deeply meaningful significances—to be patted in approbation, or beaten in punishment, or sexually approached.

Every human being has a basic need of love, which, through all its vicissitudes, retains, in greater or lesser degree, its original pristine character as need of love from his parents. Every physician (and most patients) have recognized how efficacious is a placebo, and how often pharmacologic products produce beneficial results far removed from their textbook properties, and how even a prescription carried in the pocket produces unlooked for palliation. This is because, in so far as his ailment represents a neurotic need, he has been given *love*—someone is concerned about him, and cares enough about him. It may not be a prescription. It can be just sheer time, or even a benevolent or interested question. The infantile demand for love is never "grown-out-of"—it is repressed or despaired of, or gratified in fantasy, or extracted from a more or less indifferent environment. In the ideal doctor-patient relationship, this need is experienced as *supplied* with the accompanying euphoria and effect on symptoms.

Every infant lives in a more or less threatening world—threats of harm or deprivation by stronge people and by inanimate, hurtful objects—threats against which he is helpless and against which he is protected only by the physical presence of his parents. The world of fear in which the infant lives is likewise never given up, but is mitigated by repeated adult appraisal of the relative harmlessness of the environment and ones own relative strength. In extreme situations, these mitigating factors fail—and the cry goes up, usually tacitly, for the protecting parents. The boy in the foxhole calls involuntarily on his mother or on God as the representative of his father; the ill person or the parents of the ill child call on the doctor. The doctor's service is, in a strictly literal sense, his *presence*. And it is this, in the patient's mind, as much as his medicines, for which he is being paid. The patient attributes to his doctor, because he must, the omnipotence he once attributed to his parents, and is reassured. One has only to note the peace that comes to the patient and his family with the words, "The doctor is here."

Frequently, what the doctor achieves for his patient in the course of his practical and useful medical attention is simply and purely to relieve guilt. Informed psychological observations of children never fail to impress the observer with the boundlessness and all-inclusiveness of his hostilities and aggressions directed in the first instance against his parents. A large portion of this non-specific aggression is eventually turned, in a socially acceptable manner, to manipulation of the environment for the satisfaction of economic, social and sexual needs. The remainder is handled in a variety of ways, but there is frequently a residue of unacceptable hostility which does not come to consciousness and is represented by a vague, troublesome feeling of guilt. Similarly, guilt arises from the repressed and forgotten fantasies or transgressions stemming from the sexual side of the original drives. On the basis of this continuous, thin, unrecognized sense of guilt, illness is often interpreted as a punishment* (not to speak of instances in which illness or accident are self produced as punishment on the same basis). The non-judgmental, objective effort of the physician is, therefore, correspondingly interpreted by the patient as forgiveness for his sins and as a pronouncement that his guilt is unjustified. No part of this process need be conscious, and usually is not, but it is almost mechanical and uniformly efficacious. The patient says: "It hurts me here," and may actually be suffering from organic illness. (He means, as he psychologically interprets his illness: "I have been hostile or sexually sinful and this is my punishment, imminent or already here.") The doctor says: "It is nothing serious," or if necessary proceeds to treat (meaning to such a patient—in either instance "I, your parent, regard your sins as of no importance and forgive them readily.")

---

* See also chapter on Internal Medicine.

The mitigation of the symptom or the progress of the illness, in so far as it is unconsciously motivated, then follows as a matter of course and is accompanied by a lifting of the spirit corresponding to a lifting of a sense of guilt. Every physician has patients who return regularly with a variety of symptoms only in order to hear the doctor pronounce, tacitly or vocally, the reassuring formula. Because the unacceptable fantasies are continuous and unrecognized, the need for assurance is repeated and persistent. That is what the patient wants and that is what he pays for. He is suffering from something very real and very much deserving of respect, and to the extent that the doctor is aware of what is going on and what he is doing, he can avoid impatience and hostility. He is here treating an illness just as surely as when he is setting a fracture.[3] This is to say that the doctor's ministrations are the same as they have been throughout the ages—the supplying of the same unchanging, unrecognized, imperative childhood needs.

It is in this area that perhaps may be sought at least part of the explanation for the fact that patients will frequently wander from doctor to doctor, all with, approximately, the same training and skill, until they find one whom they like. A sociologist's study on the subject found that many families did not name a doctor (as family physician) in their nearest trade center, but would go to one whom they liked or became acquainted with even though his office was in a more distant town or city.[4] This study suggests that the "psycholocical factor in doctor-patient relationships may be more important than convenience in the process of selecting a family doctor." This can mean only that, other things being equal, one doctor supplies more readily or in greater measure than another the unrecognized needs of his patients, some of which have been described above. Wolf[5] says: "Most of the time of the average physician is occupied in seeing psychologically diseased patients. That is in the main what makes him a busy physician. If he is not sympathetic to the idea that these people are at least as worthy of help as those in whom he can diagnose organic disease, he will either waste his time in examinations and with presenting and administering useless medications, or he will send the patient away in a frustrated frame of mind."

It is obvious that the doctor is able to help these patients who desperately need help because of his position in the eyes of his patients; that is, to the unconscious of his patients he represents the parents of his infancy. The objective circumstances of the doctor-parent identification are such that this attitude is almost automatically and invariably produced in the patient (in the absence of complicating or strongly negative factors against it). The doctor is big (socially, intellectually) like the parent of childhood. He is in a position of authority and his function is to render aid. The general pattern of behavior on the part of physicians that may impair this process is discussed elsewhere. What interests us here is how this relationship, which arises spontaneously, may be interfered with in the work of the general practitioner. Here we must appraise a very large and important relatively recent phenomenon: namely, the change in the position of the general practitioner.

The Change in the Status of the General Practitioner

Much has been said and written about the changing place of a general practitioner in the picture of the distribution of medical care. The change is due to a variety of conditions: the growth in the body of medical knowledge and skill which demands that it be split up into small divisions for mastery by individual specialists; the lure of greater income; the greater prestige of the specialist. For purposes of this discussion, the extreme aspects of this change and its effects will be described. For large areas, geographic and social, this description applies in relatively minor degree or not at all; but even in these areas it must be recognized as a tendency.

The emergence and growth of the specialties has given rise to erroneous attitudes on the part of patients toward the general doctor. They tend, particularly in urban centers, to regard him as an emergency man, to be consulted primarily for self limited disorders; as a temporary and provisional attendant, to be supplemented or replaced by the specialist if everything does not go right; as being entitled to fees lower than those that specialists are granted. The general practitioner lives in the neighborhood in much the same style as his patient and frequently has been known to his patients from boyhood on. These factors give rise to an attitude which militates against the patient's own need for a figure omnipotent and omniscient, and supplying in adequate degree the illusion of the parents. This tends to rob the patient of many of the unconscious effects which the patient-doctor relationship is designed to produce. One thoughtful medical observer puts it as follows:[6]

"In urban centers, the general practitioner's patients are a reserved population, skeptical, unwilling to entrust its confidence, or to ask for advice other than that bearing strictly upon the matter at issue. This reserve, this unwillingness to place oneself in the hands of his doctor, makes it impossible for the latter to justly measure the patient for the mental symptoms of the disease."

This is the problem, stated extremely and almost exaggeratedly in its superficial aspects, and appears to give the whole story. If it were entirely true, or exclusively true, it would be most discouraging. It is the opinion of this author, however, that it is not the whole story—that another possibly equally powerful factor is at work to produce the same unfortunate result; and that this latter factor is, happily, not inevitable but avoidable.

The element of avoidability changes the entire picture and entire outlook immeasureably for the better.

The fact is that the additional factor at work in impairing the psychological effectiveness of the general practitioner is his own frequently derogatory attitude towards himself *which he falsely ascribes to his patients*. Analysis of physicians and numerous interviews with doctors and patients makes this statement appear most probable. The patient longs for the maintenance of the old attitude and finds frequently that the doctor's own feelings about himself do not allow this. The patients, by and large, are not nearly as conscious of, or sensitive to, the changing situation as is the doctor. There are instances in which the doctor himself feels himself a failure by comparison with his specialist colleagues; he feels there are gaps in his knowledge and skills and because he deals with every variety of illness, he expects himself, frequently just below the level of consciousness, to have achieved the impossible task of knowing as much about each speciality as the specialist. Unconsciously, he derogates himself for not having achieved this. Being succeptible to the general social climate in which he lives, he, himself, equates his smaller fees with smaller worth. He then, of necessity, becomes defensive and sometimes almost consciously hostile.

In this psychological framework, the conditions under which he works become, in smaller or greater measure, acts of imposition and exploitation. In this framework, the long hours, the crowded waiting room, the constant demand, the odd hour disturbances and the night calls—difficult as they are by their very nature—are felt as greatly more intolerable because they are experienced as something that is imposed upon him callously and cynically by his patients only because he is not a specialist. In these circumstances, a certain impatience naturally ensues. Probably, this is at the roots of the patients' most frequently voiced complaints: "He doesn't give me any time, "He's gruff," "He tells me nothing" or "I'm not angry because Doctor Z diagnosed the case wrong . . . after all, doctors are human and everyone can make mistakes, but I am good and mad because he treated me as if I were a low-grade moron and brushed me off when I wanted to talk to him."[7] Put most baldly, in these instances, the doctor may be hitting back. This leaves patients bewildered and disappointed—bewildered because they do not understand what has happened and disappointed because they did not find the "good" parent they sought. A study called "Choice of Doctor,"[8] reports these findings:

1. Families make numerous, varied and uncoordinated choices among physicians.

2. Economic and *psychological* factors combine in motivating choice and change of physician.

3. The family doctor is a vanished ideal among two-thirds of the families and very imperfectly represented among the remaining third.

It may well be that the effect of the great change on the doctor is in itself promoting the change. This is because to some degree, which it is not possible to measure, the doctor is reacting to what he conceives to be the derogatory attitude of his patient. The patient's actual estimate of the doctor is, perhaps, best summed up by the following quotation from Dr. Karl Menninger:[2]

> The lowliest general practitioner, in however a shabby little office in the remotest country town has an authority and prerogative which few kings ever have, which the Pope of Rome does not have, which the highest judge in the highest court of this land never has.

This is the way the general practitioner's patients would like to have it if they could.

SPECIAL PROBLEMS OF GENERAL PRACTICE

It may be appropriate here to discuss some examples of the psychological overlay that covers many of the situations encountered by general practitioners. Because there are unrecognized, apparently irrational concomitants in every aspect of the patient's contact with his doctor, it is important to recognize their existence, and, in so far as time allows, their nature. This is because the patient can then be better served. Also, and this is more important, such understanding would obviate impatience for the doctor and make for greater gratification and sense of completeness in his work.

The instances cited are all from one general physician's practice. No deep psychological data on them is available and they are, therefore, discussed just as they appeared in the doctor's office. But they will, perhaps, serve to illustrate the deep and powerful unconscious urges that distort the rational elements in the relationship between the patient and his family doctor. The situations cited are sample situations and similar distortions occur in innumerable others.

The Physical Examination

Patients come for a check-up ostensibly as a sane, precautionary measure and an exercise of rational good judgment—which it certainly is. Every doctor has noticed, however, certain peculiarities in connection with this demand. Some patients ask for check-ups repeatedly, or on minimal provocation, or none at all. Others—equally sensible—seldom come or do not come at all. Some require that every test be made, omitting none; others place spoken or tacit limitations upon the examination. Some demand examination of only one organ system, the choice being based, apparently, on nothing real.

These observations can be understood only in the light of certain aspects of child development. Fear of bodily mutilation or disease are frequently products of infantile ideas of punishment for misdeeds or are projections of hostile, childhood wishes. There are those in whom these repressed fantasies and wishes continue to demand punishment. Their fears of illness are a reflection of their unconscious estimate that illness is deserved. What these patients come for is reassurance and, for this reason, only the most thorough investigation will serve. What these patients want is literally "a clean bill of health," i.e., really to be pronounced "clean."

A patient who came for repeated heart examinations insisted upon complete physical examinations, but would not allow ECG tests and would not hear of referrals to a specialist. He confessed that this procedure was enough to reassure him, without running the risk of undesirable findings in "the specialist's hands."

He was afraid that the specialist might really find something! In these circumstances, the reassurance must be absolutely positive and unequivocal. Anything less is worse than nothing and is bound to be interpreted as the imminence of the long awaited punishment.

Every psychiatrist regularly sees patients in whom potential phobias relating to heart, eyes or sanity have been precipitated into clinical phobias by inconsequential (though thoroughly correct) criticism of these systems from a physician.

Types of Medications

Some patients peremptorily demand oral medication; others demand repeated injections in the face of the most positive statement that injections are not indicated. These aberrations are the products of various unconscious fantasies; getting medicine may mean getting special attention and love (see chapter on Internal Medicine) and may revive, in the antagonistic patient, childhood fears of poison—none of these fantasies being recognized by the patient himself.

One young woman who refused medicine by mouth because it invariably made her gag and vomit, remarked laughingly in a social situation, that she had believed—as a child—that babies came from the father's transferring saliva into the mother's mouth during a kiss.

Injections are often preferred because they seem a more dramatic interference—the doctor seems to be trying harder. In other patients, this very same idea of being passive recipients may be extremely anxiety-arousing: an injection into the gluteus may revive fears of having an enema nozzle painfully inserted. To hysterical subjects, any puncture anywhere on the body may have the symbolic equivalent of being over-powered, hurt or raped. Such are the factors that often make strong men keel over in the course of a simple venepuncture.

Demands for Abortion

Pregnancy has powerful and unconscious implications which can bring about a great deal of anxiety (see chapter on Obstetrics) and sometimes, may even bring the wish for an abortion, rationalized as necessary because of ill health, lack of money, etc. Anxieties are probably the most frequent motivation—fear of becoming unattractive, of being damaged physically, of giving the husband cause for infidelity, etc. Such fears are usually quite conscious and can often be elicited by simple questioning; sometimes they can be counteracted by simple discussion and reassurance.

In other cases, guilt feelings about being pregnant may exist as though this result of intercourse were sinful even though it was sanctioned by matrimony.

A married woman urgently demanded curettage with her first pregnancy and insisted that though she knew several doctors who could perform it, she would go only to one recommended by her family doctor. When he said that he would not recommend anyone, stating that, in his judgment she should have the baby, she promptly and cheerfully dropped the demand. Apparently she nee ed the doctor's "absolution" and "forgiveness" to retain her really desired pregnancy.

Sometimes, unconsciously sensed hostility toward the prospective child creates an imperative demand for termination of pregnancy.

A young woman demanded curettage because she "only wanted a girl and this may be a boy." She made repeated, unsuccessful attempts to abort herself and to find an abortionist. Her baby was a boy and shortly after his birth she required psychiatric help for fears that she would injure or kill him. She, herself, had a younger brother born when she was aged two, towards whom she had had very mixed feelings.

The Problem of the Consultant

This relationship between the general practitioner and his patient, with its content of these unconscious significances, must frequently—from the necessities of the situation—admit a third person: the consultant or specialist. The meaning of this "intrusion" to the patient will depend on what it means to the doctor, and it has important consequences. Where the doctor's attitude toward himself, in this situation, is unconsciously self depreciating, the referral will mean a defeat for him, possibly accompanied by resentment. He will then, actually or psychologically, surrender the patient into the hands of the consultant with the unspoken formula: "I cannot help you—go to him." The doctor may feel that he has done the patient a service and the patient will understand and be grateful. Actually, in this author's experience, this is seldom true. Far from being appreciated, this is almost invariably resented by the patient even though he may be most eager for the specialist's services. This is true because he has come to rely upon his doctor for all the unconscious values of the relationship and wishes very much to continue them. He experiences the severance of the relationship, even in the one particular illness, as an abandonment and even as punishment for his illness; he is faced with the task of finding gratification for the infantile need for protection and acceptance in a new and unknown person.

The practitioner in this situation has made the error of mistaking the part for the whole; because he feels he cannot supply the *organic forms* of treatment (e.g., the diagnosis or the operation), he cuts off the more intangible and, from the standpoint of the patient, the equally valuable emotional therapeutic elements. Patients fear this abandonment and their protest is evidenced in the frequently heard: "But you'll be present at the operation, won't you?" or "But you'll visit me at the hospital?" or "*You* call the specialist, and make the appointment." The protests point to the psychologically correct procedure of having the specialist as an *extension of the* practitioner, an additional tool of his, like another laboratory test or another instrument, thus preserving the original relationship intact with all its therapeutic potency.

Frequently, fears that the patient expresses about specialists are not only fears of what he will find or do, but fears of abandonment by the "parent" person that he desperately needs.

On the other hand, patients may demand a consultant even if there is no realistic need. Sometimes this is meant as a form of aggression by the patient against this figure of authority. At other times, relatives of a patient may demand a consultant, feeling that lest they do absolutely everything imaginable for the patient, they would have to blame themselves for a demise.

A man in moderate circumstances demanded that the most expensive consultants (the more expensive, the better) be called in at the terminal illness of his father who lived with him, clearly causing great inconvenience by that fact. After the death, the man was heard telling how much money he had spent in trying to save his father's life.

In the case cited above, the doctor was offended at the apparent lack of faith in his skill until he recognized that the demand was based on the son's sense of guilt over the imminent death of a parent whose death had been quite consciously wished.

Unreasonable Demands on the Doctor's Convenience

There are some patients in every practice who routinely turn up outside the office hours or who repeatedly demand to be seen as emergencies at night. Such hostile behavior towards the doctor is sometimes based upon real or fancied conscious grievance, but more commonly it is the manifestation of infantile attitudes toward the parents. As M. Ralph Kaufman put it:[9]

There are two aspects to the patient-physician relationship. Most of the time we see only one aspect—the positive. That we do not see the negative aspect is not because it isn't there. If we search for the basis for the hostile reaction, we find that the patients are merely repeating with the physician their previous patterns of behavior.

If such behavior is checked by its recognition, and the doctor refuses to comply, patients may find a way around the prohibition.

A woman who repeatedly called the doctor at night for trivial illnesses was told that he would no longer respond. She called again at night several days later to say: "I don't want you to come now. I just wanted to know what's the earliest I may call you in the morning so that you won't consider it a night call?"

Not all demands for help at night are expressions of hostility. Some calls are, of course, most appropriate. Others again, are the result of an increase of anxiety as the hour progresses. From childhood on, all fears seem to loom larger at night. Furthermore, around midnight, the patient may feel this to be the last chance to catch the doctor—that once the real night has settled nobody will be available and he will be alone with his terror.

Among unreasonable demands of patients may be those for *operations* (see chapters on Surgery and Plastic Surgery). Physicians recognize overt signs of psychotic or neurotic disease but these are sometimes disguised behind apparently rational demands.

A young woman, a stranger to the doctor, came to ask for referral to a plastic surgeon for nose correction. The nose appeared to be in no need of correction, and the doctor's suspicions were aroused by the fact that she refused to give her name, saying it didn't matter. He refused to make the referral suspecting some psychological disorder. He heard, subsequently, that she developed openly paranoid symptoms and was hospitalized.

Hospitalization

Irrational demands for hospitalization or irrational refusal of hospitalization are frequently encountered. In the latter case, what is commonly discovered is the original childhood fear of separation from the mother. Often adults require the same kind of patient and detailed preparation for hospitalization as is now routinely given to children. Fear of hospitalization may be on many grounds.

A young married man would demand hospitalization for the most minor illnesses. The maintenance of perfect physical health had always been a preoccupation with him. It turned out, quite consciously in this case, that alongside his love for his wife, he believed that all women, including her, are hostile and rapacious and that any weakening of his condition would make him defenseless against her. He had to be "safe from her" while ill. He recognized the irrationality of this idea but could not avoid the fear.

CONCLUSION

1. There are unconscious elements in the relationship between the patient and his doctor which are therapeutically potent, and which the patient justifiably expects.
2. When these expectations are frustrated, patients will seek these values elsewhere, regardless of the realities of the organic medicine provided.
3. Classically and optimally, these values are provided by the general practitioner in the course of his utilization of his resources—of which the specialist is one.
4. The recent tendency of the decline in the status of the general practitioner may, to some unknown degree, impair his powers. The general practitioner's own reactions to this reduction in status deepens and increases this impairment.
5. An understanding, on the part of the practitioner, of these unconscious elements, makes for better service to the patient, and greater gratification for the practitioner.
6. Many symptoms, therapeutic procedures, demands upon the doctor, have unconscious and irrational aspects in addition to, or instead of, reasonable ones.

BIBLIOGRAPHY

1. Delore, P.: Des relations entre malades et medecins; avant-propos. Gaz. med. France. *58:* 1039–1070, 1951.
2. Menninger, Karl: A guide for psychiatric case study. Bull. Menninger Clinic. *14:* 192–201, 1950.
3. Rome, Howard F.: Doctors; drugs; patients. Med. Clin. N. Amer. *34:* 973–979, 1940.
4. Hoffer, Charles R.: The family doctor sociometric relationships. Sociometry. *11:* 244–245, 1948.
5. Wolf, William: The problem of the psychosomatic patient. Am. J. Psychotherapy. *2:* 438–440, 1948.
6. Flagg, Paluel G.: The Patient's Viewpoint. Milwaukee, Bruce, 1923.
7. Russell, Katherine: Collecting medical fees. New York J. Med. *7:* 23–24, 1951.
8. Swackhamer, Gladys V.: Choice and change of doctors. A study of the consumer of medical services conducted under auspices of the Committee on Research in Medical Economics. New York, The Committee, 1939, 48 p.
9. Teaching Psychotherapeutic Medicine. Commonwealth Fund. H. L. Witmer (Ed.) New York, 1947.

CHAPTER 3

Psychiatry Applied to Internal Medicine*

ERNST HAMMERSCHLAG, M.D.

Dr. Hammerschlag received his M.D. at the University of Vienna and further medical eduation in Vienna, Heidelberg, Frankfurt and Berlin. He was on the staff of the Department of Medicine at the Franz Joseph Hospital and at the Vienna Polyclinic, as well as at the S. C. Childs Hospital in Vienna. He was Assistant and Senior Clinical Assistant in Medicine at Mount Sinai Hospital from 1939 to 1950. There he worked in the Gastric Clinic, the Nutrition Clinic as Internist, and from 1944 to 1950, was also psychiatrist in the Psychiatric Clinic. Since 1948, he has been a Psychiatric Consultant in the Mount Sinai Consultation Service.

Dr. Hammerschlag is Associate Clinical Professor of Medicine at New York Medical College. He has worked in the Gastrointestinal Clinic at City Hospital and is Associate Attending at the First Medical Division of City Hospital. He is Senior Clinical Assistant in the Psychiatric Outpatient Department of Lenox Hill Hospital, New York. He has attended lectures at the Psychoanalytic Clinic for Training and Research, Columbia University, and at the School for Applied Psychoanalysis, of the New York Psychoanalytic Institute.

CERTAIN PSYCHIATRIC ASPECTS of many internal diseases are well known. The mental changes accompanying cerebral disease of various origins, (vascular, degenerative, infectious) pernicious anemia, various intoxications, and vitamin deficiencies have been extensively described and are in the realm of the common knowledge of every physician. Similarly, psychogenic factors in such disorders as peptic ulcers, mucous colitis, asthma, etc., have received much attention in the past decade. Some excellent recent discussions of the subject matter can be found in Alexander,[1] Weiss and English[15] and Cantor.[7]

* In this largest of all medical fields it is, of course, impossible to offer an exhaustive treatment of the topic. Certain general aspects and illustrative problems of the various organ systems are discussed. Some problems which might also fit into this chapter can be found in the chapters on general practice, on pediatrics and in the introduction.

I am indebted to Dr. Herman Lande, Chief, Consultation Service, Mount Sinai Hospital, N. Y., for having given me permission to use case material from the Service. I am also very grateful to Dr. Sandor Rado, Chief of the Psychoanalytic Clinic for Training and Research at Columbia University, N. Y., for instruction in lectures and for stimulating personal contact.

This chapter will deal primarily with the emotional role internal disease may *secondarily* play. An illness may mean different things to different people; different diseases—the impact of illness on different organ systems—carry differing connotations to various patients. These images of the illness often determine the patients' reactions to the disease, to the doctor, to the therapeutic procedure, and may, therefore, be a most decisive prognostic factor.

In various parts of this book and particularly in the introduction, the concept of the body image has already been mentioned. We will, therefore, restrict ourselves here to but a brief restatement: Schilder[12] has pointed out that each person carries with him a barely conscious notion of his body and its various parts. "The image of the human body means the picture of our own body which we form in our mind; and is to say, the way in which the body appears to ourselves . . . ." People may see themselves totally differently from the way other people see them—better, or worse, or just plain different. Sometimes people's bearing will clearly connote certain aspects of self image to the observer. It has been said that whether a woman is considered attractive or not depends primarily upon whether she *feels* herself to be good-looking: if she does, she bears herself in such a way as to elicit interest, and if she does not, the prettiest may slink about—slightly hunched forward—and will not impress the men as well as she might. The man who considers himself muscularly powerful has a characteristic swagger. In his novel, *The Picture of Dorian Gray*, Oscar Wilde has intuitively perceived the idea of the body image and the self image: Dorian Gray sees himself—or his picture—the way he imagines himself to be. He collapses the moment he realizes the discrepancy between image and reality. We are in danger of transcending from the concept of the strictly bodily image to the wider one of a self image (the sort of person one considers oneself to be) if we pursue this line of thought any further—but perhaps this example helps to communicate the concept.

The fact is that people invest emotion in their body and its well being, and that they feel disturbed and anxious if external or internal changes of size, shape, or function occur. The amount of anxiety will vary with the previous make-up of the person, and the notions about the organ and its illness. Therefore, it will be useful to discuss the subject matter as it relates to organ systems and some specific disorders later in this chapter.

Before this, however, there is yet another aspect of illness that bears discussion, namely, the *use* the patient makes of his illness. The most gross form of misusing an existing illness (or inventing one, or accentuating an existent one) is known as malingering. Much subtler means are employed in the patient who demands attention or tyrannizes the environment. In his novel, *The Nigger of the Narcissus*, Joseph Conrad has given a classic description of the undue advantage a man derives from his illness: a sailor, suffering from tuberculosis, succeeds—by direct means of his illness—in dominating an entire ship and its crew.

Other individuals may use shortcomings as mainsprings of special ambition. The examples of Demosthenes and of Theodore Roosevelt are commonplace. The same process, though less successfully, may be used by the patient who is afraid of appearing ill and dependent, and responds to his illness with denial of any concern and defiance of doctor's orders. There are, of course, those who take to bed with alacrity and need super-human efforts to remove them from what is for them a comfortable haven of security and freedom from care. The multiplicity of human nature unfolds itself in some of its richest colors under the impact of physical disease.

The Gastrointestinal Tract

The gastrointestinal tract is the organ system which—aside from the skin—is involved in the earliest and main contact with other people and, by that token, is related to experiences and expressions of earliest emotion.

Intake of food (and sometimes of medicine[11]), gains a significance far beyond the mere metabolic one: to be fed by the mother or her substitute, becomes synonymous with being cared for and loved generally. Every doctor is familiar with the person who, under stress or disappointment, will eat and over-eat—as though food would indeed be equated with love and satisfaction and have a pacifying and sedating effect. Some cases of hyperacidity—and the possibly related ulceration—have been conceptualized as due to constant psychic appetite secretion of an individual who wants to be "fed" (and loved) all the time. Obese people may be people who do play mother with themselves and feed themselves well at all times. A particularly exhaustive study of the gastro-intestinal tract is presented in Cantor.[7] Fairly non-neurotic individuals learn to direct their needs for gratification into more adult and socially useful channels than that of direct gratification from eating. Socially useful forms of the need for approval find expression in drive for achievement, pride in work and emotional warmth of family life. But if gastrointestinal illness strikes, the normal gratifications, even of the emotionally relatively stable person, will be disturbed and cause emotional repercussions.

Diet. Most gastrointestinal illnesses—of any origin—involve a diet. A diet may mean restriction; these restrictions may arouse (unconscious) anger in the patient—as though the doctor were a restrictive mother. The patient may not follow the diet to spite the doctor (consciously or otherwise) unless the doctor can make the rationale of it clear, possibly discussing with the patient the fact that the diet may have such emotional meanings for him. On the other hand, some people may be quite happy to have a special diet to follow. It gives them a chance to fuss with themselves; may give them an avenue for special demands upon wife, parents, etc. Some dependent people may behave according to a formula of: "food is love, special food is special love." These are the patients who are punctilious in following every prescribed diet and who tyrannize their environment to get it. It is as if they wanted to force their feeders to "love them on doctor's orders." Occasionally, the physician will be made a party to this scheme. The patient may demand exaggerated concern with his diet, and may produce more symptoms in order to obtain it. In such cases, the doctor must be aware of the special use the patient is making of his illness, and be wary of playing into the hands of this wish for illness and treatment.

In some patients, the idea of a reduced or limited food intake, creates anxiety: it is as though they were afraid of not getting enough. They may have notions of wasting away, of losing strength. Others, again, may be primarily concerned with the social aspects of dieting: since eating is often done in a group, they may be embarrassed about being different and having to be considered ill. A totally different variety of patients are those who impose diets upon themselves or those who are so happy about having a diet as to overdo the doctor's orders. In such people, not eating is often a form of atonement. Fasting, as a form of atonement, is encountered in many religions, and some neurotic patients may feel gratified by such restriction as though out of a sense of expiation (for usually deep-lying guilt feelings about all kinds of things for which they may be blaming themselves). For by purifying themselves by fasting, they expect their bodies to grow healthy.

Peptic Ulcer. As mentioned, this illness has received a great deal of attention from the standpoint of psychogenesis.[1, 15] Once the ulcer has been diagnosed it is invested with various meanings and propositions in the minds of the patients. Some think of it as a hole in the stomach, or as an ever-threatening perforation which may cause them to bleed to death. While this may not be a manifestly distorted picture by itself, such patients may experience such emergencies as much more imminent a threat than is the case. Moreover, the idea of the "bleeding hole" may conjure up childhood images related to the difference between men and women and may actually connote—to a man—that he now "bleeds like a woman," thus adding a great deal of irrational strain. Others, again, who have had some experience with leg ulcers, for example, may imagine the stomach lesion as something putrid and festering and may greatly suffer from disgust over their internal "dirtiness."

Diarrhea and Constipation. The loss of control over a function which is subject to the will of the individual under normal circumstances, is the common factor in anxiety concerning many disturbances including those of the gastrointestinal tract (see also the chapter on Neurologic Disease). This loss, and often the fear of loss of control, of course, enters into such disturbances as diarrhea and constipation whether they are primary condions or secondary to infection or obstruction, etc.

This, however, is only one aspect of the problem. The control of elimination is acquired only slowly, and often painfully in the course of a child's development. Many a parent punishes the child for a lack of regulation; diarrhea then, particularly, will rouse long ago repressed fears and will make the patient feel childish, embarrassed and dirty. The more entrenched the need for cleanliness, the more disturbed a person would become when struck by amebic dysentery, etc. Organic obstruction of the bowel, fistulae, artificial openings, and other afflictions which make the usual cleanliness impossible, cause the breakdown of long established habits and means of dealing with unpleasant matters. This, in turn, causes people anxiety and upset. Such a breakdown of established behavior patterns always causes discomfort and embarrassment and the patient may come to think of himself as despicably dirty.

Defecation may, as is expressed in the vernacular, be experienced as a form of aggression—say, against the person nursing the patient (a chronic one especially) and may lead to guilt feelings on the part of the patient and counteraggression by the environment (the literature is rich in discussions of the expression of unconscious hostility by diarrhea as a "functional" symptom). The "nurse" may behave as though the patient would have his bowel disorder just to spite her, and the patient may feel that way himself and be apologetic!

On the other hand, *constipation* may give rise to a number of disturbing—more or less conscious—thoughts. Some patients are imbued with the notion that if they do not have a daily bowel movement, poison accumulates within them. They experience a sense of illness which disturbs them often far beyond rational comprehension. Illness there, as elsewhere, creates special awarenesses and special fantasies about the diseased organ. The majority of people—even the highly educated ones—are often completely unaware of the location and function of their organs, particularly those within the abdominal cavity. The concept of the organ frequently has more to do with its imagined function than with its natural role. For instance, many patients simply refer to the entire region below the belt as the "stomach." Since children often believe that babies come from the stomach and got there through the mouth, many abnormalities of eating (anorexia nervosa) and swallowing, as well as many abdominal disorders—including some cases of constipation—are unconsciously and irrationally related to such notions of impregnation. Ascites frequently creates such ideas, usually mentioned in a humorous vein. Needless to say, such fantasies are greatly disturbing to patients, particularly in men, whose entire set of childhood fears concerning the "difference" between men and women, may become revived.

Ano-Rectal Illness. What has been said above about diarrhea, holds true for other ano-rectal diseases. Long repressed concern with bodily cleanliness is forced to the surface again by the physical illness, and the patient is deeply disturbed by the change in habit patterns.

However, certain special aspects pertain to such disturbances as pruritus ani, hemorrhoids and the instrumentations and medications applicable to them.[10] Psychoanalysis has long ago made us aware that bodily excitation is not restricted to the genitals proper. The homosexual is the extreme example of anal sexual excitation. For other people, the anus may play a similar role to a lesser extent.

This has a number of implications (as is also discussed in the chapter on Urology). On the one hand, certain cases of intractable itching may be the expression of misplaced sexual excitement. On the other hand, proctoscopy and suppositories may fulfill infantile needs for stimulation. The physician may have to recognize the lack of organicity in such cases and may have to realize that frequent medication and instrumentation are contraindicated lest they lead to an accentuation of symptoms on a psychological basis.

Of even much wider significance is the fact that in the "normal," too much examination, medication and manipulation of the anus may arouse undue embarrassment and fear related to the stimulation of such unacceptable infantile pleasures. Thus, a patient may resist "to the death" the order for an enema, or may avoid a simple hemorrhoidectomy or harbor excessive fears about a sigmoidoscopy.

Gallbladder Disease. Diseases of the gallbladder are complex in their origin, in their symptomatology and in their consequences for the diseased individual. The most common disease, cholelithiasis, shall be discussed here because it serves the purpose of this study well.

Constitutional, infectious, metabolic, neuro-vegetative and emotional factors are of importance in the formation of gallstones. This formation takes place without the individual's knowledge. The awareness of the condition usually begins with the first attack of pains. From then on, the attention of the individual will be directed toward the diseased organ with its actual greater or lesser disturbance of normal function; and last, but not least, the fantasied impact of the disease will begin to take its toll. Only the latter shall be discussed here.

The constitutional and metabolic factors frequently encountered in stone formation imply that many stone-carriers have outspoken oral leanings; they are big eaters. It depends on the premorbid personality how one reacts to the restriction of food intake concerning quality and quantity. This type of patient often has mood swings. He can react to the disease with depression or with denial of concern, and with defiance. Eating has been for him a means to ward off anxiety. Oral frustration, dictated by the disease, will increase tension. These patients will derive a considerable satisfaction (or secondary gain) from their disease (as far as special care, diet, restriction of activities go) and will behave like self-styled "gallbladder invalids."

In many women, gallstones are formed in connection with pregnancy. Although there is probably a neuro-endocrine and metabolic factor responsible for this coincidence, the disease is, in many instances, highly emotionally charged. The woman's attitude towards pregnancy and childbirth specifically, and towards sex, in general, is often reflected in the unconscious fantasies about the significance of the gallstones. She identifies this indwelling growth with the pregnancy and exhibits towards it the mixed feelings and fears she entertained for the fetus.

This short and sketchy survey of various possible reactions towards gallbladder disease demonstrates that the same organic disturbance can have different meanings and consequences for different individuals. It will, therefore, be of no therapeutic value to tell the patient that emotions have a great impact on the function of the gallbladder and that he should try to avoid them. He knows that, anyhow, and cannot do anything about it willfully. It is more important to find out about the specificity of the patient's emotions, about his personality structure and his defense mechanisms. The highly personalized attitude of patients who respond to organic disease with superimposed neurotic symptoms is reflected in the way in which they discuss their diseases. They will say: "My ulcer forces me to keep such and such a diet" or, "My gallbladder prevents me from doing such and such a thing." Thus, the patient's description of his symptoms will give valuable hints to the physician concerning the prognosis as far as a potential neurotic reaction is concerned.

CARDIOVASCULAR DISEASE

The psychiatric implications of cardiovascular disease have much in common with the above described potential reactions to gastrointestinal disorders. Regression to an earlier developmental emotional stage, dependent attitudes, anxiety created by the disease and defense mechanisms brought to bear against the fear can be observed. The diseased organ will acquire, here, too, an exaggerated importance within the body image. But a basic difference from the reaction to gastrointestinal disease can be observed. The psychological impact of organic change, as has been stated previously, depends upon the symbolic significance of the organ function in the patient's fantasies and upon the way in which the individual deals with them. Intake and elimination, two important functions of the gastrointestinal tract, are subject to the individual's will and the way the individual deals with them has a great influence upon his character formation and vice-versa. Disturbances of this developmental process, often unnoticed under normal circumstances, come to the surface in gastrointestinal disorders. In contradistinction to this aspect of gastrointestinal function, the cardiovascular tract (as the respiratory tract) functions automatically. (However, it must be mentioned that respiration can be controlled within certain limits; breathing can be increased in frequency or held back; but basically, it is an automatic function.)

Furthermore, the anatomic and physiologic concept of the heart and the lungs are much better known to the average person than the concept of gastrointestinal organs. Location and purpose of the former are no secret to most people. The heart is usually looked upon as the source of life; it has to beat permanently; its function cannot be controlled; it cannot be removed or replaced (yet) (while even large parts of the gastrointestinal tract can be removed without too great an impairment of the functioning of the whole organism). Every cardiac affliction is, therefore, directly experienced as a severe threat to life.

Thus, the heart and its ailments, or imagined ailments, lend themselves admirably as the battlegrounds for anxiety and panic. As the seat of possible sudden death, the heart literally serves as the center for fears of "suddenly dropping dead."

The *fear of death* is a highly individual thing and one that appears closely enough related to the practice of medicine and particularly to cardiology, to warrant some discussion here. Some thoughts of death are actually related to notions of freedom from care and from active striving. This notion is the one probably responsible for most of the suicide fantasies—especially in adolescents—which, by themselves, never lead to actual suicide. The religious representation of this type of wish to be dead is found in the various conceptions of paradise. Nevertheless, the idea of being passive and being taken care of can also have its frightening aspects; for some people the stress is on being passive and *powerless*. This creates within them fears of being unprotected and prey to any attack. Of course, this is an irrational way of thinking about one's status as a dead person, but it is the live person who worries about it, in the terms of a live person.

In such people, we often find difficulties with sleeping, too; a fear of what might happen to them while asleep being very much akin to what they are afraid of in death. Such fears very often go back to childhood days when one was afraid of darkness and its evils: these childhood fears, themselves, psychoanalysts have found to be related to the child's early ideas of what father is doing to mother. Children frequently overhear the intercouse of the parents and misinterpret it as a fight. The child, then, feels afraid that it, too, might be attacked and such early fantasies survive in neurotic fears concerning any state in which one feels similarly helpless.

The religious representation of these ideas of death can be found in the various concepts of hell—a place where one is helplessly tortured.

A fear of *dizziness and fainting* is often associated with concern over heart disease and has a similar psychological basis as the fear of sudden death. When one has a chance to hear the patient elaborate in fantasy, it appears that the fear of fainting is primarily concerned with lying prostrate and helpless. These patients resemble most what psychoanalysts know of patients with agoraphobia (the fear of being in open spaces, on the street, etc.). There, too, the patient is afraid that if he were alone he might faint and fall. When the unconscious content is examined, one finds that the patient wishes to be in that position because with it go fantasies of being sexually attacked. The seclusion at home, then, serves the purpose of avoiding streets of temptation—of street-walking, one might say. As has been said, there is nary an old maid who—afriad there might be a burglar under the bed—doesn't hope there is one!

Physiological factors play an additional role in cardiac anxiety because anoxia can be anxiety-provoking. Anxiety can produce anoxia and changes in cardiac rhythm. Conversely, cardiac anoxia can cause anxiety. The various cardiac disturbances have differing psychological implications. A simple and clinically insignificant arrhythmia, such as extrasystoles, is often overrated in its significance. The concept of the normal "internal body image" implies that the organs function automatically and rhythmically. Every disturbance of automatism and rhythm creates apprehension and anxiety out of proportion to its physiologic consequences.

Cardiac failure, of whatever origin, has an organic symptomatology. However, how the individual will deal with the anxiety provoking dyspnoe with the enforced restriction of activities or with temporary immobilization, depends upon the premorbid personality structure of the individual. The dependent, passive patient will give in and this surrender can have, in turn, an unfavorable effect upon the course of the disease. The aggressive individual or the one with repressed cravings for dependency may be defiant and so endanger himself. (Cerebral edema can be an aggravating factor because it may increase the patient's irritability and impair his judgment.)

Edema of the internal organs or of the extremities may occasionally induce the patient to experience the afflicted part of the body as a separate entity and thus lead to a severe distortion of the body image with resultant anxiety. This holds especially true for ascites, a condition which the patient cannot control by reduction of intake or increase of elimination and which can often have anxiety-provoking symbolic significance. ("I look as though I were pregnant," a patient might say.)

Coronary disease creates complex problems for medical as well as for psychiatric reasons as Arlow[2] and Bellak[4] have pointed out. The first coronary attack with its overwhelming pain and the accompanying feeling of imminent death, is a severe trauma for the patient. The fear connected with the attack is a real and legitimate one. Once the acute danger situation is passed (the knowledge of this disease being widely publicized) the patient starts to realize the nature of his affliction within the framework of his established reaction pattern to danger situations. He may feel—albeit mistakenly—that he is doomed and his attitude towards life will change. Some may accept the restrictions of activities imposed by the disease. But sufferers from coronary heart disease are frequently overactive, ambitious individuals; it is especially when their overactivity had been employed as a compensation for inferiority feelings, that the imposed limitations will create new anxiety and often give rise to an either overly immobilized or defiant behavior pattern.*

Coronary heart disease is widespread. Every sufferer of it has had ample opportunity to observe it in others. The emotional attitude towards relatives and friends is, often consciously, and more often, unconsciously, very mixed; in case of a previous affliction of near ones with the disease (which our patient now has himself) repressed anger, death wishes, etc., may be brought out and will create severe guilt feelings. He may feel: "I wished this illness on uncle, and now it happened to me!" These guilt feelings, in turn, can lead to anxiety and depressive states and thus may have an unfavorable effect upon the course of the organic disease.

The coronary attack needs immediate medical attention. Underlying and superimposed psychological factors must then be considered during the course of the disease after the organic aspects have been properly dealt with. However, in many cases of anginal pain without infarction, the psychological factors deserve foremost attention.

Identification with people and events emotionally close plays a great role in this affliction. In addition, when anxiety—which is frequently created by unconscious guilt feelings—becomes chronic, it can possibly create organic changes. Psychotherapy must play the role of preventive medicine.[5, 13, 17–19]

A short case history will illustrate this problem:

A woman in her forties had been suffering from attacks of precordial pain for several years and had been taking nitroglycerin for an assumed anginal syndrome. Psychiatric examination revealed that she had been forced, by external circumstances, to nurse her father (with whom she had always had a poor relationship), during a cardiac illness which led to his death. She remembered a frightening dream in which she had poisoned her father. In the associations to this dream it appeared

---

* See the Introduction.

that she had to administer medication to her father during his illness and that she had been aware that either too much or too little of the drug administered might have a fatal effect upon him. Although she had never made a mistake in the dosage of the drug, the guilt feelings about her unconscious death wishes against her father had been so strong that she tried to atone after his death in experiencing the symptoms which she had observed during his illness. From the patient's viewpoint, it seemed easier to have, and to be treated for, an "organic disease" than to admit her unconscious death wishes against her father to herself.

In other words, this patient had experienced a natural resentment over the fact that she had to spend so much time and energy in caring for her father. Unconsciously, the thought that if he would die, she would be better off, must have crossed her mind. Since, however, such thoughts are personally and socially unacceptable, she had to repress them, even from herself. In fact, she behaved as though she was such a mean person to have these thoughts about her own father, that she deserved to die of heart trouble herself.

Hypertension has become a controversial subject in the days of so-called "psychosomatic medicine." All extremes of approach can be found in the prolific literature. Certain personality types have been described which are believed to have a disposition for the development of hypertension. The role of repressed aggressive impulses has been widely stressed. One could think of this concept in the following way: chronic anger causes not only chronic vascular constriction directly, but also continuous muscular tension, and these two factors in combination with the increased adrenalin output may cause hypertension. It has been pointed out that emotion can only change the systolic pressure. Others feel that the renal vessels may be thus affected and, in turn, cause the change of the diastolic pressure, as well.

While it is impossible to discuss these issues in any detail here, it can be said that undoubtedly a variety of factors play a decisive role: constitutional factors, the state of balance of the autonomous nervous system, organic vascular changes of whatever origin, the personality structure with its inherent reaction to, and defense against stress, and finally—environmental circumstances. To single out one of these factors as the most important and to minimize the importance of others, is bound to obscure the issue. One can safely state that existing hypertension with its threat of sudden death and its requirement of continuous inactivity and diet—whatever its origin may be—creates increased psychological tension and irritability. If previous conflicts, especially those of an unconscious nature, have been an additional factor for the development of the disease, then a vicious cycle sets in. It is here, therefore, that psychotherapy—regardless of the nature of the hypertension—can be useful.

RESPIRATORY DISEASE

Respiration sets in with birth. It has been assumed that the transition from placentar to lung oxygenation is an overwhelming experience for the newborn and that it may be one of the factors contributing to what is called the birth trauma. The act of breathing is so closely connected with the feeling of living that every impairment of respiration must cause a very basic anxiety—primarily without symbolic significance. That the impairment of breathing, as such, is an extremely threatening experience, can be observed in every patient with severe dyspnoe. His face expresses, indeed, the terrific struggle between life and death.

The child discovers soon that breathing can be influenced to an extent by the will; it can be accelerated, slowed down, or held back temporarily. Tachypnoe can be observed by the child during sexual excitation—in adults as well as when the child, himself, is aroused—and then acquires a sexual connotation. Holding back the breath brings upon a slight blurring of consciousness, a sensation which—under certain circumstances—can be experienced as pleasurable. In such a way the change of rhythm in respiration can have the meaning of either pleasant excitation, of loss of control, or even of death. Most respiratory diseases are accompanied by a change in the physiologic rhythm and—as stated previously—every change in the physiologic rhythm of body functions can produce anxiety. Here again, the premorbid personality structure and the established defenses against anxiety will determine what type of superimposed anxiety symptoms the patient with diminished respiratory capacity will produce.

Asthma has a special place among the respiratory diseases. Even if due to organic causes, it is hardly ever devoid of concomitant aggravating emotional factors or of emotional reactions to the attack.[15] Environmental and situational factors, therefore, warrant careful consideration.

In many respiratory diseases the patient produces purulent or sanguinolent sputum. The production of pus can easily gain special significance. The patient may feel that there is something dirty inside him which is coming out, and he may irrationally—and without being aware of it—identify dirt with feces and react with undue disgust. On the other hand, some patients can regress to a childhood level and will become careless in expectorating, behaving almost like a smearing infant. They may occasionally use their unclean habits to punish the environment for their disease. In other instances, coughing and spitting can be used to express the feeling of utter despondency and to attract the attention of the environment.

The *loss of blood* has a special significance (and this holds true not only for hemoptysis but also for melena, hematuria and other blood loss). The reaction to it is frequently out of proportion to the amount of blood lost.

The sight of blood is threatening because it evokes unconscious fantasies of violence; such harm is either fantasied as being inflicted upon the patient or as the patient wanting to inflict harm upon others. The defenses against such repressed sadistic or masochistic drives are often easily shattered and anxiety results. Another anxiety-provoking factor in the loss of blood is caused by the connotation of blood as a substance indispensable for the living process. Loss of this substance—even in small quantities—can bring fear of death.

Diseases Without Manifest Organ Changes or Disturbance of Function

Diseases of the gastrointestinal, cardiovascular and respiratory tracts have a definite clinical symptomatology. But there are diseases which, at least in their initial stages, have vague clinical manifestations or none at all. Among them are various blood dyscrasias, diabetes and other metabolic disorders as well as some renal diseases in their early stages. These diseases are either discovered during a routine check or they may have created minor unspecific symptoms such as fatigue or slight malaise and may thus have induced the patient to seek examination. The fact that the disease can, at that stage, be diagnosed only by laboratory methods often creates a typical reaction. The possibility of making a diseased organ the center of attention —in a direct or symbolic way—is not present in these cases. There is no tangible change of a part of the body, no pain, and no manifest disturbance of function. The awareness of such disease creates, therefore, a vague though deep anxiety which can lead either to attempts of denial of the existence of any disorder, or to excessive hypochondriacal behavior.

In these diseases, defiant reactions are generally more frequent than hypochondriacal ones. The strict diet necessary in metabolic and renal disorders will be experienced as incomprehensible, an unfair deprivation, and can engender defiant behavior. This can be observed especially in diabetes and gout, diseases which frequently afflict individuals with outspoken oral needs.

The asymptomatic course of these illnesses deprives the patient of all warning signals and creates a general uneasiness. The magic concept of disease (as an evil force)—present to some degree in every individual— necessitates bodily manifestation; in its absence the patient is at a loss as to where to attach his anxiety.

Infectious Diseases

Probably the most common psychological denominator of these afflictions is the feeling of having been attacked by "bugs" which one cannot see and feels helpless against, and to which all sorts of anthropomorphized notions are ascribed. However, this general feeling rarely leads to any psychiatric complications of consequence except where the infection leads to secondary structural changes that lend themselves to irrational elaboration.

Chief among this latter group, is tuberculosis. It often causes patients to have the feeling of being attacked *unaware*. This, as in the common cold and other such afflictions, leads to much retrospective self-accusation about one's mode of living, things one should not have done, and conduct for which the illness is conceived of as punishment.

Young people may frequently feel that they should not have gone dancing "that night" and should have obeyed mother's wishes in this and other respects. Such superficial guilt feelings usually cover up deeper ones. It may be that an adolescent patient actually feels that masturbation has weakened him so much that he fell easy prey to the illness. Disobedience to parents and drives for sexual autonomy and aggression may create feelings of guilt and many a patient changes from a mature person to a childlike one under the impact of the trauma.

Such reactions to disease are not limited to tuberculosis, of course, nor only to infectious disease. Venereal diseases are certainly particularly used for such interpretation. Seguin[12] points out that in the middle ages and later, and in contemporary primitives, an animistic and punitive theory of disease existed: evil spirits invade the patient, frequently as punishment or a form of the wrath of gods, and only atonement can bring improvement.

Many irrational and exaggerated responses to illness can be understood as just such unconscious notions of illness as punishment for any number of imagined misdeeds. Attempts at atonement by fasting, unnecessary limitations of sexual and social life, change of character from an outgoing to an introverted one may be consequential to this concept of a major illness.

More specifically pertinent to tuberculosis, is the fact that patients have fantastic notions of cavities and tuberculous activity.[3] Germs and sperms are associated in many an individual's mind—both conceived of as invaders who cause growth, pain and possibly destruction. While many female patients think of pregnancy as a threat of bursting, many males may associate their cavity and bloody sputum (unconsciously) with menstruation and "bleeding like a woman." This may sound fantastic to the non-psychiatrist, but excellent evidence exists that the unconscious can easily substitute symbolically one body opening for another.

Another general characteristic of infectious disease of all kinds is the fact that they make the patient feel like a social outcast, a leper. He suddenly is a dangerous person of whom others have to beware. Especially warm feelings of loyalty are felt for the visitor who dares to disregard the danger to himself, and some hostility is felt for the ones staying at a safe distance.

Diseases with visible eruptions of the skin are particularly likely to make the patient feel unclean and revolting (see chapter on Dermatology). The *fever* usually accompanying infectious diseases may give the patient a feeling of strangeness—of unreality—be it that the fever makes him feel unusually good or unusually bad. The body does not feel and behave the way one is accustomed, and all such changes are anxiety-arousing, as we remarked before. The fever may impress the patient as something running wild and rampant, of being out of control, thus arousing unreasonable fears.

PARASITIC DISEASE

As in infectious afflictions—but much more so—particularly with macroscopic parasites, the patient often has the feeling of being invaded. He anthropomorphizes the parasites, thinking of them as a personal enemy. Even more disturbing may be the identification of this live being in the body—a worm in the intestines—with an embryo. On this unconscious basis, a great deal of anxiety may be experienced. The itching of intestinal parasites produces at times, sensations in the anal mucosa which are akin to sexual excitation and may—without the patient's awareness of this kinship—arouse strange and thus, frightening sensations.

CHRONIC DISEASES

In the attitude of patients toward chronic disease, all the previously mentioned factors can be found, plus an additional one: the legitimate fear of chronic invalidism. This fear creates a peculiar and specific atmosphere. The chronically ill will live in a world of his own, isolated in his fantasies and in the hot house conditions of his reality situation. The atmosphere has been described beautifully and with great understanding and sensitivity by Thomas Mann in his novel, *The Magic Mountain*.

Chronic diseases are not necessarily incapacitating and the functioning of the patient depends to a high degree upon the kind of adjustment he makes to his affliction. The well integrated person will often be able to make up for his restrictions on one level and may even develop different and often better abilities and capacities. The dependent individual's increasing passivity will, in turn, have an unfavorable effect on the course of his disease. The present trend of organizing the rehabilitation of invalid persons is, therefore, of great importance because it forces them out of this despondency and passivity and gives them, simultaneously, the feeling that the community is interested in their well-being and functioning and does not consider them to be useless burdens. When the effort of practical rehabilitation is combined with the endeavor of studying the specific chronic disease, then the outlook for good results is even better. This approach is gaining ground and many societies have been organized for the purpose of studying and combating certain diseases such as rheumatism, rheumatic heart disease, tuberculosis and poliomyelitis.

This type of collective approach to disease serves a dual purpose: the concerted effort to study the disease at the hand of a great and well-observed material is bound to yield practical results which, in turn, alleviate the threat of the disease; beyond this accomplishment, it serves as an efficient group therapy on a large scale. The invalid recognizes that he is not an outcast anymore, emotionally, socially and economically, but that he "belongs" somewhere and that something constructive is being done for him.

Summary

Much understanding of the psychiatric implications of organic disease has been gained in recent decades by the use of psychoanalytically oriented methods. In his *Introduction to Narcissism*, Freud[9] described the withdrawal of the sick person's emotion from people and objects, and the development of a self-centered attitude. S. Ferenczi[8] was one of the first to study this subject more extensively. He called the neuroses which are consequences of somatic disease, "pathoneuroses." Many contributions to this subject have been made since.

Within the context of this new approach the common denominator in the evaluation of the psychiatric implications of organic disease is the symbolic significance of the organically altered organ or organ function. The lowering or breaking down of the physiologic resistance leads to a weakening of established ways of dealing with anxiety and frustration. A regression to infantile emotional levels may take place. When the ability to counteract the psycho-physiologic impact of disease is not completely impaired, secondary reactions set in which attempt to ward off the threatening anxiety.

Thus, the organically sick person rationalizes, denies concern, defies doctor's orders or exaggerates his need for care. As with other stresses, when disease is the precipitating trauma, the premorbid personality, the emotional make-up, the timing and the severity of the trauma play an important role. The defense mechanisms used to ward off the anxiety created by the traumatizing effect of organic disease, may have a more crippling effect than the disease proper.

Emotional elaboration of organic symptoms can lead to a complex and colorful symptomatology. One must be aware of these possibilities because the neurotic not only "fools himself," but may also mislead the physician who—sometimes for reasons of his own—cannot see beyond the organicity of symptoms.

However, the physician's understanding of the underlying dynamics does not necessarily imply that the patient should share in this knowledge. The doctor's insight may be helpful by his handling of the patient rather than by free interpretation to the patient. A patient who is anxious to make all possible use of his illness may be discouraged from doing so—or the doctor will at least be especially careful not to play into the hands of this unconscious desire. An exploration of the meaning of the disease for a specific patient may lead to a rational discussion of the actual process involved and may prevent or decrease irrational overlay. One must restrain oneself, in most instances, from direct interpretation and certainly from painful and premature interpretations—premature in the sense that the patient is not emotionally prepared for it. The psychiatrist makes interpretations only after the ground has been carefully prepared, and increases the depths of insight as carefully and cautiously as the internist increases doses of a potent drug. The desire of man to take refuge from psychological conflicts in organic disease is tremendous. Interpretation of the mechanisms involved, at the wrong moment or in the wrong way, is, therefore, bound to increase the patient's resistance and can—particularly in patients on the borderline of psychosis—have most unfortunate consequences.

Hypochondriasis is often a means of avoiding psychotic episodes and organic disease becomes a legitimate outlet for this type of patient. Their "rehabilitation" belongs in the realm of psychiatry. But when simpler emotional mechanisms are involved in the secondary elaboration of organic symptoms, then the understanding of these mechanisms will enable the physician—who has learned to handle these situations—to help the patient to speedier and more complete recovery.

BIBLIOGRAPHY

1. Alexander, F.: Psychosomatic Medicine. New York, W. W. Norton & Co., 1950.
2. Arlow, J.: Identification mechanisms in coronary occlusions. Psychosom. Med. 7: 195–209, 1945.
3. Bellak, L.: Psychiatric aspects of tuberculosis. Soc. Casework. May, 1950.
4. —— In: Haselkorn, F. and Bellak, L.: A multiple service approach to cardiac patients. Social Casework. July, 1950.
5. Blumer, G.: Psychiatry in general hospitals. Current Med. Dig. June, 1951.
6. Braceland, F.: Psychosomatic Medicine and the General Practitioner in Medical Clinics of North America. Philadelphia, W. B. Saunders Co., 1950.
7. Cantor, Al. J.: A Handbook of Psychosomatic Medicine (with Particular Reference to Intestinal Disorders). New York, Julian Press, 1951.
8. Ferenczi, S.: Disease or patho-neurosis. Chap. V. In: Further Contributions to the Theory and Technique of Psychoanalysis. London, Hogarth Press, 1926.
9. Freud, S.: On Narcissism. Collected Papers, Vol. IV. London, Hogarth Press, 1946.
10. Granet, E. and Hammerschlag, E.: Anal eroticism and certain ano-rectal syndromes. Rev. Gastroenterol. 16: 549–563, 1949.

11. Rome, H. P.: Doctors; drugs; patients. *In:* Psychosomatic Medicine and the General Practitioner in Medical Clinics of North America. Philadelphia, W. B. Saunders Co., 1950.

12. Seguin, Alberto C.: Introduction to Psychosomatic Medicine, New York, International Universities Press, 1950.

13. Symposium. Should the general practitioner diagnose and treat psychoneurosis? Current Med. Dig. 28–37, June, 1951.

14. Weiss, E.: Psychosomatic aspects of hypertension. J.A.M.A. *120:* 1081, 1942.

15. Weiss, E.: and English, O. S. Psychosomatic Medicine. 2nd Ed. Philadelphia, W. B. Saunders Co., 1949.

16. White, B. V., Cobb, S. and Jones, C. M.: Mucous Colitis. Psychosomatic Medicine Monograph. I. Washington, D. C., National Research Council, 1939.

17. Whitehorn, J. C.: Basic psychiatry in medical practice. J.A.M.A. *148:* 329–334, 1952.

18. Witmer, H. L.: (Ed.) Teaching Psychotherapeutic Medicine. New York, Commonwealth Fund, 1947.

19. Ziskind, E.: Training in psychotherapy for all physicians. J.A.M.A. *147:* 1223–1225, 1951.

CHAPTER 4

Psychiatric Problems of Malignancy

JOOST A. M. MEERLOO, M.D.
ADOLF ZECKEL, M.D.

Dr. Meerloo received his Medical degree from Leyden University, in Holland and his Ph.D. at Utrecht University. He took his psychiatric and psychoanalytic training in Holland where he was established in private practice since 1934. During the war he was Chief of the Psychological Branch of the Netherlands Army and also served as High Commissioner of Welfare.

Since 1946, Dr. Meerloo has been practicing in New York as a psychoanalyst. He is an Instructor in Psychiatry at Columbia University and a Lecturer in Social Psychology at the New School for Social Research. He is a member of the American Psychiatric Association, a member of the Royal Academy of Medicine and of the Psychosomatic Society.

The affiliations for Dr. Zeckel are given on page 142.

THE DIAGNOSIS OF MALIGNANCY carries with it many severe emotional problems in addition to the strictly medical-surgical ones. The physician is faced with both problem areas. The emotional implications themselves can be subdivided into three groups.

In the first group we are interested in the *subjective attitudes of* patient, family and environment and in the psychological management of the case by the physician and the surgeon. Increasing understanding of dynamic psychology, and insight gained from the study of psychosomatic phenomena have increased the physician's awareness of the patient with malignancies. Of course, the physician who deals with these diseases as one human being dealing with another who is suffering and who may die, is in the psychological limelight.

A second group of problems deals with the *meaning that an organ* which has been invaded by a neoplasm has for the patient not only in a realistic sense, but also in a symbolic sense. Unrealistic, neurotic attitudes towards organs and their functions have been described in other portions of this book. These reactions depend on the specific personality of the patient and in each case a certain amount of insight on the part of the physician is requisite.

The third group of problems that we merely want to mention deals with psychosomatic aspects of cancer. As with other diseases, personality patterns have been observed and reported in different forms of cancer. These

45

observations have led to questions regarding how the mind and the body work together in the field of malignancies.

As stated before, these problems have a common denominator and form, therefore, a special group in clinical medicine. The malignancy group is characterized by: (a) *greater chance of death;* (b) *greater chance of destruction or removal of organs (loss);* (c) *greater chance of pain, suffering and fearful anticipation.*

Of course, it must be remembered that in cancer study too much emphasis on psychological implications may be just as disturbing for the general practitioner and the surgeon as total neglect of psychological aspects would be for the psychiatrist. However, the summing up and analysis of problems involved may give us new leads on how to expand and apply our observations to the ultimate benefit of both patient and physician.

A. The Patient

Concerning the malignancies, the gamut of emotion may run from the delusion of having cancer (cancerophobia in otherwise healthy people), to the complete denial of the disease in those who are already seriously afflicted. All kinds of irrational attitudes may come to the fore. In accordance with our own experience these emotions are dependent upon the patient's attitude toward danger (only one among a multitude of other elements with which we cannot deal in this brief context). One person may completely break down under his fears, while another may imagine symptoms he does not have, and a third may accept his fate with equanimity and/or resignation.

Aside from the patient's general capacity to tolerate anxiety and danger, the specific notions which he may have of the neoplasm may be grossly irrational and, therefore, unduly anxiety arousing. It has often been remarked in many fields of human activity that the worst fears are those of an unknown or irrational nature. Soldiers have been known to brave the worst enemy fire only to withdraw under the impact of screeching noise machines which revived their childhood notions of evil spirits and the like. During the air raids of the last war it was found that panic could be controlled if the dangers were clearly outlined and rational countermeasures provided. The same psychological attitudes hold true for medical dangers. As has been pointed out in the Introduction, the chapters on medicine, surgery and others, the *meaning* of the illness to the patient may determine his emotional reaction.

It is, therefore, the task of the physician, to impart rational information to a patient, after he has carefully elicited the patient's own ideas about the illness. This presupposes, of course, that the physician saw fit to tell the patient of the diagnosis at all. Most people in whom a malignancy is diagnosed, even if not told, know about it unconsciously or consciously, anyhow. Unless there are special reasons, it will be advisable to share the diagnostic findings with the patient, stating concepts in common sense terms.

Images which patients may have of malignancies may range from those of having a body riddled with holes to an anthropomorphisation of the invading cells. Psychiatrists have found that patients may conceive of themselves as helpless and passive against the cancer enemy, the way they felt passive and helpless as children against the bogeyman in their nightmares. Doom stalks them in the form of the worst imagings. Giving them an active part in their treatment often may decrease this feeling of utter defenselessness and greatly change the patient's entire outlook. Such active treatment and patient participation (by taking medicines and treatments, etc.) may even be indicated in terminal cases as some form of placebo and support.

Subjective reactions may intrude into the therapeutic management of the patient, especially in the case of one who refuses to be operated upon when the prognosis at a given time is still good. The emotional situation of the cancer patient has to some extent become more difficult because of a general artificial cancerophobia as a result of increased publicity about cancer and other malignancies. Campaigns aiming to enlighten the population about malignant growths are in many cases used by neurotics to increase their fears. They may also prevent some people from visiting their doctors.

Fear is a very paradoxic propagandist; it may alert people, but it may also paralyze them. Many people definitely do not want to know the truth about themselves. This attitude can be conscious and it can be unconscious. They look upon every examination for cancer as though there were already the certainty of a *fatal verdict*.

This magic attitude toward the diagnosis of cancer, as a verdict, as a death sentence, is the center point of the psychodynamics of the patient. It has often been observed that after the diagnosis of cancer has been established, the patient suddenly becomes much worse. The combination of the tumor plus the fear or the illusion that the diagnosis means a fatal verdict, brings the patient to a state of melancholy and compulsive preoccupation with his symptoms, setting off a vicious circle that brings him sooner to the end of his resistance. He may make his life intolerable for himself and for his family.

In many such cases, psychotherapy has to be seriously considered as an accompaniment to the total arsenal of medicine and surgery. In some cases, treatment by means of hypnotic suggestion has lead to an alleviation of pain and of the patient's anxiety.

The following case (treated until death) may illustrate a few points.

A woman of 43 had had an amputation of her left breast eight years before. She was well for a long time. A year ago, the scar from the mastectomy was traumatized and metastases, visible to the eye and palpable in many different places, began to develop. She became depressed, waiting for her death. Reading about psychosomatic medicine, she came upon reference to the cancer problem and asked her surgeon to refer her to a psychiatrist. Explorative psychotherapy enabled her to deal with her problems at home. She had always been an over-conscientious person and her guilt feelings toward her children and her husband had to be worked through. She became able to face her problem regarding the family. Following this conflict, her fear of death was discussed. It emerged that death was seen as mutilation: she had heard that sometimes, in cancer, an arm or a leg had to be amputated and she found this a particularly repelling idea. Her death fear was linked with her fear of mutilation and was successfully dealt with. The patient felt mentally much better and this improvement profitably affected both her family and her surgeon. Psychotherapy continued until a day before her inevitable death. She finally had lung metastases with dyspnoe. In the last visit of the psychiatrist to her home, she was completely resigned to die, did not want to impose any last wishes on her husband, and passed away in a tranquil frame of mind.

Cases have been observed in which psychotherapy was even more indicated than in the above mentioned one.

Twenty-five years ago, one of the authors saw a patient who was referred with a severe depression in connection with impending death. Shortly before the psychiatric referral, a surgeon had found an inoperable breast cancer, proven by biopsy. From the first session on, the patient went more and more into her very difficult psychological problems. After a brief treatment she was able to start on a trip that she had longed for all her life and had never before felt able to indulge herself in. Now she wanted to enjoy it before her death. After two years of traveling, she returned, feeling well and full of vigor, though with her tumors . . . and she is still alive. The patient refused to go back for renewed histologic examination.

Of course, one knows of similar cases of apparently unequivocally diagnosed malignancies which never progressed. We do not want to draw any conclusions from this case other than to point out that wherever anxiety exists it is—in one way or another—always profitable to remove it, if we can. What the results will be upon the soma, we do not know. Like the old surgeon who applies the dictum: ubi pus, ibi evacua (where there is pus, remove it), we psychiatrists believe that anxiety should not be left untreated whenever and wherever we come upon it.

THE INVASION OF SPECIFIC ORGANS

As has been mentioned in various chapters (see Introduction, Internal Medicine, etc.) the emotional significance of an illness varies, among other things, with the part of the body and the type of function affected. Therefore, malignancies will constitute varying problems related to (in addition to other elements) the site invaded and the function affected.

Breast cancer obviously afflicts an organ in which a woman invests much pride; as an erotogenic zone, it is particularly invested emotionally. Amputation of a breast may involve a total change of a patient's image of herself as a woman. It definitely alters her role as a sexual object to her husband, and it alters her appearance to the world somewhat. One of the authors treated a girl in whom the amputation of a breast precipitated a psychotic reaction. Renneker and Cutler[8] wrote a valuable study on the problems of the adjustment to breast cancer. Some form of psychotherapy is nearly always indicated.

Patients with a malignancy of the *gastrointestinal* tract are exposed to all the deprivations of diet discussed in the chapter on internal medicine. The patient with anus praeter has to face uncleanliness which was taboo ever since his earliest childhood and which may deeply upset him. The idea of a growth inside the body may revive irrational childhood fears of pregnancy (as a form of internal growth) and notions of a bleeding opening in the body may again arouse primitive concepts of bodily mutilation discussed in various chapters. Cancer of the *larynx* and the resulting disturbances of communication is discussed in the chapter on ear, nose and throat diseases.

In *pulmonary cancer* we often find early anxieties associated with a vague feeling of danger: it is as though even breathing were not safe anymore.

In cachexia (of at first unknown origin) tumors of the head of the *pancreas* are often involved. Infantilization of the patient is frequent. Hunger and fear of death break through the ordinary control of emotions; anger is easily and unreasonably expressed and the psychological disturbances may be so severe that the patients may be diagnosed as catatonic and hospitalized in a mental institution.

Thus, each neoplastic affliction is related to specific problems aside from the common denominators mentioned earlier, and the reader is referred to the various other chapters for a systematic discussion of problems inherent in the various tracts and organs.

B. THE PHYSICIAN

Of necessity, contact with any patient arouses some feelings in the doctor, just as the doctor arouses some feelings in the patient. Working with a patient suffering from a malignancy causes special problems for the physician.

For one thing, doctors are human beings too, with their fair share of fears and failings. Though medical practice of necessity hardens one to much of human tragedy, the patient with a malignancy belongs to those most likely to engender anxiety concerning death—even in the doctor. At the same time, this type of patient constitutes a serious frustration to medical ambition. As a result, a doctor may react less unemotionally and objectively than in other areas of activity. He may, at times, be carried away to more optimistic statements than are warranted, and, at other times, his own concern may make him more pessimistic than necessary. It is as though he would want to steel himself and the patient to the worst.

As a result of feeling frustrated in his wish to help, the doctor may have moments of annoyance with the patient, be "sick of the hopeless case. . . ." After a gruelling day in the office, one may feel most inclined to want to avoid this type of patient. Under the impact of lack of results one may feel driven to desperate measures.

As in all patient-physician contacts, the patient perceives the finest nuances of the doctor's attitude unconsciously if not consciously. Thus, the maintainance of the patient's relatively unneurotic attitude toward his illness presupposes a doctor who can be aware of inappropriate emotions aroused in himself by the patient. Once one is aware of one's own problem, one can either exclude it or at least control it in such a way as to cause minimal interference.

C. The Family

The emotions which we discussed for the case of the physician also hold true, and even much more so, for the family. They have strong emotional ties to the patient to start with, and are most likely to take his fate and fears personally. Panic often strikes them.

Whatever guilt feelings they may harbor toward the afflicted—for whatever reasons—(see chapter on medicine and orthopedics) emerge to plague them: they wish they would have been pleasant and good to the patient, and now are doubly struck by every injustice they feel they may have done. Hypochondriasis in members of the family of the one afflicted with a malignancy is very often the result of some unconscious thought such as: "I have been so unkind to him, that I, too, deserve to be fatally ill." The alert physician has to understand these and other ramifications of the emotional identification of the family with the patient.

There are many frustrations for the family of a person afflicted with a malignancy. To the emotional strain, one must add the financial and particularly the physical demands which especially advanced illness may impose. The patient with a neoplasm may develop extreme weakness, incontinence and ill odors. The pressure of all the problems is likely to arouse resentments and, in turn, guilt feelings on the part of those who have to do the nursing.

The tendency to keep the diagnosis of a malignancy a secret from the patient while it is shared with a family member, produces many difficulties. A daughter who has been told secretly that her mother suffers from cancer suffers a great deal of anxiety, and probably communicates that fear and concern whether she wishes to or not. It must be seriously doubted that a policy of secrecy succeeds very often.

It must be the task of the doctor to evaluate what type of approach to use with the personality of each patient or relative. In the vast majority, probably, a rational exploration of impending problems with patient and family, will be most useful.

It is with the family, particularly, though also with the patient, that skilled social workers attached to a hospital or a community agency can be of great help in easing the burdens of malignant disease.

SUMMARY

The importance of the psychological meaning of somatic affliction for its therapeutic management could hardly be greater in any field than in that of malignancies. The fear of mutilation, of drastic change, and of death, which malignancies arouse, make it very important that the doctor be aware of psychological aspects of his patient, the patient's family, and himself, as well. Medicine, surgery, psychiatry and social work must constitute a united team to deal appropriately with neoplastic illness for the benefit of the afflicted.

BIBLIOGRAPHY

1. Blain, D.: Are There Dangers in Public Education for Cancer Control? Lecture for the Am. Cancer Soc., New York, 1948.
2. ——: Elements in Motivation for Cancer Examination and Treatment. Lecture for the Am. Radium Soc., Atlantic City, 1949.
3. Conklin, G.: Cancer and environment. Scient. Am. Jan., 1949.
4. Gagnon, F.: Cancer due to emotional upsets. Science News, March, 1952.
5. Groddeck, G.: The World of Man. London, Daniel Company, 1934.
6. Kline, N. S. and Sobin, J.: The psychological management of cancer cases. J.A.M.A. 146: 1951.
7. Meerloo, J. A. M.: The initial neurologic and psychiatric syndrome of pulmonary growth. J.A.M.A. 126: 1944.
8. Renneker, R. and Cutler, M.: Psychological Problems of Adjustment to Cancer of the Breast. J.A.M.A. 148: 1952.
9. Rose, S. M.: Transformed cells. Scient. Am. Dec., 1949.
10. Tarlau, M. and Smalheiser, I.: Personality patterns in patients with malignant tumors of the breast and cervix. An exploratory study. Psychosom. Med. 13: 117, 1951.
11. Trawich, J. D.: The psychiatrist and the cancer patient. Dis. Nerv. System. II, Sept., 1950.
12. West, P. M., Blumberg, E. M. and Ellis, F. W.: Correlation between emotional make-up and growth rate of cancer. Lecture in the Am. Assoc. for Cancer Research, New York, 1952.
13. Witmer, H. L. (Ed.): Psychotherapeutic Medicine. New York, Commonwealth Fund, 1947.
14. Wright, S.: I had cancer and lived. Everybody's Digest. Aug., 1951.

CHAPTER 5

Psychiatric Problems in General Surgery*

————————————VICTOR H. ROSEN, M.D.

Dr. Rosen received his M.D. at the College of Physicians and Surgeons, Columbia University. He was an Assistant in the Department of Pathology at Mount Sinai Hospital; had a Rotating Internship at the Brooklyn Jewish Hospital, and a residency in Neurology at Montefiore Hospital in New York. He was Fellow in Psychiatry at the Henry Phipps Clinic of the Johns Hopkins Hospital and graduated from the New York Psychoanalytic Institute.

Dr. Rosen was Chief, N.P. Section, 98th General Hospital (ETO) from 1943 to 1945; was Attending Psychiatrist, Bronx Veterans Hospital, New York; was Adjunct Neurologist at Mount Sinai Hospital, New York, and is now Adjunct Psychiatrist at the same Hospital, where he has served as liaison psychiatrist to the Surgical Service and later as Chief of the Tuesday-Friday Clinic.

He is Fellow of the New York Academy of Medicine; Fellow of the American Psychiatric Association; Member of the New York Psychoanalytic Society, Member of the American Psychosomatic Society, and a Diplomate of the American Board of Neurology and Psychiatry. In addition, Dr. Rosen is a Member of the American Academy of Neurology and the New York Neurological Society.

SINCE THE ADVENT of dynamic concepts in modern psychiatry, the word "psychological" has come to be equated with the idea of "inner conflict," thus neglecting the continuous series of disturbances that constantly impinge upon the individual from the external world. In this series of events a surgical operation stands as a major threat to anyone who must undergo it. It carries certain similar dangers for all, no matter how well or how poorly their personalities are integrated.†

These realistic dangers may be listed as: the threat to life itself, the loss of important body parts or functions, the danger of chronic invalidism, postoperative pain or suffering, the delay of important plans, questions concerning the surgeon's skill and competence, economic dislocations due

---

* Cases, unless otherwise specified, have been taken from the Psychiatric Service of Dr. M. Ralph Kaufman and the Surgical Service of Dr. Arthur S. W. Touroff, both at Mount Sinai Hospital, New York.

† For those to whom psychoanalytic terminology is not a barrier to understanding, an excellent account of the deeper psychodynamic problems imposed by surgery is available in papers by Helene Deutsch[12] and Karl Menninger.[34]

to the period of unemployment and the expense of the operation, hospital care and postoperative treatment.

Two variables must be evaluated in order to understand the part played in the psychic life of the patient by these more or less constant factors incident to any major surgical intervention. One is the present actual life situation of the patient and his specific conditions of living. The second is his special psychological make-up which is largely determined by his historical development with special reference to his particular susceptibilities and idiosyncrasies. The skilled clinician, as time goes on, will more and more be not only a surgical technician, but a humanistic physician who has the knowledge and the personality to assess the interplay of these various factors.[1, 3, 6, 7, 14, 15, 18, 25, 26, 34, 36, 50]

EMOTIONAL RESPONSES TO DANGER

Anxiety is an appropriate "warning signal" of the approach of a danger that threatens the integrity of the individual. One of the important contributions of psychoanalytic psychology has been its recognition that anxiety can be stimulated not only by forces which threaten the individual from the outside world but also by impulses that arise from within the individual which would compromise his safety if they were to reach the bodily apparatus for motor discharge. Both types of anxiety are stimulated in varying degree in different individuals by the threat of surgery.

As a general rule the need for surgery presents itself to the individual either as an emergency problem for which there is no time to make either adequate external plans nor inner emotional readjustments, or it presents itself as an elective procedure with ample time for reflection and anticipation.

The emergency operation has its closest analogue in other life experiences to sudden accidents, injuries or war traumas.[2, 29] Deutsch[12] likens it, in this respect, to the "fright" or traumatic neurosis wherein the suddenness and overwhelming nature of the stimuli involved cannot be integrated by the psychic apparatus. The event sets off a chain of events which represent the attempts of the mental apparatus to master the anxiety produced by the event. All individuals, to a greater or lesser extent, can be expected to show a vulnerability to such traumatic events. The familiar symptoms which represent the psychological process of mastering the anxiety produced by the injury are: general irritability, insomnia, anxiety dreams, nightmares and attacks of palpitation or respiratory distress which are usually nocturnal. The more acutely indicated the surgical procedure and the less the time to prepare the patient for his experience, the greater is the likelihood as well as the intensity of this response.

It is important for the surgeon to understand the etiology and the manifestations of the "fright" neurosis. The apparent lack of anxiety on the part of the patient who is about to undergo emergency surgery should not mislead the surgeon. It is likely that the patient who has had time to assimilate the situation and to develop an appropriate anxiety will fare better during the postoperative period, so far as the manifestations of "fright neurosis" go, than the patient who is apathetic or too cheerful. Since the symptomatology of "fright neurosis" may closely resemble those of certain organic postoperative complications such as pulmonary embolus, atelectasia, etc., the surgeon who has performed an emergency operation will be in a better position to evaluate these symptoms as they are encountered when he is aware of the important difference in this regard between the "unassimilated" anxiety of the emergency procedure as contrasted with the "assimilated" anxiety of an elective operation.

The Preoperative Period

A preoperative period can be defined both surgically and psychologically as the time which elapses from the moment that the decision to operate is made until the time of the actual incision. For the reasons stated above, however, a preoperative period in terms of psychological preparation would have meaning only where the operation is an elective one or one in which there is sufficient delay so that problems involved in the patient's life situation and personality structure can be assessed and dealt with.

Foremost among the reality problems that the surgeon is expected to handle are the threats of death and bodily mutilation. There is insufficient interest at the present time, among surgeons, in the technical problem of giving a patient information that is pertinent to his manifest and latent anxieties and yet sparing him the necessity of dealing with problems which are outside his (the patient's) ken. The errors in regard to this technical problem fall equally into two categories; those of giving too much information and those of giving too little. An example was encountered in a man who was about to undergo nephrectomy for a stag horn calculus in a chronically infected kidney with a normally functioning kidney on the other side. The surgeon, apparently to reassure the patient of his technical ability, discussed with him some of the surgical problems in nephrectomy due to the incidence of anatomic anomalies of the kidney. This was also thought to be a frank and open way of answering his questions concerning the mortality rate in nephrectomy. The effect upon the patient was to increase his anxiety. Actually, the patient would want only two questions answered in this regard: one would be his statistical chances of surviving such an operation, and the second would be the effect upon his vital urinary function of being left with a single kidney. To discuss the fine points of renal anatomy produces an unnecessary burden on the anxiety-assimilating process of the patient, while to give him nothing but a blanket reassurance about his real anxieties would also have the opposite effect from the one intended.

The problem for the surgeon is to separate his own special preoccupations in regard to the pending procedure from those that would concern the average layman and his patient in particular. A simple, forthright description of what is to be expected concerning recovery time, postoperative pain or discomfort, and the overall expense that is likely to be incurred is usually sufficient for most individuals. In regard to these practical everyday considerations it is a good general consideration never to take any knowledge on the part of the patient for granted no matter how apparently sophisticated he may be.

The handling of the ordinary expectations and concerns of the patient has a double meaning. The interview is not only a medium for giving facts which are the best antidote to the anxieties that are mobilized by the real dangers, but it is also indirectly establishing for the patient a rapport with the surgeon as an individual, thus implicitly dealing with his questions concerning the man who is going to perform the operation.

The situation of suddenly having to place one's bodily safety entirely in the hands of another individual is fraught with many problems. It is bound to resurrect many feelings from the period of childhood no matter how "emotionally mature" the individual involved. In most instances, the patient feels at least an intellectual trust in the surgeon who has been recommended to him or has been chosen by him. The intellectual confidence, however, should not give the false assurance that no underlying doubts exist. The surgeon is usually a stranger. Toward all strangers there is always a varying amount of skepticism and distrust. In the initial stages of the patient's relationship with his surgeon we can expect this underlying struggle between confidence and distrust to seize upon small and seemingly insignificant impressions to augment one or the other of these opposing feelings. Thus, without intending to do so, the patient will often be on the alert for signs in the "character" of the surgeon that he can interpret as circumstantial evidence of his insecurity or ineptitude. He is likely to equate indecision in the discussion of the surgeon's fee, or other practical problems concerning which the surgeon must impart information to him, as evidence of inexperience in the surgical procedure itself. Thus, in this subtle area of interpersonal relationships, we can also expect that the surgeon who gives too much or too little information about the operation is not only increasing the patient's anxiety about the procedure but is also increasing his uncertainty of the surgeon himself. The patient, and who can blame him, wishes the surgeon who performs the operation upon him to be an omnipotent and omniscient human being. But he is also capable of realizing the unreality of such a wish; thus, much as he will equate indecision and hesitation with ineptitude, so is he likely to interpret any undue display of self-confidence on the part of the surgeon who wishes to gratify the patient's wish, not as evidence of strength, but as something to add to the feelings of distrust. The channel between Scylla and Charybdis lies in simplicity, explicitness and directness.

The Surgeon as Psychotherapist

Ebaugh[13] stresses the importance of the surgeon himself taking the time to discuss the patient's problems concerning surgery and not relegating this task to assistants. Many experienced surgeons have achieved the same point of view. Finney[15] states, in regard to the often made plea that if surgeons gave time to such details they would not be able to operate upon as many cases, "no surgeon has the moral right to undertake to do more than he can accomplish." *The proper handling of the preoperative preoccupations of the patient have an important bearing on the avoidance of residual states of psychological invalidism in the post-operative period.* Elman[14] stresses the need for surgeons not only to develop skill in the handling of interpersonal relationships with the patient, but also with nurses, ward personnel and anesthetists as well. Observations by liason psychiatrists[5, 6, 47] on surgical wards indicate that the surgeon is too prone to handle the patient's questions in a somewhat routine and mechanical fashion. Not enough importance is attached to the individuality of the recipient of the information. When such a need is apparent and the services of a psychiatrist are available in the hospital organization, it is too often felt to be his responsibility to deal with questions on the part of the patient concerning surgery. Ebaugh[13] points out that the surgeon meets too many minor psychiatric problems to permit sending any significant portion of them to the psychiatrist. Even if he could, it is doubtful that the best results would be obtained in this fashion. There is an important psychological need in having the surgeon himself fill this role. The patient usually suspects second hand information and frequently reveals this by having the information repeated from the surgeon's own lips even after it has been exhaustively dealt with by an assistant. The leisurely-answered query also has an implicit meaning for the anxious patient,[14] who feels himself at the moment to be at the center of the universe.[9] Anything that diverts the surgeon's attention from a continuous concern with the patient's problem is felt to be a threat to his safety. A busy surgical service is often a reassurance to the patient's relatives that he is in competent hands but to the patient it is likely to stir up fears of being overlooked or neglected in the general bustle. The fact that the surgeon himself has time for the patient's problems is a reassurance that he is no mere cog in a busy machine but that he is an individual who will be cared for.

In other chapters the art of listening to the patient has been dealt with. This is a sine qua non of any professional relationship between a technically trained individual and one who is unsophisticated about the service he is receiving. In the relationship between the surgeon and his patient it has a special significance since the surgeon's highly developed degree of sophistication concerning anatomy and physiology tends to produce in him a loss of contact with the inaccurate and fantasy-like concepts that the patient has —to a greater or lesser extent—regarding the form and function of his body. The art of listening in its most developed sense will take the form not only of understanding his manifest gaps in knowledge but also the latent ignorance that is revealed.

A 37-year-old woman of meager educational background had been told that her menorrhagia was due to small "growths" in the wall of her womb and that removal of the womb was necessary. The patient had asked many questions about the operation. During the period of recovery she continued to complain of persistent pain in the lower abdomen. No adequate physiologic cause for these symptoms could be found. Six months after the operation the patient was interviewed by a psychiatrist. She described her pain and feelings of fatigue[30] as being due to "something that must have gone wrong with the operation." She felt quite sure of this in spite of all previous reassurance from the gynecologist. Further listening "between the lines" elicited the astonishing information that the patient was awaiting the return of her menstrual periods. She had conceived of the removal of the womb as being necessitated by the "growths."

In her conception of the function of menstruation it was quite apparent that she had never fully comprehended this as part of the cycle of ovulation with its relation to child bearing, but as one of the body's methods of getting rid of "poisons." She had never connected the removal of the womb with the cessation of her menses and no one had thought it necessary to make this connection explicit for her. One can suspect that the original failure to anticipate her fear and anger at being thus exposed, in fantasy, to the destructive process of slow autointoxication, came from not having listened to what lay behind the original questions.*

It is patently impossible for the surgeon to be able, on short notice, to undertake the kind of understanding that such "special listening" involves. A greater awareness of such problems, however, without the necessity of becoming a psychoanalyst, will attune his ear to tones he has not heard before.

THE OPERATION

According to elementary surgical teaching, the surgeon's four tasks in the operating room are concerned with the technical features of the opera-

* Case from the Gynecological and Psychiatric O.P.D. of the Mount Sinai Hospital, New York.

tion itself, successful hemostasis, prevention of infection and prevention
of postoperative shock. The first three depend largely upon mechanical
skills. The role of psychic stimuli in the production of surgical shock is
becoming increasingly apparent.[23, 24, 32, 43, 44, 51] The factors which influence
the shock mechanism are important in the problems of anesthesia as well.
Raginsky[43] has produced experimental data showing that the degree of
anoxia in nitrous oxide-oxygen anesthesia in the human is not predictable
in quantitative physiologic terms as it is in lower animals but is profoundly
affected by psychological disturbances which do not necessarily produce
conscious or strong manifest emotional reactions.

The variations in patient's attitudes and feelings in regard to anesthesia[12]
is second in importance only to the profound feelings toward the operation.
Indeed for some, the problem of anticipating the anesthesia—whether
local, spinal, or general—is greater than the anxiety produced by the anticipation of the bodily mutilation itself. The state of being unconscious has
deeper meanings to most individuals. For many unconsciousness is equated
with death. Although modern methods of anesthesia with all the technical
improvements in mechanical equipment, blood transfusion methods and
pharmacologic agents, reduce anesthesia mortality, most patients and surgeons are likely to treat this fear only in its rational terms. Yet these are
not the kinds of fears that can be dealt with by logical persuasion. *The
irrational element in the reaction is also the one that produces the greatest influence on autonomic neural mechanisms[44] and is thus the significant factor
in the problem of shock.*[51]

The fear of death evoked by the idea of general anesthesia is the resurrec-
tion of an almost universal childhood anxiety which does not differentiate
between death and the separation from or abandonment by parental
figures.[12] Where such fears are outstanding they should be taken quite
seriously. When they are accompanied by evidence of overt anxiety or
panic they should be an important indication for the use of spinal or local
anesthesia if this is surgically possible. The preservation of consciousness
in such individuals allows for continuous contact with the anesthetist and
the surgeon, thus reducing the element in the fear that arises from "separation" anxiety. There seem to be cases, in the experience of many physicians, of patients who have expressed the conviction that they would die
on the operating table and whose fears have subsequently proven to have
been justified. Although a carefully controlled study of such cases is not
possible, and in many it is quite probable that the prediction and the fatal
outcome were merely coincidental phenomena, it is still likely in some that
the depth and the intensity of the fear of separation from protecting figures
played a crucial role in producing a fatal autonomic imbalance. In many,
such fears may not be conscious and the only manifestations are in the

autonomic lability that becomes evident during the operative procedure. Where general anesthesia must be used in such patients, careful preoperative preparation is indicated. The anesthetist should become acquainted with the patient and become a definite personal figure in his eyes instead of a distant shadow in white. This is perhaps even more important than the necessary preoperative sedation. The anesthetist's role should be characterized throughout by a particularly "maternal" attitude.[9] Deutsch[12] is of the opinion that the "separation" fear of general anesthesia is more characteristic of female patients while other reactions to be described below are more characteristic of the male.

Another frequent meaning of the anesthesia to patients may be the threat of having to give up "control." To some individuals who show this quality to an exaggerated degree, anything is tolerable so long as he (the patient) has a hand in influencing the outcome. To these individuals the anesthesia may portend an intolerable state of passivity which must be fought, albeit against the patient's conscious intentions in the matter. These are probably the patients who struggle during the induction period and develop tense musculature which makes retraction of tissues difficult whenever the anesthesia becomes lighter. They require larger amounts of anesthesia than usual. Here, too—where possible—some of the difficulties may be avoided with local or spinal anesthesia. The patient's feeling that he is in partial control of the procedure acts as an alleviant to his anxiety.

There are other individuals in whom psychological considerations would indicate the use of general anesthesia rather than one that permits the retention of consciousness. These are people who show a marked incapacity to deal directly with unpleasant facts. They tend to shut their ears and eyes to external events that might arouse painful feelings within them. Any discussion of death or injury is avoided by them. They cannot stand the sight of blood and do not want to know anything about the inner workings of the body. Such patients would probably do better under general anesthesia and it is well to consider the advisability of starting the induction before they go into the operating room. Excessive anxiety is produced in these patients by the impressions of the operating room perceived even remotely through vision, hearing or smell.[13] It is well, also, for operating room personnel to be aware of the fact that during the induction of general anesthesia, hearing is the last sense category to be obliterated[44] and that profound impressions can come by way of the partly narcotized hearing apparatus.

The surgeon and the anesthetist cannot rely completely on good routine methods and intuition alone in planning the preparation of the patient and the type of anesthetic to use. It is necessary to augment these with a knowledge of the particular personality involved.

The Postoperative Period*

The careful preparation of the patient and the correct handling of the personality problems in relation to anesthesia and the operating room set the stage for a smooth convalescence. It is inevitable, however, that new problems will arise which are characteristic of this period. The demands upon the patient as an individual have grown with newer surgical concepts of postoperative care that have arisen during the period of World War II and its aftermath. These are characterized by early mobilization of the patient and other active rehabilitation routines that place a large premium upon active cooperation and participation by the patient himself. Psychological as well as physical disturbances should be sought out in all cases where the usual active strivings on the part of the patient to aid in his recovery are inadequate. They should also be sought out in those cases in which the patient's activity and attempts to participate in the recovery process outrun those of the surgeon and nursing personnel.[42, 45, 47, 48]

Clothier[9] in a significant psychological discussion of the convalescent period likens its deeper meaning for the patient to a kind of condensed emotional re-growing up. She reminds us that a universal reaction to the pain and physiologic disturbances that are present in the immediate postoperative period shows itself by an intense withdrawal of interest from the outside world onto the self. This intense preoccupation with internal sensations produces a state of being which is reminiscent of early periods of infantile life. It shows other similarities in this respect in the patient's unaccustomed petulance and inability to withstand even brief periods of frustration of immediate needs. During this period, Clothier feels, the significance of the special nurse goes far beyond her immediate role of the routine or special care of the patient's physiologic needs. She reminds the patient of a kind of early mother figure for whom he is willing to perform. Her mere presence during the first few post-operative days may mean the difference between his being able to carry out eliminatory functions, or the taking of fluids spontaneously, or the need for mechanical procedures in this regard. It is also probable that the return of interest from the self onto the objects and people of the outside world is enhanced by the nurse's presence[9] and forms a very significant part of the psychological readiness to get well.

Clothier also points out that the process of getting well is not always one that has the patient's full psychological cooperation. There are many advantages to being taken care of. Just as it is retarding in the development of the child to have his mother's indulgent care past the period when he is

---

* Toxic deliria are important postoperative psychiatric reactions but they will not be dealt with here since they are major reactions which are not within the scope of this symposium.

able to do things for himself, so it may retard the psychological recovery of the patient to have the special nurse past the period of immediate need. The process of recovery at this stage will be furthered by the transference to floor care where several people become involved in the patient's recovery, thus expanding the area of his interest in the external world and aiding him in the relearning process of delayed satisfaction of physiologic needs which is such an important part of the growing up process for adults as well as for children.

The personality attributes of the patient will become increasingly important in the pattern of convalescence toward its later stages. For many patients the problem will not be one of mobilizing interest in re-participation in the getting well process, but of somehow getting them to realize that they are sick and that some part of the convalescent process must be allowed to remain in the hands of others. These are the individuals described briefly above as being unable to give up control. They tend to deny the facts of their illness[47] and tolerate the restrictions of convalescence poorly. Their behavior is often like the "know-it-all" child.[9] Often, in spite of the best attempts on the part of the surgeon to make the illness and the operative procedure clear, these patients manage to elude the full emotional significance of what they are about to undergo. If the surgical procedure involves major bodily mutilations, or loss of a function, or a prolonged period of recovery, one can expect that the sudden affectively-charged realization of what has occurred, will produce in these patients, at some time during the period of recovery, a profound emotional effect. The following case illustrates this problem:

A 64-year-old messenger for a brokerage firm was seen two weeks after an abdominal-perineal resection of the rectum for carcinoma. The operation and postoperative course were uneventful and the colostomy opening was functioning well. About eight days following the operation the patient's mood changed from one of cheerfulness and habitual good spirits to a gloomy despondent attitude. The nurses complained that he cooperated poorly in getting out of bed and in the usual ward procedures although he had been up on the second postoperative day and had given them little trouble. His spontaneous remarks at the first interview were, "I feel generally discouraged. I keep wondering what is to become of me. I suddenly realize that I am a sick man." He was often found in bed with the covers pulled over his head but he was quite eager to discuss his personal problems.

His past history revealed the following pertinent data: He came from a large family, being the fifth of seven siblings. His father was a hard working factory machine operator. The mother was an uncomplaining woman who was constantly busy with the household chores and had little time for the children outside of their routine care. Early independence and the need "to make one's own way" were constantly stressed in the family. The father treated the world as a grim place where "you took care of yourself because no one else was going to do it for you." At the age of eight, the patient was already saving money toward his education by working as a delivery boy for a grocer after school hours. At the age of 22, the patient flunked out of law school after working his way through much of his college career. His friends were struck by the unperturbed manner in which he reacted to this set-back. His attitude was "as long as I have my health, nothing else matters." He married a young woman of his own age and then took a relatively menial job as a Wall Street messenger. After several years of this employment the patient saved and borrowed enough money to start a small dress manufacturing business with a partner. The business thrived and he became moderately wealthy. During the economic crisis of the early 1930's the business failed and the patient was once again destitute. He said, "I took it with a grin. Other men were blowing their brains out but I thought, 'I've got my wife and family and my health.'" He refused to seek any help from a wealthy brother and went back to his former job as a messenger maintaining his household in reduced circumstances.

A year before his present hospitalization he had begun to notice rectal bleeding but it was some time before he sought medical attention. After his first examination, hospitalization was advised but the patient said: "In my blessed foolish ignorance I didn't believe the doctor; I couldn't imagine that anything could really be wrong with me." Six months later when the bleeding had become worse, he returned for proctoscopic examination. This time he was told that he probably had a tumor of the rectum. Once again, however, he told himself that the "doctor was making a mountain out of a molehill." It was four more months before combined family and medical pressure convinced him to seek surgical relief.

His course in the hospital is described by the patient as follows: "The surgeons told me I had a tumor in the rectum and that the operation was a pretty big one, and still I really didn't believe it was anything. They said I would have to readjust my way of life. I thought to myself that it wouldn't be the first time."

After recovery from the acute effects of the operation the patient was agreeably surprised at the dispatch with which he was gotten out of bed. The procedure of early mobilization seems to have reinforced his constant tendency to minimize and deny the reality of his illness. This period coincided with a general light-heartedness. On the eighth postoperative day, it appears that the patient clearly visualized the colostomy opening on the abdominal wall, with fecal contents oozing out, for the first time. He says, "I was shocked—it suddenly came to me that I was a very sick man." His discouragement and depressive symptoms dated from this undeniable realization of the change in the appearance of his body and his bowel functioning.[47]

In similar cases, the dramatic emotional realization does not take place. These are the patients who demand discharge from the hospital before they are ready to leave and generally make things difficult for the surgeon because of their unwillingness to take any kind of passive role in the process of recovery.

In addition to depressive symptoms, undue elation, hostility, apathy, hypochondriacal complaining, exaggerated demands for attention and negativism should make the surgeon look for a discrepancy between what the patient seems to know about his operation and what he really feels about it.

Some recent experiences have indicated that certain specific emotional problems encountered in surgery are not only the product of the personality involved, but are also likely to be provoked more by certain kinds of surgical procedures than by others.

CHEST SURGERY

The chest is a more important part of the patient's "body-image" than is usually conceived. For the male it has many associations to ideas of virility, strength and endurance. Competitions in chest expansion are not uncommon in adolescent boys. For women it is intimately associated with the breasts and attitudes that relate to feminine attractiveness and the maternal feeding function. For both sexes the chest and breathing functions are connected with deep primitive fears related to suffocation and death. The most violent and generalized physiologic defensive reflexes are set in motion by the threat of suffocation.

Amputation of the breast in the female can never fail to be an intensely disturbing procedure no matter how resigned the patient may seem. It can be expected to be followed by a depressive affect of some degree. Any operation, but even more particularly those that involve changes in the surface appearance of the body, should be carefully described in advance along with a clear statement of the necessity for the procedure. This is especially true of breast amputation. Thoracoplasty in both sexes has similar implications. If the surgeon knows in advance that breast amputation or disfiguring chest procedures are necessary, it is poor psychological technic to avoid the unpleasant task of imparting this information to the patient. In the case of breast masses, the patient often goes under the anesthesia with the fate of the breast dependent upon the frozen section. In such cases the patient has agreed to leave the extent of the procedure to the surgeon's judgment. The effect of a radical mastectomy in such cases is always a profound disappointment for which the surgeon must be prepared. This is the reality of the problem of undiagnosed breast masses, but wherever possible, the patient should have a clear picture of what to expect if the radical procedure should prove necessary.

Hartz[20] has called attention to the frequency of claustrophobic symptoms following thoracoplasty. He feels that these are related to the fantasy of being crushed which arises from the patient's mental picture of the procedure. It is significant in these cases that the symptoms of being unable to stay in the hospital room, dyspnea which is out of proportion to pain or encroachment on respiratory reserves, is often partly a secondary phenomenon to the neurosis itself. Thus, the patient who is only aware of a vague feeling of oppression and difficulty in breathing does not know that he is suffering from symptoms with a thought content which is related to being in an enclosed space. He is likely to feel that something has gone wrong in the operation or the process of healing. There can be considerable relief, when the syndrome is recognized, if the patient is told that he is suffering from a well recognized emotional reaction to the ideas aroused by chest operations. Similar cases have been observed following pulmonary lobectomy and pneumonectomy. Test of vital reserve in these cases reveal that the feeling of oppression and the dyspnea are out of proportion to any physiologic disturbance. It is well in all such cases to see whether there is a relationship in the symptoms to the feeling of being enclosed.

Abdominal Surgery

Most surgery of the abdominal viscera has rather different psychological implications from those procedures affecting the surface of the body. Even in the most sophisticated and "balanced" individuals where the direct perceptual recognition of phenomena is obscured, the fantasy function of the psychic apparatus takes over.* This is true also of simple procedures such as appendectomy which would appear to be easily conceptualized even if not seen. Where complex gut anastomoses are performed or operations on visceral organs which the patient has never clearly conceptualized, the area of fantasy can be expected to be correspondingly widened, within the framework of the patient's personality and previous life experience.[5, 12, 41]

The patient's need to fill in his conceptual deficits with a fantasy of the rearrangements that have taken place within him, is not in itself a pathogenic process. But to the extent that the fantasy which fills the void is the residual of some early set of childhood traumatic experiences, is it likely that psychogenic symptoms will appear. Unusual opposition to early ambulation, distrust, repetitive needs for reassurance, bizarre sensations in the operative area, unduly prolonged urinary or bowel retention following operation should be looked upon—barring sufficient evidence of mechanical or physiologic disturbance—as possibly consequences of unspoken fantasies concerning the operative procedure. It is usually not sufficient to reassure the patient that nothing is wrong. More lasting alleviation of the symptoms is frequently possible if the patient can be induced to verbalize the fantasy involved. The following is an illustrative case:

A middle-aged man had undergone splenectomy for thrombo-cytopenic purpura. The spleen as an organ and the whole meaning of the operation were very poorly understood by him. He continued to require enemata and was unable to have a normal bowel movement long past the time that a reflex atony of the bowel would be a plausible explanation. Investigation revealed that certain deep sensations in the region of the healing operative site had been interpreted by him as indicating the possibility that the surgeon had left instruments inside of him. These, he supposed,

* See discussion of eye surgery and psychological effects of temporary interference with visual function (Linn).

might have been clamps to keep him from bleeding internally, and not due to an oversight. He feared that being a ward patient he might be receiving inferior care. He did not want to talk to anyone about this because he thought it would sound foolish and the surgeon might also be insulted. He solved his dilemma by refraining from using his abdominal muscles in defecation thinking in this way to avoid the hazardous consequences of causing himself some internal injury by excessive straining, if his suspicions were correct. And by keeping the whole matter to himself, he would avoid hurting the surgeon's feelings by his distrust of him if his suspicions were wrong. There was rapid return of normal bowel function after the fantasy was discussed in a mutually friendly atmosphere.

On other occasions, patients may be having some organic postoperative complications. Fantasies which will further complicate the postoperative course are inevitable if the surgeon treats the patient with the false reassurance that everything is in order. Most patients can sense a physician's dissatisfaction with the process of convalescence no matter how well he may think he is hiding this from the patient. Sick people are especially sensitive to minimal signs in this regard and will use them for the elaboration of fantasies which may be more anxiety producing than the actual state of affairs. A middle-aged woman who had suffered from a saddle embolus of the aorta following a coronary attack developed an ischemia and subsequent gangrene of both lower extremities. During the subsequent course of her illness no one would admit to the patient that she would inevitably have to lose both lower extremities. The patient developed a manic episode during which she expressed the fantasy that she was an experimental subject whose legs were being encased in ice as a special form of treatment that was going to preserve them. The manic episode was rapidly terminated by telling her the truth.[47]

Many postoperative fantasies that follow laparotomy cannot easily be verbalized by the patient because their content is sexual in nature. Frequently these involve fears of sterility in women and impotence in men. The greatest tact on the part of the attending surgeon would be necessary in bringing them to light.

Amputation of Limbs

Amputations of limbs are operations in which the "reality" factor far outweighs the problems of individual reaction in most patients. The evidence indicates that lower extremity amputations produce a greater feeling of helplessness than those involving the upper extremity.[45] Since amputations are starkly visible changes of the body surface they are operations about which the patient should never be left in doubt. An overprotective surgeon may feel that he has described the result of operation to a patient when actually he has left him with quite a different concept than the one intended. I once had the experience of hearing a surgeon discuss amputation of a leg with a female patient. It was striking that the site of the amputation, which was to be in the mid-thigh region, was never mentioned so that the patient might have expected to find a stump, on awakening, anywhere from the ankle to the groin. The patient's insistence on this point finally brought a reluctant definitive answer from the surgeon but even when thus "put on the spot," he was unable to let go of his need to minimize and indicated a site just above the knee joint.

One hundred soldier amputees were studied by Randall.[45] The striking feature of the study was the high incidence of psychopathology in a group of individuals who seemed superficially adjusted to their mutilation. Men with upper extremity amputations, married men, and men in the older age group seemed to have less difficulty in social readjustment than single men. Ninety-five per cent of the group had phantom limb sensations. Psychological symptoms which interferred with occupational readjustment far outweighed in number the ones complaining of sexual difficulties.

The practical difficulties which interfere with freedom of movement or manual manipulation thus cause the greatest disturbances; but it is also observable that a great deal of an individuals "narcissistic" feelings are invested in the limbs. Mitscherlich[20] stresses the almost universal reaction of loss of self esteem following amputation of limbs. This is probably an important factor in the large proportion of so-called "social" maladjustments in amputees. Pride is an important factor in the independence and productivity that motivates work. The significant number of amputees, still capable of work and with job opportunities, who seem to prefer to "beg for a living," is probably in large part related to the problem of loss of self esteem. It seems likely that in the future greater cognizance will be taken of the social problem of the amputee. The United States Army, Navy, and Veterans Administration[21, 31, 53] have gone a long way in developing such a program but the individual in civilian life who must lose a limb is not the recipient of the same kind of team treatment.[11, 27] The future total therapy of the amputee of civilian as well as of military origin will probably devolve upon a team of individuals rather than upon the surgeon himself. This team should comprise the surgeon or orthopedist, the physical and corrective therapists, who will be responsible for the learning process in the use of the prosthesis following surgery, and a skilled social worker with experience in the social and occupational readjustment problems of amputees. In many cases, the supervision of a psychiatrist will be necessary in the preparatory and rehabilitation stages to help with those patients for whom the amputation mobilizes not only reality problems of the present but traumatic emotional experiences of the past.

The Council on Physical Therapy of the American Medical Association[11] has suggested that amputees be divided into three groups: (1) those previously intact individuals for whom amputation is a sudden confrontation of an entirely unexpected loss; (2) those with chronic diseases of an extremity where the saving of life is the primary consideration in the amputation, and (3) those patients with functionless limbs for whom amputation is performed in order to provide a useful prosthesis. In the first group, psychological problems are likely to be the most extreme. Explicitness on the part of the surgeon concerning the type of stump to be expected and what it holds forth in terms of the possibility of a useful prosthesis is of the greatest immediate psychological help to the patient. This report stresses, for the physical therapist's attention, that the evidence of emotional readjustment to the loss of the limb is a shift in the patient's attitude from "how do I look" to "what can I do."

In all amputation problems the surgeon and auxiliary personnel should avoid falling into the trap of the patient's narcissistic problem. While the patient is talking about appearance, the surgeon and his assistants should be patiently emphasizing function.

"Cryptic" Symptoms in the Recovery Period

The persistence of certain kinds of vague complaints during the period of convalescence, such as anorexia, backache, headache, malaise, etc., without explanatory organic pathology, should be looked upon as indices of possible "relationship" problems.[14] Often such complaints are an indirect way of bringing attention to the patient's fear of getting well and taking on his usual responsibilities again. Or it may be one patient's way of expressing dissatisfaction with family relationships. One elderly woman recovering from a minor surgical procedure complained of generalized aches and pains that kept her in the hospital a week longer than necessary. This was her way of reacting to what she felt was the neglectful attitude of her children in visiting her in the hospital. By intensifying her illness she unconsciously hoped to make them feel guilty for their negligence. Similar difficulties may express a patient's desire for more sympathy and attention from the nurse. But often overlooked is the role of the surgeon in producing these "relationship" complaints.

Clothier[9] points out that during the immediate postoperative period and, to a diminishing extent, until recovery is complete, the surgeon becomes the most important figure in the patient's life. He is the maker of miracles who has brought the patient safely to death's door and back again. His visit each day is usually the great event in the convalescent's life. For this reason, incidents that may appear small in the surgeon's eyes may have an exaggerated emotional significance for the patient. The surgeon who habitually stops at the adjoining bed first, or who always makes his rounds in one direction, or seems to have a slightly greater interest in another case, or who has reason to scold the patient, or who exhibits more interest in the condition of the wound than in the patient's picture of her twelve-year-old boy, may find that the patient's protest is expressed in terms of "cryptic" symptoms. The patient's gratitude to the surgeon and his fear of arousing his antagonism, make it very difficult in most cases to give direct expression to these feelings. The surgeon should try to become aware of the possible chronologic connection between the onset of such complaints and minor incidents that may have occurred between the patient and members of the family or between the patient and himself.

When such observations are made it is frequently possible to bring them into direct discussion with the patient in such a way that he is made to feel that his jealous or hostile reactions to the surgeon or ward personnel can be verbalized without jeopardizing the surgeon's interest in him. *In such a discussion it should never seem that the surgeon is treating the patient's feelings as a joke nor that he means to imply a direct connection between the symptoms and the subject under discussion.* Such an implication will usually be interpreted by the patient as a veiled attempt at discipline or a desire to "talk him out of some imaginary complaint." Unless the patient's protest is real and justified the discussion of his "gripe" does not necessitate giving in to it. The ill-considered indulgence of a patient's unreasonable demand will only produce more symptoms in anticipation of similar treatment. By the same token, unnecessary anger or abrupt rejection on the part of the surgeon will similarly augment the symptoms. A friendly discussion of the surgeon's bill or his reasons for not being able to see the patient on a certain day when his visit had been eagerly awaited, can often produce a dramatic change in the patient's attitude and somatic symptoms.

"SURGICAL ADDICTION" AND POLYSURGERY

A considerable literature has arisen in both psychiatric and surgical journals which attest the widespread interest in, and awareness of this problem.[3, 4, 8, 17, 19, 28, 34, 35, 39, 52, 54, 57] Patients who look for operations as a solution to their emotional problems are more common than the literature indicates.

Menninger,[34] in an excellent psychoanalytic study of the problem, cites Jelliffe's observation of a 21-year-old woman who had already obtained for herself 28 different operative procedures. Numerous anecdotes in fiction and folklore give testimony to the widespread belief in the ability of the knife to influence the mind. The primitive roots of this idea have been culled from anthropological sources by Sigerist:[49]

If we look at Australia first, we remember that the cause of disease was considered to be the intrusion of a foreign object into the victim's body by means of magic. The purpose of treatment, therefore, was to remove the object from the sick man. To that end the Kurnai medicine man inquired where the patient felt the pain. He then touched the sick part, rubbed it gently until he suddenly declared that he felt the object under the skin. He covered the part with a piece of cloth from which, after a while, he produced a bit of quartz, a splinter of wood, a glass bear or whatever the object may have been. In other cases, he rubbed the sick part energetically and sucked it with his mouth. Then suddenly, he would spit the foreign object out.

Add modern steel instruments, anesthesia and asepsis, and some surgical procedures would not look very different.[8, 12, 34]

Most surgeons are well aware of this problem when faced with the patient who displays a "gridiron" abdomen, gives a history of numerous surgical procedures, or shows signs of unmistakable psychopathology. There are many less spectacular instances, however, where the operation fills a psychological need much more than a surgical need. The surgeon's suspicion and further study of the matter should always be aroused by the patient who attempts to influence, in a positive direction, his decision to operate, or who appears to have visited too many other surgeons with negative results.

Many deeper emotional needs can be temporarily satisfied by a surgical procedure:* (1) The operation gives the patient the opportunity to avoid something that he fears more than surgery. It is striking how many impending marriages or divorces or even a visit to a psychiatrist are delayed by a surgical procedure. (2) At times, it represents the need on the part of the patient to put himself in the hands of a strong, paternal figure who will still his feelings of doubt and indecision by taking positive and definitive action. (3) In the female patient (less often in the male) the surgery is a magical method of solving the problem of an ungratified wish for impregnation and a child. (4) At times, an unconscious punishment wish is being satisfied. By giving up what the patient feels to be the offending organ, he escapes a fate that he considers worse than surgical mutilation. Menninger[34] cites the case of a young man who, after many attempts, finally succeeded in finding a surgeon to remove both his testicles. He was a young scientist who felt unfulfilled in his research work and thought that his work inhibition was due to interference with his research interests by his sexual drive. It is stated that curiously, his sexual potency was not impaired nor his research capacity increased by the operation. But he lived to regret the surgery when, in a second marriage, he desired to have a child. (5) Sometimes the operation, with its preoperative attention, the drama of the surgical amphitheatre, and the increased interest and solicitude of friends and family, satisfies the exhibitionistic needs of the patient. Where this is the case one should not expect to find a flamboyant, dramatic individual but more likely a shy, socially uneasy person who seeks surgical exhibition

* Based on Menninger's paper "Polysurgery and Polysurgical Addiction."[34]

because other avenues for the satisfaction of this drive are blocked to him. (6) Many operations give the observer the strong impression of a "partial" suicide. The expression of such attitudes on the part of the patient as "I don't care if I come out of this operation dead or alive," should point in this direction.

In all cases where these deeper psychological mechanisms are at work, surgery becomes a welcome method of solving the inner conflict because it has the special quality of displacing the responsibility for the act onto the person of the surgeon. In this lies one of the great dangers in surgical addiction to the surgeon himself when he is wittingly or unwittingly drawn into the patient's plan. It is most likely that in the initial phases of the relationship established with such a patient, the surgeon will be able to bask in the sunshine of the patient's gratitude and admiration. As soon as the discovery is made, however, that the inner conflicts have not been resolved and that life is still unsatisfying, then the patient's anger may be expected to be turned in all its force upon his erstwhile benefactor.

Both Menninger[34] and Deutsch[12] emphasize the bilateral unconscious needs in the surgical addiction problem. The truism that "at least two persons are involved in a surgical procedure" is frequently ignored. Elman[14] expresses some shock that these two psychoanalytically oriented writers on the subject allude to the psychological theory that surgery is a "sublimation of sadistic drives." The expression of sensitive feelings on this score is an unnecessary misunderstanding of this formulation. Neither of the above writers implied that surgery was "sadistic." The specialty of surgery is a highly skilled art in the general body of medical science. In its most developed forms it has exactly the reverse qualities of destructiveness for its own sake. This is what makes it a "sublimation." But the sublime must evolve from baser sources. Thus, it is casting no stones in the direction of these honored specialists to say that at one time, what may have been more than a usual interest in pain and injury, has now become just as strong a drive in the opposite direction. That at some time, in some surgeons, the original drive can threaten to reassert itself in disguised form, is something that the psychiatrist must be as much aware of in himself as the surgeon. If the psychiatrist appears to take a holier-than-thou stand in this regard, it is not because he is not made of the same clay, but because his failures are less exposed and less irreversible.

Lastly, an appeal for caution in the decision to operate would be remiss if it did not point to the danger signal in the reverse direction. The health and life of a patient who needs surgery can be jeopardized by one who is overly impressed at such a time with his psychological mechanisms. The fault of not operating when it is needed, because of the patient's manifest neurotic difficulties,[42] may not be as widespread a danger as the problem of surgical addiction, but it is certainly more hazardous. There is no easy solution to the complexities and pitfalls that beset this many-sided problem. Mechanical formulations[40] are not likely to serve this purpose. There is no substitute for ever expanding knowledge and research both in the refinements of surgical diagnosis and the effects of psychic conflict upon organ pathology.

BIBLIOGRAPHY

1. Altaf, J.: Psychic examination of the pre-operative period. An. Cong. Inter. Am. Med. *1:* 119–126, 1947.
2. Bakwin, H.: Psychic trauma of operations. J. Pediat. *36:* 262–264, 50.
3. Barnacle, C. H.: Pain in relation to personality disorders. Rocky Mountain M. J. *39:* 197–199, 1942.
4. Bennett, A. E. and Engle, B.: Faulty management of psychiatric syndromes simulating organic disease. J.A.M.A. *130:* 1203, 1946.
5. Blanton, S. and Kirk, V.: A psychiatric study of 61 appendectomy cases. Ann. Surg. *126:* 305–314, 1947.
6. Brooks, B.: Psychosomatic surgery. Ann. Surg. *119:* 289–299, 1944.
7. Brown, W. T.: Psychiatry and surgery. Ann. Surg., *131:* 445–447, 1950.
8. Clarke, R. B. and Ziegler, L. H.: Survey of surgical operations among psychiatric patients. Dis. Nerv. System. *3:* 198–201, 1942.
9. Clothier, F.: Some thoughts on the psychology of post operative convalescence. Dis. Nerv. System. *2:* 266, 1941.
10. Crampton, H. P.: Factors other than anesthetics affecting anesthesia. President's Address. Proc. Roy. Soc Med. *28:* 91–96, 1934.
11. Council on Physical Therapy. Am. Med. Assn. Psychologic and Physiologic Principles in Amputation. J.A.M.A. *115:* 1719–1720, 1940.
12. Deutsch, H.: Some psychoanalytic observations on surgery. Psychosom. Med. *4:* 105–115, 1942.
13. Ebaugh, F. G.: The psychiatrist in relation to surgery. Surg., Gyn. & Obst. *68:* 372–376, 1939.
14. Elman, R.: Psychogenic factors in surgery. S. Clin. North America. *30:* 1391–1409, 1950.
15. Finney, J. M. T.: The human side of surgery. Arch. Surg. *41:* 296–298, 1940.
16. Gervasio, L.: Su alcuna caso di psico-nevrosi reattive ed intervento operatoria. Arch. psicol. neurol. e psichiat. *12:* 70–74, 1951.
17. Gordon, R. G.: Psychogenic pain. Edinburg. M. J. *55:* 596–611, 1948.
18. Gossett, J. and Mary, P.: Surgery and psychosomatic problems. Bruxelles-méd. *30:* 246–261, 1950.
19. Hart, H.: Displacement guilt and pain. Psychoanalyt. Rev. *34:* 259–273, 1947.
20. Hartz, J.: Thoracoplasty and claustrophobia. Psychosom. Med. *8:* 344–346, 1946.
21. Hughes, J. and White, W. L.: Amputee rehabilitation; emotional reactions and adjustment of amputees to their injury. U. S. Nav. M. Bull. Suppl. pp. 157–163, 1946.
22. Iosset, G. I.: Psychic trauma sustained by patients in surgical clinics and wards. Vestnik. khir. *59:* 315–322, 1940.
23. Jackson, K.: Psychologic preparation as a method of reducing the emotional trauma of anesthesia in children. Anesthesiology *12:* 293–300, 1951.
24. Jacobson, J.: Psychiatric aspects of surgery with special reference to post operative psychic shock. Virginia M. Monthly. *77:* 25–31, 1950.

72   PSYCHOLOGY OF PHYSICAL ILLNESS

25. Kennedy, A.: Psychology of the surgical case. M. Press. *214:* 254–257, 1945.
26. ——: Psychology of the surgical patient. Brit. M. J. *1:* 396–400, 1950.
27. Kessler, L. H.: Psychological preparation of the amputee. Indust. Med. & Surg. *20:* 107–108, 1951.
28. Krapf, E.: Accidentes y operaciones como expresion auto-destructivas. Rev. méd. d. Hosp. brit. *1:* 36–40, 1944.
29. Levy, D. M.: Psychic trauma of operation in children and a note on combat neurosis. Am. J. Dis. Child. *69:* 7–25, 1945.
30. Lindemann, E.: Observations on psychiatric sequellae to surgical operations in women. Am. J. Psychiat. *98:* 132–139, 1941.
31. Luck, J. V. and Smith, H. M. et al.: Orthopedic surgery in the Army Air Forces during World War II. Psychologic problems, convalescent care and rehabilitation. Arch. Surg. *58:* 75–88, 1949.
32. Mechling, G. S.: Psychologic Approach to the patient for anesthesia. South. M. J. *35:* 83–84, 1942.
33. Meier, C. A.: Chirurgie-Psychologie. Schweiz. med. Wchnschr. *73:* 437, 1943.
34. Menninger, K. A.: Polysurgery and polysurgical addiction. Psychoanalyt. Quart. *3:* 173, 1934.
35. Miller, N. F.: The abuse of pelvic surgery in the female. Surgery. *22:* 976, 1947.
36. Mira, N. F.: Cirurgia y psicologica. An. d. cir. *6:* 223–232, 1940.
37. Mittelman, B., Weider, A., Brodmann, K., Wechsler, D. and Wolff, H. G.: Personality and psychosomatic disturbances in patients on medical and surgical wards: Survey of 450 admissions. Psychosom. Med. *7:* 220–223, 1945.
38. Ochsner, A.: Importance of psychiatry in surgery. Digest Neurol. & Psychiat. *18:* 91–96, 1950.
39. Oltman, J. E. and Friedman, S.: Role of operative procedure in the etiology of psychoses. Psychiatric Quart. *17:* 405–422, 1943.
40. Palmer, H.: Pain charts. A description of a technique whereby functional pain may be diagnosed from organic pain. New Zealand M. J. *48:* 187–213, 1949.
41. Pearson, G. H. J.: Effect of operative procedures on the emotional life of the child. Am. J. Dis. Child. *62:* 716–729, 1941.
42. Pollak, A. and Thompson, G. N.: Common surgical lesions causing mental disturbances. J. Nerv. & Ment. Dis. *110:* 400–412, 1949.
43. Raginsky, B. B.: Mental suggestion as an aid to anesthesia. Anesthesiology. *9:* 472–480, 1948.
44. ——: Some psychosomatic aspects of general anesthesia. Anesthesiology *11:* 391–408, 1950.
45. Randall, G. C., Ewalt, J. R. and Blair, H.: Psychiatric reaction to amputation. J.A.M.A. *128:* 645–652, 1945.
46. Rawlings, N. W.: The psychology of induction in anesthesia. Brit. J. Anesth. *7:* 126–129, 1930.
47. Rosen, V. H.: The role of denial in acute postoperative affective reactions following the removal of body parts. Psychosom. Med. *12:* 356–361, 1950.
48. Schneider, R., Gray, J. S. and Culmer, C. U.: Psychologic evaluation of surgical patients; correlation between pre-operative psychometric studies and recovery. Wisconsin M. J. *49:* 285–290, 1950.
49. Sigerist, H. E.: A History of Medicine; Primitive and Archiac Medicine. New York, Oxford University Press, 1951, Vol. I.
50. Stajano, C.: Influence of the psyche in surgical disease; concept of functional

unity in physiology and the unitary concept of the "sick man" in clinical surgery. Bol. Soc. cir. d. Uruguay. *18:* 4ь–492, 1947.

51. Stern, M.: Anxiety, trauma and shock. Psychoanalyt. Quart. *20:* 179–203, 1951.

52. Ulett, P. C. and Gildea, E. F.: Survey of surgical procedures in psychoneurotic women. J.A.M.A. *143:* 960–963, 1950.

53. Von Werssowetz, O. F. and Baum, M. W.: Rehabilitation of the amputee. Mil. Surgeon. *107:* 3–19, 1950.

54. Witt, G. F. and Cheavens, T. H.: Psychiatric contraindication to surgery. Texas State J. Med. *35:* 681–684, 1940.

55. Zaki, Ali: Les psychoses post-operatoires. Schweiz. Arch. f. Neurol. u. Psychiat. *47:* 1–25, 1941.

56. Zanelotti, G.: Le psicosi post-operatoria. Minerva chir. *2:* 301–305, 1947.

57. Zeno, L.: Errores psicologicos in clinica quirurgica. Semana méd. *1:* 1267–1274, 1942.

58. Zugliani, J. A.: Psiquismo e anestesia. Rev. Brasil de cir. *18:* 123–128, 1949.

CHAPTER 6

Psychiatric Aspects of Plastic Surgery*

LOUIS LINN, M.D.

Dr. Linn received his M.D. at the University of Chicago, Rush Medical College, and—after internship—was a Psychiatric Resident at State Hospital, Trenton, New Jersey and at New York Psychiatric Institute. He was a resident in Neurology at Montefiore Hospital, New York and is a graduate of the New York Psychoanalytic Institute.

Dr. Linn had extensive psychiatric experience with the United States Army overseas, and is at present an Adjunct, Department of Psychiatry, Mount Sinai Hospital, having been attached as Liaison Psychiatrist to the Plastic Surgery Service. He is currently associated with the Neurologic Service there.

Dr. Linn is a Diplomate of the American Board of Psychiatry and Neurology, a Fellow of the American Psychiatric Association, an Associate Member of the New York Psychoanalytic Society and a Fellow of the New York Academy of Medicine.

THIS CHAPTER WILL DEAL exclusively with the patient who presents himself for surgery for cosmetic reasons. Cosmetic operations are always elective and rarely, if ever, endanger the life of the patient. There may be associated disturbances in function which will also be benefited by surgery. However, these improvements of function are only incidental to the patient's main concern, which is improvement of appearance. It is clear even from superficial consideration that the psychological problems with which one is confronted are quite different from those encountered in other surgical patients.

The plastic surgeon is often warned, "Beware of the patient who comes to you for psychiatric reasons." This injunction is not very weighty since, with few exceptions, all patients who come for cosmetic surgery are, in effect, psychiatric patients. They are at the very least more or less anxious, depressed and obsessively preoccupied with themselves. With these as presenting symptoms they are unequivocally in the psychiatrist's domain in spite of the fact that they turn to the plastic surgeon for relief.

THE PSYCHIATRIC SYNDROME OF THE PLASTIC SURGERY PATIENT

Psychiatric study of these patients reveals a broad diagnostic spectrum ranging from relatively mild psychoneurotic reactions, at one extreme, to

* Cases are from the Psychiatric Service, Mount Sinai Hospital, N. Y.

overt schizophrenia with delusions and hallucinations, at the other. What these patients have in common is a large element of narcissism which contributes significantly to the total clinical picture.

This was well illustrated in a large number of rhinoplasty patients who displayed with great regularity a striking constellation of symptoms.[8] These patients, as a group, believed that people look down upon them because of their appearance. They were shy and seclusive. In social situations they suffered from considerable anxiety. They would go through special maneuvers to avoid presenting to others what they regarded to be the unfavorable view of their face (usually the profile). This would give rise to a certain awkwardness of bearing. They would often develop peculiar mannerisms with the hand for the purpose of hiding the nose during conversations. They were never able to apply their attention fully to any situation since an important part of the attention would be distracted laterally. This distracted manner would communicate itself to others as an attitude of boredom or unfriendliness, which would in turn elicit correspondingly rejecting attitudes from the environment. Because of the conviction that they were physically unattractive these patients would dress in a self-effacing manner. Women would wear only the plainest clothes. They would wear one style of hat for years in the conviction that only the style in question blended with their nose. For the same reason they would confine themselves to a single type of hair arrangement. They would be unable to enjoy a movie or a play because of the feeling throughout the performance that they were being critically scrutinized by their escort. Many would suffer work disturbances. Thus, students complained that they could not concentrate on their reading when working in a library or classroom. Salesgirls, teachers, secretaries, entertainers in this series complained that the quality of their work suffered because of their inability to apply to their work their undivided attention.

Although the foregoing observations were made primarily on rhinoplasty cases, similar phenomena were observed in patients who presented themselves for other types of cosmetic surgery—"flop ears," harelip and disfiguring facial scars, for example. One man with a rather sinister looking facial scar and another whose face was given a strikingly brutal appearance by a fractured nose complained that people would frequently react to them with fright or hostility. They reported that people seemed to expect violent behavior from them and often maneuvered them into unlooked for altercations. Purely on the basis of his fierce appearance one of these patients was persuaded to become a professional prizefighter, a career for which he was most unsuited and which to his own good fortune he soon gave up. Other patients have reacted to such disfigurements with criminal careers. Nicknames referring to facial disfigurements, such as "monkey face," "one-eared Dago," "fish face," "dog ears," etc., are not infrequently encountered among delinquents and criminals.[10]

In addition to facial disfigurements one encounters cases calling for cosmetic surgery elsewhere on the body. Deformities of the genitalia, whether congenital, such as hypospadias, epispadias and undescended testicles or acquired as a result of trauma, have a profound effect upon the emotional life of the individual. Hypertrophic breasts are not uncommon offenders. A simple lipoma on the back may cause a young man to dread disrobing in a gymnasium. Congenital deformities of the hands or feet, such as webbing or the presence of supernumerary digits, can occasion severe emotional trauma. Improvement of a limping gait or strabismus is often as important as a cosmetic measure as it is from a functional point of view. The obese patient and the patient with malocclusion may show psychological evidences of their physical deformities.

What these patients all develop is a more or less severe constriction of the personality. They are constricted in their bodily movements, in the flow of their attention, in their capacity to relate warmly to other human beings and in their capacity to concentrate on their work. This contributes significantly to the general psychiatric picture which the plastic surgery patient presents. However, it is repeated, the diagnostic categories and the severity of the problems involved vary from case to case.

The Immediate Effects of Plastic Surgery

When the cosmetic surgical procedure has been carried out satisfactorily the patient's immediate reaction is, with rare exception, one of elation. There is a rapid reorganization in the patient's mental image of himself. In a matter of weeks following the operation patients no longer clearly recall what they looked like prior to surgery. They express surprise at their appearance when they look at old photographs. With this change the preoccupation with the former physical defect disappears too. The former sense of self-dissatisfaction is replaced by a feeling of pleasure. They no longer feel that people are looking at them except possibly in admiration. The inferiority feelings are replaced by feelings of self-confidence. In social situations the patient becomes aware of a hitherto undiscovered sense of physical freedom. Anxiety and awkwardness diminish. Patients display new warmth in their social contacts. Female patients, after rhinoplasty, indulge in experiments of dress and haircomb which result in an over-all heightening of their self-confidence, on the one hand, and in their actual physical desirability to the environment, on the other. Several of our patients found themselves precipitated into marriage (with varying results, to be discussed subsequently) in a matter of months following the operation. Improved level of employment was often seen. Previously ineffective people sometimes found themselves in positions of leadership in their social organizations as an immediate sequel to the operation.

THE LONG-TERM EFFECTS OF PLASTIC SURGERY

Many patients were carried by their initial reaction into depths for which they were psychologically unprepared. Sexual situations predominated in this regard. As a result, a period of reaction would set in. The patient would gradually work out a level of adjustment which lay somewhere between the preoperative state of maladjustment and the initial postoperative period of enthusiasm. But some advance in the level of adjustment was maintained in a surprising number of cases. The following case histories are instructive.

Case 1. A. B., a 31-year-old married woman had a rhinoplasty performed at the age of 21 because of a somewhat excessively developed fleshy nasal tip. The defect was not a great one, and members of her family opposed the operation. However, the patient was deeply self-conscious about it. She felt it made her look old beyond her years, and because of this "old feeling" she felt "robbed of her youth." In social situations she protected her profile from the view of those about her. A brother, three years younger than herself, was an extremely handsome boy and was definitely favored by both parents. She describes herself as having been in general an unhappy child with a hostile attitude towards her mother.

After the operation a striking change occurred in the patient. She says, "I felt free. I felt young. I felt like an adolescent. It changed my personality from that of a sober person to that of an exuberant one. I became capable of having fun unself-consciously." She experimented in dresses, hats and hair arrangements, and emerged considerably changed in her overall physical appearance. Then she started to have trouble. Whereas men used to leave her to herself they began to make advances. She found that her high spirits and seductive dress caused men to force intimacies upon her that repelled and frightened her. She said, "It caused me to be more careful about how I dressed and what I said. I had to tone down, but am still much more relaxed and buoyant in my spirits than I used to be."

One year after the operation she entered upon a very congenial marriage which, although childless, has gone on successfully for nine years. Perhaps, as shall be seen later, we should say that it has gone on successfully *because* it has been childless. During periods of excessive responsibility she develops "nervous indigestion." Her husband describes her as an excessively sensitive person who has few close friends. He has made it possible for her to lead a rather sheltered life. She would probably benefit from psychotherapy. However, she feels too content with the status quo to make the necessary effort.

Case 2. C. D., a 35-year-old married woman had a rhinoplasty at 19 years of age. From early adolescence she had deep inferiority feelings which she related to the excessive size of her nose. She developed the usual syndrome of social withdrawal and protection of her profile. After the operation she was transformed. She says, "I felt as if a great burden had been taken away. I wasn't ashamed anymore. I mingled with people in the community freely and happily." Socially, the patient became aggressive and self-confident. Her marriage five years after the operation threw her into a series of personal complications. She found herself in an unfamiliar social milieu which brought out many of her old inferiority feelings. The problem of motherhood (she had three children) added to her inferiority feelings. She never told her husband of her nasal plastic. She developed the fear that her secret would be exposed in the noses of her children. This fear, incidentally, was encountered in one other case in my series. In this setting she became anxious and depressed. In treatment she gained considerable understanding of some of the origins of her inferiority feelings. She left treatment much improved.

The degree to which a patient slips back after the initial stage of improvement depends on many factors, some of which are accidental. Some of our patients, for example, entered upon congenial marriages during this first stage, went on to have children and to experience the satisfactions of motherhood, and over a period of years underwent a process of progressive maturation. More frequently the advent of children disrupted what had been an apparently satisfactory psychological adjustment up to that time. However, in one of our patients, plastic surgery improved her performance as a mother.

Case 3. This patient, age 32, was a shy unhappy housewife obsessed with inferiority feelings about her oversized nose. Her daughter, age 10, developed a rather severe behavior disorder because of the patient's rejecting attitude. The latter was based, in part, on the patient's competitiveness with this daughter who was a pretty child. Following rhinoplasty there was a change in the mother's behavior. She became cheerful and tireless. The change in the attitude towards her daughter was so striking that the child guidance department commented on it spontaneously and expressed the feeling that this change facilitated their work with the child. The patient took an active role in her parent-teacher organization and rapidly assumed a place of leadership. When last seen, about a year after the operation, she was somewhat discouraged as a result of financial difficulties and a disagreeable housing situation. However, she maintained the largest part of her early improvement.

How Plastic Surgery Helps

In order to understand how plastic surgery is capable of effecting any lasting psychological changes it is necessary to refer to three basic concepts:

1. The body image
2. The unconscious
3. Psychic energy

We turn first to the body image. This is a concept which was formulated by Schilder.[12] According to this idea each one of us carries about a mental image of his own appearance. Normally this image is a pleasing one. When it is not personally pleasing, the individual is more or less ill from a psychiatric point of view.

The body image is based on two sets of factors. First, are our actual sensory experiences concerning the body; what we actually see and feel concerning ourselves, and what we perceive of ourselves in the reactions of others. For example, the child who is teased by his companions because of some disfigurement will necessarily tend to have a different image of himself than the child who is favored with admiration and affection. The perceptual impressions of early childhood are the most powerful factors in helping a child to decide what sex he belongs to. The childhood visual discovery of the physical difference between the sexes has profound and far-reaching implications in the subsequent psychological development of the individual, implications which are part of the basic structure of psychoanalytic psychology.[2, 3] There is a second group of factors which enters into the formation of the body image; psychological factors which are an outgrowth of personal emotional experiences. The disfigured child who is adored by its mother will tend to develop a more pleasing body image than the comely child who is rejected. The girl who grows up wishing she were a boy, and the boy who grows up wishing to be a girl will tend to develop psychological distortions of the body image in response to wishful thinking, psychological distortions of great tenacity most difficult to remove by means of psychotherapy.[4] Men frequently grow up with a deep feeling of inferiority concerning the appearance of their penis, which is primarily the result of psychological experiences in early childhood.

These complicated psychological factors are in the long run the most important ones in determining the "structure" of the body image. Certainly, we encounter people every day who have achieved happiness in spite of severe physical limitations, and we have all seen neurotics whose debased estimate of themselves is strongly out of keeping with their potentialities or actual achievements. However, the great importance of these purely psychological factors should not lead us to overlook the importance of contemporary physical reality. Modifications in actual appearance of the body can cause rapid and sometimes far-reaching changes in the body image. And by causing changes in the body image, surgical improvement in the appearance of the body can be of psychotherapeutic importance.

The following quotation from Schilder[12] is pertinent. "We should not underrate the importance of actual beauty and ugliness in human life. Beauty can be a promise of complete satisfaction and can lead to this satisfaction. Our own beauty or ugliness will not only figure in the image we get about ourselves, but will also figure in the image others build up about us and which will be taken back again into ourselves. The body image is the result of social life. Beauty and ugliness are certainly not phenomena in the single individual, but are social phenomena of the utmost importance. They regulate the sex activities in human relations, and not only the manifest heterosexual activities, but also the (latent) homosexual ones, which are so important for the social structure. . . . Our own body image, and the body images of others, their beauty and ugliness, thus become the basis for our sexual and social activities."

During World War II I questioned several infantrymen, recently returned from active combat duty, concerning what type of physical injury they feared most. A surprising number answered that they feared mutilating injuries of the face most of all.[9] Further inquiry indicated that the major concern of these men was not only the loss of desirability to the opposite sex which would result from such mutilation, but also the isolation from fellowmen in general which would ensue if the mutilation were horrible enough. It is noteworthy that more men expressed concern over facial mutilation than over direct injury to the genitalia.

Because the face is constantly exposed to society, disfigurements of the face are of particular psychological importance. And the nose, as the most conspicuous structure on the face, is of particular importance in this regard. Furthermore, there are certain social factors which make the nose a matter of special concern to the plastic surgeon. Where anti-Semitism and xenophobia are widespread (among our patients were several Spaniards, Italians and Greeks) specific nasal configurations add to feelings of loneliness and rejection in certain susceptible individuals. Alteration of the features in the direction of greater conformity to the social average and in keeping with certain culturally determined esthetic norms helps overcome this sense of "not belonging."

Probably of greatest importance is the fact that the nose is an organ with secondary sexual characteristics. At puberty there begins a period of increased nasal growth[7] which continues through adolescence. The "cute," relatively bridgeless nose of childhood becomes transformed into a structure which is capable of being exquisitely feminine or clearly masculine in its contours and proportions. Ideally, this final product blends harmoniously with the rest of the body. However, this does not always occur. A large, masculine-looking nose can mar the beauty of an otherwise lovely woman. An otherwise virile-looking man can be made to look ridiculous by an oversized nose or a disproportionately small one. Very frequently nasal deformities which are congenital or the result of fractures in early childhood are not at all noticeable prior to the period of accelerated nasal growth which occurs at puberty. It is for this reason that psychological disturbances centering about the nose rarely begin before puberty. In patients in whom there already exists a distortion in the body image based on difficulties in sexual identification, a deformity in the nose which appears at puberty can be a critically disturbing force, complicating the already difficult sexual problems of this period. Two of our female patients described their feelings in almost identical words, "There's nothing wrong with the shape of this nose," they said, "provided it were on a man." One of our male patients with strong homosexual leanings drew a picture with the statement, "This is how I'd like to look after the operation." What he drew was the profile of a girl! The sexual implications of the changes effected by rhinoplasty were most strikingly evident in our female patients in whom a satisfactory cosmetic result was followed by thoroughgoing changes in the patient in the direction of increased femininity; changes involving haircomb, speech and general deportment. One of our male patients had a dread of physical conflict from early adolescence. He felt that his oversized nose was too provocative a target to others. As a result he was overanxious to avoid situations that might result in fist fights. He did not participate in rough sports. After the operation there was a considerable improvement in his self-confidence. He spoke with more assurance. He felt more at ease in the company of other men. He got a better paying job. In short, he acted in a more manly fashion.

For many psychiatric reasons rhinoplasty was more apt to be successful in women than in men. First of all, preoccupation with physical appearance is more normal in the psychology of the female than it is in that of the male.[1] The man who is so disturbed by his appearance that he comes for rhinoplasty is more likely to be severely ill to start with than is his female counterpart. Secondly, the basic normal role of the female is more frequently a passive one.[1] Her goal is to be admired and loved. Provided she does not develop too much anxiety in response to the normally aggressive advances of the male she will achieve this goal without too much difficulty. As will be presently elaborated, with the onset of motherhood and the need to assume a more active loving role with respect to her offsprings, she may develop difficulties.

The problem is more complicated in the case of the man. An active aggressive role is demanded of him from the very outset. Rhinoplasty may help him to achieve a more normal, active attitude by improving his self-esteem. However, the overall psychological effects of rhinoplasty are less satisfactory in the case of the male.

Extensive personal experience with rhinoplasty patients justified, I believe, detailed discussion of the concept of the body image in this group of patients. However, it is quite clear that the same general principles apply in plastic surgery problems involving other parts of the body.

We turn next to the concept of "The Unconscious." It is not possible to understand many of the reactions of plastic surgery patients unless one realizes that in addition to the conscious part of the mind there is also an unconscious part, "The Unconscious." The latter is much the larger. In fact, the mind has been compared to an iceberg in which the small part that we see above the water is the conscious mind, and the vast unseen mass that floats below the surface of the water, the unconscious. The contents of the unconscious are unknown to the patient. We known of its existence in various ways, through experiments with hypnotism, the study of dreams and the symptoms of mental disease. Most of all, we know about the contents of the unconscious by the method of psychoanalysis. By this method one endeavors to make known to the patient the contents of his unconscious for the purpose of relieving him of his symptoms.

In the discussion of the body image we confined ourselves primarily to the conscious reality factors involved, to what we called "contemporary physical reality." For example, the secondary sexual characteristics of the nose can be regarded as part of contemporary physical reality. However, in the unconscious the fact that the nose is an orifice and is subject to bleeding gives it a special symbolic feminine significance. Because the turbinates have erectile tissue which are responsive to certain emotional states, the inner nose has in addition special masculine significance.[11] Because the nose is an organ of smell it plays an important role in the child's interest in its bowels, which in turn has great significance for the subsequent structure of the character of the adult.[5] For all these reasons, instrumentation of the nose by the plastic surgeon may have unexpectedly stormy psychological consequences, for example, paranoid reactions which are not understandable without referring to the unconsicous meanings involved. One patient had a satisfactory cosmetic result following rhinoplasty but discovered to his horror that the bridge of his nose was no longer broad enough to support his glasses. The now excessively small bridge became a symbol, unconsciously, for his penis which he felt for many years was excessively small, a symbol of his shame for all the world to see. The intensity of this man's anguish and his dissatisfaction with the surgical result were certainly not understandable by referring to conscious factors only. A young woman felt guilty and depressed following a sexual indiscretion. She became obsessed with the feeling that a minor deviation in the bridge of her nose indicated to the world her sinfulness. She reacted to the painful surgical procedure as to a punishment, and emerged from the operation minus the small nasal defect and with a vast sense of mental relief as if having expiated a sin. We have no follow-up on this patient, and I do not know how long her state of mental well being lasted. With this sort of "magical" result, one would anticipate that the psychiatric prognosis in this case is not good. However, the main point at this time is that the degree of her mental relief from this minor corrective procedure could not be explained by reference to conscious factors alone. Sometimes a woman comes for plastic surgery with deep unconscious longings to be a man. If in her unconscious she hopes to secure a penis from the operation, her disappointment with the procedure, no matter what the cosmetic result, is inevitable and understandable.

Case 4. S. P., a 28-year-old woman, had a rhinoplasty at the age of 19. She was a painfully shy individual, given to serious, scholarly pursuits. In this respect she resembled her father, as contrasted to her more vivacious sister who resembled the mother. After the operation she stated with manifest displeasure that her nose still resembled her father's. In spite of her expressed dissatisfaction she became more active socially. However, symptoms of agoraphobia appeared for the first time. After a long period of courtship and considerable indecision she got married. Her agoraphobic symptoms increased, and when she had a child two years later these symptoms became so bad that she became completely confined to her home. Psychotherapy over a period of several months produced no improvement. Material which emerged during the period of treatment revealed an almost complete inability to accept herself as a woman. She identified herself either with her child or with her father. In this case the inability to accept the adult feminine role was so great that rhinoplasty was of no avail. In fact, this can be regarded as one of the few cases I have seen in which rhinoplasty made the patient worse by forcibly thrusting upon her an adult feminine role which was unacceptable to her.

Further observations on the role of the unconscious in the formation of the body image are to be found in an illuminating paper by Friedman.[6]

The concept of psychic energy. When we ask a patient about his nose several months post-rhinoplasty, a very frequent response is, "My nose? Good gracious, I never think of my nose any more!" If the patient is no longer preoccupied with his nose it can only mean that he is free to think of other things. It is as if the operation in this way makes available a supply of energy to the individual for further efforts at adjustment. Of course, basic conflicts in life are not solved by plastic surgery, but the manner in which the individual deals with these conflicts is very often changed as a result of the operation. Morbid mental mechanisms tending to draw the individual away from reality are often replaced by others which are more benign and which make possible an improved contact with reality. The patient may need psychiatric help at this point. However, the changes effected by plastic surgery will often facilitate psychotherapy.

This release of "psychic energy" does not always result in the happy course just outlined. Sometimes the new channels of action opened to the patient are frightening to him. This new access of energy may lead, not to new solutions of conflicts, but to overwhelming anxiety. Such patients may develop sleep disturbances. Two rhinoplasty patients stated that they could not sleep for fear they would "accidentally" injure their nose during sleep. In this fear they were expressing a hostility towards the altered nose. In three other cases this hostility resulted in actual injuries as a result of which the operated nose was deformed again by fracture.

CONTRAINDICATIONS TO RHINOPLASTY

Implicit in the foregoing discussion of the possible adverse effects of plastic surgery is the fact that a cosmetic deformity may be utilized by a patient in a psychological mechanism of defense, and that with the surgical removal of the deformity a vital psychological process may be undermined.

In certain rigid individuals the removal of a previous system of defense is *not* followed by the evolution of new defenses, and as a result the ego is left defenseless. It becomes flooded with unmanageable anxiety, and in the resultant psychological turmoil, a malignant psychosis may emerge. While this complication undoubtedly occurs from time to time, it was striking how rarely it was encountered in actuality.

Case 5. One patient developed an acute schizophrenic psychosis two days before a projected rhinoplasty. She had toyed for years with the idea of having a nasal plastic, and several times in the past she had cancelled her appointment for surgery at the last moment. She was a withdrawn unmarried woman of 32 given to many eccentricities of behavior. This patient apparently had a chronic schizophrenic psychosis of many years duration that erupted into an acute phase prior to her last appointment with the surgeon. Obviously, surgical alteration of the nose did not precipitate the psychosis.

Case 6. A young woman described by Goldman,[7] a concert violinst, presented herself for a rhinoplasty. The surgeon refused to operate because he felt she was too disturbed psychiatrically at the time of the first consultation. Several months later this young woman, without having been operated on, developed an acute psychosis for which she had to be hospitalized. If surgery had been carried out, the acute psychosis would have been attributed to the operation. It is necessary, therefore, to consider the natural history of the psychotic process itself before evaluating the specific role of the surgical intervention.

It is fortunate indeed that psychosis is a rare complication of plastic surgery since "schizoid" personality changes are so frequently encountered in these narcissistic patients. Weeding out the pre-psychotic personalities may not always be easy. The following case histories show how wide a margin of safety is actually present as far as psychiatric complications are concerned.

Case 7. M. L., a 35-year-old single automobile mechanic, presented himself for rhinoplasty because of a nasal deformity due to an old fracture. The surgeon was so impressed with his bizarre behavior that he insisted on psychiatric consultation. The patient was a markedly withdrawn individual with few friends or social interests. He complained to the psychiatrist of physical weakness, sexual impotence and a feeling that girls regarded him with contempt. He was depressed and preoccupied with his nasal deformity. He was unable to work. Two months of intensive psychotherapy produced no change and he was given a course of nine electroshock treatments. Following this he improved considerably as far as his depression and complaints of physical weakness were concerned, and he was able to return to his work. However, he continued his demands for rhinoplasty and after much hesitation this was carried out. The operative result was good and patient was pleased. He started going out with a girl. Six months later he was still sexually impotent and inadequate. However, he continued at his work and maintained the improvement in his social adjustment.

Case 8. A. M., a 16-year-old schoolboy, was brought for psychiatric treatment because of unreality feelings, inability to concentrate on his schoolwork because of homosexual fantasies and because of feelings that people were laughing at him because of his ugly nose. Several surgeons had refused him rhinoplasty because of the severity of his psychiatric difficulties. After a year of psychotherapy he showed some improvement in his general adjustment. Because of his continued insistence, rhinoplasty was carried out. His initial reaction was one of euphoria. He said, "Wait till I get back to school. I will be admired by everyone." On return to school he found little change in the attitude of his schoolmates. He soon lapsed into his preoperative schizoid state. He no longer discussed his nose; instead he blamed his sallow complexion for his social difficulties. Interestingly enough, during the ensuing two years the patient started a homosexual relationship which he himself interpreted as a sign of psychiatric improvement. Along with this overt expression of his homosexual impulses there was an improvement in his schoolwork. He entered college and at this time is doing fairly well.

Case 9. L. P., age 16, complained of a burning sensation in the eyes, which was without evident organic basis. He was unable to make friends. He suffered from tormenting doubts about everything. He was unable to hold a job. He blamed all his difficulties on the fact that his nose looked Semitic. Rhinoplasty produced no change in the patient's behavior. However, he stated that following the operation he had a feeling of inner contentment which he lacked before. Two years later he was referred for psychiatric treatment. Psychotherapy brought out the fact that there was a strong tendency in the patient to identify himself with women. He was treated on several occasions for a chronic sinus infection. In his fantasies the nasal probing of the surgeon represented sexual intercourse in which the patient played the feminine role. He has had several nose bleeds which in his fantasies represented menstruation. He has improved somewhat in his social adjustment, although he continues to be a basically lonely, inadequate person.

Case 10. L. S., a 21-year-old unmarried woman, with a somewhat prominent nose, presented herself for psychotherapy in a state of anxiety and depression. These symptoms arose during a homosexual relationship with an older woman. During treatment she brought out marked feelings of inferiority as a woman and expressed the belief that she was incapable of attracting a man. At the end of a year of treatment she decided she wanted to have a nasal plastic, stating that this procedure would make her a woman. The result was satisfactory from a cosmetic standpoint. The transformation was even more striking from a psychiatric point of view. Whereas she had previously dressed in an unattractive rather juvenile fashion, she now took to a more strikingly feminine style of dress. She started using cosmetics for the first time. She entered college, achieved an excellent scholastic record, and participated normally in heterosexual social activities. She is engaged to be married at this time. She still suffers from periods of anxiety and it was the recommendation of the psychiatrist who treated her that she consolidate her gains by entering upon a psychoanalysis.

Case 11. M. N., age 38, female, separated, had inferiority feelings from early childhood. She had few friends. She was irritable in her relationships with members of her family. She was subject to frequent episodes of mild depression. She attributed most of her difficulties to the fact that her nose was too large. She entered a hospital in 1941 for rhinoplasty, but at the last moment she became so terrified that the operation had to be cancelled. In 1942 she entered upon an uncongenial marriage. Six months later she developed pulmonary tuberculosis and had to go to a sanatorium. While she was in the hospital her husband deserted her, taking all her money with him. She became severely depressed at that time. She got well gradually over a period of a year. She attributed this improvement to Christian Science. She continued to be dissatisfied with her nose. Finally, in October 1947, she had a rhinoplasty done. She was very pleased with the result. She underwent a marked elevation of mood which was still present when she was examined psychiatrically one year postoperatively. She states that she has more confidence in herself and more happiness than she has ever felt. She goes out more frequently with men. She was able to work as a salesgirl without suffering from painful self-consciousness—an unprecedented accomplishment for her.

In each of the foregoing cases there was present a severe psychiatric problem. Rhinoplasty was carried out with trepidation. Yet the final outcome was not a harmful one. On the contrary, unanticipated psychiatric improvements occurred. These cases are not unusual and help to bring out the fact that cosmetic surgical procedures are not as hazardous as they are sometimes regarded to be. However, it may be stated as a fair warning that psychiatrically harmful results *are* encountered clinically, and surgery should not be done indiscriminately. Here, as elsewhere in the practice of medicine, the slogan should be "primum non nocere." Above all do not harm the patient! The surgeon should beware of the temptation to correct minimal asymmetries and deformities. Too frequently the surgeon sets out to correct a nasal asymmetry, for example, and ends up creating one even more disturbing to the patient.

A final word of warning should be said about the "repeater" patient. Whatever skill and discrimination are exercised in the selection of the patient who comes for a first operation, they must be even greater in considering the patient who has had previous plastic surgery. Some of the most distressing psychiatric complications were seen among patients who cajoled surgeon after surgeon into a succession of futile operations in search of a psychological will o' the wisp. There are indications for multiple interventions in plastic surgery; for example, when a bone graft resorbs, or when operations are carried out in several stages. However, the plastic surgeon will spare himself and his patient unnecessary grief by exercising particular caution in the case of the "repeater" patient.

PLASTIC SURGERY IN CHILDREN AND ADOLESCENTS

Although it is usually stated that physical deformities are not of psychological importance until the child goes to school and becomes the object of the jibes of his schoolmates, it is remarkable how early in life they can begin to play a role in the psychological development of the individual. Straith[15] describes several interesting examples of this. I quote from his paper. "Only recently a mother informed me that her daughter had become aware of her harelip when little more than one year of age, and on several occasions had been observed in the act of contemplating this deformity in the mirror and noting the effect of approximating the ununited parts with her fingers. This child, when operated upon at the age of 18 months, had already gained a painful impression of her abnormality. Another child (age not given) with a double harelip always lifted the bed clothes to cover its face when persons entered the room. A 6-year-old child with a single harelip covered her face or secluded herself at the approach of strangers." A 7-year-old girl with "flop ears" was an anxious, depressed youngster. Psychotherapy, which was in progress at the time of the operation, proceeded much more effectively after the child was relieved of this physical defect.

What these cases emphasize is the fact that cosmetic abnormalities should be rapaired as soon as it is surgically feasible to do so. Adolescence is traditionally a time of storm and stress. Added to the emotional tensions and increased consciousness of self which characterize this period there are also special growth phenomena, which have already been alluded to. As a result of this combination of circumstances, hitherto subclinical malformations may become psychiatrically symptomatic at this time. It has been my impression that the best psychiatric results in a group of adolescent girls who came for rhinoplasty were obtained in those in whom the actual pubertal nasal growth was considerable and the preceding neurotic factors relatively small.[8] In a study of inadequacies of masculine physique as a factor in personality development of adolescent boys, Schonfeld[13] reported that plastic surgery was able to make a significant contribution in solving some of the emotional problems of this group. He stated, "Plastic surgery was found to be helpful in some cases of gynecomastia which persisted after puberty was fully developed. . . . The plastic surgeon was also of great help in building up the self-esteem of some of our boys by removing disfiguring scars and by correcting nasal deformities after the establishment of puberty. The orthodontist contributed to the relief of anxieties through correction of dental deformities. The cooperation of the surgeon and the urologist was useful in cases which required correction of cryptorchidism through orchidopexy."

Plastic Surgery and Criminology

In this brief section I wish to call attention to an interesting report by Pick.[10] In it he states, "The application of the resources of plastic surgery to criminology is an interesting departure from the conventional perspective of surgery." And one might add to this—"and from the conventional perspective of criminology." Over a period of ten years Pick operated on a total of 376 inmates in a state penal institution. He operated for a variety of conditions, congenital and acquired, involving almost all parts of the body for a total of 663 operations. Striking improvements in behavior were observed during the period of incarceration. The rate of recidivism among these men following liberation was much below the expected rate. The report admittedly is a preliminary one. "The ultimate sociologic evaluation of the project must await certain official statistics and developments in the future."[2]

PLASTIC SURGERY AS AN ADJUVANT TO PSYCHOTHERAPY

The value of plastic surgery as a psychotherapeutic procedure is an important, although, limited one. What it does in certain favorable cases is to initiate a chain reaction in the individual's social relationships which has the effect of hastening the process of emotional maturation. Thus, a girl who has been excessively dependent on her mother may become less so as her social activities are expanded. When the companionship secured in these circumstances is congenial the patient makes still further gains in her emotional development. Successful marriage and improved function as a wife and mother may emerge as an end result in such a chain of events. However, it frequently happens that plastic surgery by itself is not enough. Indeed, starting with the fact that almost all plastic surgery patients are psychiatric patients it would be reasonable, if not imperative, to make direct psychiatric assistance available to all patients undergoing plastic surgery. They should be warned preoperatively that the psychological gains which the operation will secure may bring new psychological problems in its wake. The infrequency with which patients are made worse by plastic surgery should embolden psychiatrists to use plastic surgery as an adjuvant to their psychological methods of therapy in cases where the patient is harassed by a correctible physical deformity. Many patients will require deep and prolonged psychotherapy to bring them to the maximum level of happiness and effectiveness. But in these cases, too, it is probably correct to say that plastic surgery will have made an important contribution in that the psychological defenses which the patient develops postoperatively are, in general, more accessible psychotherapeutically than those which were employed preoperatively.

In our discussion of children and adolescents we indicated the great potential usefulness of plastic surgery in dealing with the emotional problems of these earlier age groups. We might add, at this point, that it is in these groups in particular that the psychological advantages of plastic surgery stand the greatest chance of being of lasting value.

Since plastic surgery is part of psychotherapy, it is to be expected that plastic surgeon and psychiatrist will work in closer liaison in the future and that improved psychotherapeutic results and gains in psychotherapeutic theory will be the consequence of this cooperation.

BIBLIOGRAPHY

1. Deutsch, H.: Psychology of Women. New York, Grune & Stratton, 1944 (Vol. I); 1945 (Vol. II).

2. Freud, S.: The sexual theories of children *In*: Collected Papers. London, Hogarth Press, 1942, Vol. II.

3. ———: Some psychological consequences of the anatomical distinction between the sexes. Ibid, Vol. V.

4. ———: Analysis terminable and interminable. Ibid, Vol. V.

5. ———: Character and anal erotism. Ibid, Vol. II.

6. Friedman, P.: The nose: Some psychological reflections. American Imago. *8:* 337, 1951.

7. Goldman, I. B.: Personal communication.

8. Linn, L. and Goldman, I. B.: Psychiatric observations concerning rhinoplasty. Psychosom. Med. *11:* 307–314, 1949.

9. Noble, D., Roudebush, M. E. and Price, D.: Studies of Korean war casualties. Part I: Psychiatric manifestations in wounded men. Am. J. Psychiat. *108:* 495, 1952.

10. Pick, J. F.: Ten years of plastic surgery in a penal institution: Preliminary report, J. Internat. Coll. Surgeons. *11:* 315–319, 1948.

11. Saul, L. J.: The feminine significance of the nose. Psychoanalytic Quart. *17:* 51, 1948.

12. Schilder, P.: The Image and Appearance of the Human Body. Psyche Monographs #4. London, Kegan, Paul, French, Trubner & Co., 1935.

13. Schonfeld, W. A.: Inadequate masculine physique as a factor in personality development of adolescent boys. Psychosom. Med. *12:* 49–54, 1950.

14. Straith, C. L. and DeKlein, E. H.: Plastic surgery in children. J.A.M.A. *111:* 2365, 1938.

15. ———: Plastic surgery; its psychological aspects. J. Michigan M. Soc. *31:* 13–18. 1932.

CHAPTER 7

Psychiatric Implications in Gynecology and Obstetrics

STEPHANIE HAAS, M.D.

Dr. Haas received her M.D. from the University of Prague Medical School and had her postgraduate training in gynecology and obstetrics at the University of Vienna (Frauenklinik Kermauner). Later she was on the gynecologic staff at S.C Child's Hospital, Wiedner Hospital and Rudolph's Hospital, Vienna.

Since 1940, Dr. Haas has been associated with the Gynecologic Clinic, Mount Sinai Hospital, New York, as well as with the Gynecologic-Obstetric Clinic of Sydenham Hospital, New York. In private practice for the past two decades, she has practiced her specialty in close association with psychiatrists and psychoanalysts.

OF ALL THE MEDICAL DISCIPLINES, gynecology was the first to deal with psychosomatic medicine. Hippocrates and Galen recognized the connection between diseases of the womb and the emotional disturbances of women. Indeed, the term *hysteria*, deriving from the Greek, *hysteros* (meaning womb), still testifies to their acuity. As late as the end of the 19th century, pathology of the womb or the ovaries, was still assumed to be the cause of mental or emotional disorders.

Moebius, in 1892, was the first to claim that changes in the body which result from mental processes are hysterical. Kroenig, in 1902, according to Halban,[9] first recognized the psychogenic basis of gynecologic symptoms such as prolaps sensations, pruritus, amenorrhea and menorrhagia. He advised enlightment and clarification of the patient's misconceptions about physiologic processes, together with suggestion therapy. He claimed that the success of such suggestion therapy depended on whether or not the physician had a strong and impressive personality.

When Strassman, in 1903, drew attention to Freud's work, a new era began. Freud's contributions in the field of psychological processes illuminated many hitherto inaccessible problems and gynecology, together with all other branches of medicine, was to profit by these discoveries.

VAGINAL EXAMINATION

Regardless of the age at which it occurs, the first gynecologic examination is unquestionably of greater significance to a patient than any other physical examination. Children and adolescent girls are often subjected to such an examination because of vaginal discharge or if some suspicion of malformation is in question. Usually it is the mother and not the girl who is concerned about the symptomatology. In spite of careful preparation by the mother, as well as by the physician, the genital examination of a child is a highly traumatic experience, which is often met with the greatest opposition.

The genitals play a particularly important role in the child's mind. They are protected by the sense of shame and any interference with this attitude encounters resistance and may produce an emotional reaction sufficiently violent to give rise to profound disturbances. Though a girl at puberty or adolescence is already aware of the function of the genitals, the same reaction exists though to a lesser degree.

The defensive attitude against the examination conceals a fear of injury to the hymen or a vaguer fear of injury to the genitals, or the dread that some abnormality may be discovered. The examination is often felt to be a punishment for forbidden sexual activities (masturbation).

It is, therefore, obvious that a vaginal or rectal examination should be avoided at this early age unless there are imperative reasons for doing so. No matter how carefully the situation is handled it still may be a traumatizing experience.

The situation is altogether different with the adult girl who is seeking premarital advice. She, too, is fearful of the results, whether "everything is normal" and whether she will be able to have children. These patients usually try to conceal their fears and try to appear as fully adult women, especially if this is their first attempt at becoming independent. The relief is great if no pathology is found. Conscious and unconsicous fantasies are involved, e.g., fear of discovery of previous masturbation or imagined damage from it. These fears are the more readily activated since it is the first time (since childhood games) that the girl exposes herself to close inspection. To the child or young girl, the concept of insertion is something painful which a man does to a woman. Therefore, this fear is intensified if insertion has to be done for the purpose of examination and instruments like a speculum have to be used.

Even adult women react to a gynecologic examination with anxiety, as to a threat of being injured. Fears are centered around the genitals to a much higher degree than any other part of the body. Moreover, to the adult woman the first vaginal examination may also have connotations, since it is the first time she exposes herself to anyone but her husband. In spite of the professional setting, the experience may have a sexual meaning to the patient and, therefore, have the meaning of the forbidden.

MENSTRUATION AND ITS DISTURBANCES

Probably the most frequent symptom the gynecologist meets is aberration of the normal menstrual flow. Symptoms of disturbed menstruation form a major part of a gynecologic practice. There are a few patients in whom no pathology can be found, and for whom our endocrinologic knowledge is of no benefit. For these patients, the great varieties of our therapeutic procedures are of no avail for they do not respond to medical treatment. In such cases, one must bear in mind that menstruation, more than any other function, can be disturbed by emotional influences.

The psychological implications of menstruation and its disorders can only be properly evaluated against the background of the maturational processes which take place at puberty.

It is the impact of the somatic development on the still immature personality which results in the characteristic imbalance of the adolescent. The social prohibition to gratifying sexual impulses at this age leads to a craving to emancipate from authority. This attitude of rebellion loosens the ties to parental figures before new and stable attachments have been formed. Therefore, fantasy life has to substitute for what is still unobtainable in reality and in turn tends to reactivate former childhood fears and prohibitions. Masturbational activities will often bring these underlying conflicts to a climax. The outcome will depend largely on the course of early psychosexual development, for sexual interest and playful sexual activities are exhibited long before somatic and psychobiologic maturation.

They start in earliest childhood and come to a premature climax at the age of five to six when they subside until they are reactivated by the onset of puberty. Childish curiosity leads to discovery of the differences in the sexes, to fantasies and, frequently, even to observations of adult sexual life. Theories on parental intercourse, pregnancy and delivery are developed. Since babies grow in the belly, the little girl may imagine that mother swallowed father's seeds and urine and will push out the baby like a bowel movement. The sight of little boys genitals arouses anxious thoughts and envy and hopes that her organ will also grow. The realization that this wish will not be fulfilled leads to ideas that she may have been harmed or punished for masturbation. But normally the little girl becomes reconciled to her supposed deficiency and proud that she will bear children in the future, like her mother.

Even though the menstrual bleeding mobilizes these early fears of genital injury, normal girls consciously desire their first menstruation. It is a symbol of growing up, a point of competition with schoolmates or older sister as well as the known prerequisite for bearing children. It is essential that the mother be the one to tell her daughter about menstruation before it occur. Even though an explanation of her anatomy and physiology will not resolve all the fears and anxieties of the girl who has had early psychosexual disturbances, it nevertheless alleviates at least those which are conscious. Since preoccupation with sex is prohibited, such a talk is in itself a helpful experience in sanctioning curiosity about the function. The mother's confidential discussion is a sign that she accepts the child's growing up and tends to decrease her daughter's fear of her. The mother's psychosexual adjustment, her attitude toward her own menstruation and, most of all, her relationship to the girl, are of great importance. The mother who is not emotionally disturbed will be able to spare her daughter conflicts from early childhood on. However, the girl can hardly escape also getting information from other sources. If patients occasionally tell us that their first menstruation took them by surprise, one is justified in suspecting a previous disturbance which caused the girl to refuse to take notice of her own knowledge on the subject. Such ignorance may result from earlier curiosity which has been repressed or out of fear and guilt because of previous erotic fantasies. The emotional motives responsible for rejecting knowledge also manifest themselves in other forms. It is not unusual for a girl to respond to the first menstruation with open fear and disgust, particularly when she has difficulty in accepting her feminine role, since normally the renunciation of earlier masculine wishes is supported by identification with the mother.

The impact of physiologic and emotional factors brought about by the menarche is then responsible for a great part of the pathology of menstruation. The first menstruation, which was so anxiously expected and proudly accepted, is often followed by disappointment. The girl realizes that it did not bring about basic changes in her situation within the family; she is not being granted more liberties nor other advantages which adults may enjoy. The first pride of growing up wears off rapidly and in neurotic personalities is followed by a tendency to fight against menstruation. Intensified sexual drive which directs more attention toward the genitals leads to a more extensive struggle against masturbation. Anxiety and guilt about masturbation may pave the way for dysmenorrhea. Another meaning of mensturation is being "unclean." It is looked upon as an excretory function without sphincter control and may awaken anxieties similar to those associated in childhood with accidents of sphincter control. Everything coming from the lower part of the body is "unclean."[3] The girl is burdened with the task of taking care of her bodily cleanliness and in addition her physical activities which she has been sharing with boys will be curbed. She may react to these new restrictions in either of two ways. They may intensify her maladjustments—or the tomboy type of girl may negate her menstruation by becoming more intensely competitive with boys in sports. In this way she can deny the fact of being a woman.

Dysmenorrhea is the most frequent psychosomatic response to these common conflicts and to all kinds of specific emotional problems which may arise during the formative years of puberty and adolescence. The mechanism of the condition is unknown. Although many theories were elaborated about the organic cause of dysmenorrhea, most of them did not prove to be correct.

Clinical experience substantiated that the individual pain threshold plays an important role. The high strung nervous individual's pain threshold will be lower than the one of the well adjusted woman. The widely discussed physical reasons are:[17]

1. *The mechanical obstruction due to sharp ante- or retroflexion of the uterus and/or pin point cervix.* This might hold true for a few of the cases; however, many women who reveal these signs don't suffer from dysmenorrhea and others who don't have sharp anteflexion or pin point cervix still suffer intensely.

2. *The recently more accepted view is based on hormonal disturbance, to some sort of inbalance between estrogenic hormone and progesterone.* It is known that dysmenorrhea occurs exclusively following ovulation and never in anovulatory bleedings. The pathway is still unclear—the more so because estrogenic hormone has been recognized as a normal stimulant for uterine contractility and progesterone as the inhibitant. It seems contradictory that in unovulatory bleeding in spite of excess estrogen and deficiency of progesterone the pain is absent.

3. *The nerve pathway via autonomic nervous system.* The presacral neurectomy does not alter the uterine contractility. Often it relieves the pain by blocking the afferent pathway from the uterus. However, even this operation does not always bring about the expected result. The mechanism of dysmenorrhea is unknown and it is still an open question to what extent cervical stenosis, the hormonal imbalance, or nervous hypersensitivity is caused by emotional disturbance.

I have not referred to the organic dysmenorrhea which occurs on the basis of tumors, inflammation, endometriosis, etc. However, it should be pointed out that the empirical observation that dysmenorrhea yields to medical, physical or hormonal treatment still does not prove that the cause of it was not emotional. There may be many reasons for giving up a symptom in response to a certain kind of treatment.

Benedek and Rubenstein[1] made extensive studies of the correlation between hormonal variations of the ovarian cycle and emotional manifestations. The state of ovarian function was established by the physiologist on daily vaginal smears and basal body temperature charts. These patients were being psychoanalyzed so that it was possible to make daily observations of their psychic manifestations, their actions, dreams, fantasies and experiences. When the two sets of data were compared later it was found that the charts coincided in indicating the various phases of the ovarian cycle. Ovulation could be diagnosed on the basis of emotional manifestations. During the follicle ripening phase of the menstrual cycle, the psychological material is dominated by heterosexual interest. According to the authors if this heterosexual desire does not find adequate gratification, it builds up tension even in normal personalities. In neurotic women the tension enhances the preexisting psychological conflict with intensification of neurotic symptoms. The heterosexual desire may reach another peak in some women during the last days of the luteal cycle and not infrequently even during the time of menstruation. Since this time is not suitable for sexual gratification, the frustration may lead to excessive states of tension, rejection of menstruation and extreme dysmenorrhea. The authors have concluded that estrogenic hormones characteristically influence psychodynamic processes related to the sexual life of the individual. Moreover, the reverse relationship also exists inasmuch as frustration and disappointment were observed in association with evidence of suppression of hormone production and delayed ovulation. Thus, critical emotional experiences can adversely affect the degree of ovarian secretion, which in turn is normally dependent on the gonadotropic activity of the adenohypophysis. One may surmise that emotional inhibition of adenohypophysial activity does not result in equal degree of suppression of gonadotropic hormones, since clinical pictures of psychogenic ovarian dysfunction range from menometrorrhagia to amenorrhea.

The physiologic processes of ovulation, corpus luteum formation and menstruation can be influenced by powerful emotional forces. Markee,[14] studying endometrial transplants in the anterior chamber of the eye, observed that fright causes reopening of the arterioles at the end of the period. Within 15 to 20 seconds they deliver blood which promptly clots. Loeser[13] studied women with histories of regular menstruation, each of whom after experiencing the emotional shock of the bombardment of London, missed her period. The endometrial biopsies showed an endometrium at the stage of development it would normally have reached at the time of shock, suggesting that the shock caused an immediate arrest of development by interrupting the release of pituitary hormones.

Pseudocyesis, shock and accidents were accepted as causative factors for amenorrhea in popular belief earlier than by physicians. It was frequently observed in college girls or in the enlisted women of the armed forces during the last war, that sudden environmental influences were often accompanied by amenorrhea. How far the war amenorrheas during the First World War and the amenorrheas in concentration camps during the last war were provoked merely on a nutritional basis has not been established with certainty. The war amenorrheas frequently subsided when the husband returned despite further worsening of the nutritional condition. Inmates of concentration camps usually started to menstruate exactly four weeks after their liberation, although there had been no particular change of their nutritional condition. At any time of sexual maturity, if the emotional impact of a sexual situation is sufficiently intense, it may cause delayed onset of menstruation or amenorrhea as it did following the first menstruation—when rejection of the feminine role or fear of menstruation because of unacceptable sexual desires, brought on these disturbances. Emotional stimuli can produce alterations in the neuroendocrine system, which result in disturbances in the menstrual cycle. On the other hand, by no means all disturbances originate from emotional stimuli. The impact of the sudden endocrine changes at puberty may also cause disturbances since a perfect integration of their functioning does not always take place immediately.

Hypothyroidism, which occurs so often in puberty and adolescence, leads not only to amenorrhea or menometrorrhagia but also to mental states which may simulate emotional disturbance. If thyroid medication is indicated and administered, all the symptoms may strikingly disappear. Menstruation may become regular and learning and working difficulties may greatly improve.

Premenstrual Symptoms

Premenstrual symptoms occur in the majority of women although to a varying degree. Many individuals, probably the well adjusted ones, do not suffer from them exceedingly and their discomfort may be minimal. However, some women become depressed, irritable and emotionally unstable. They complain of crying spells, insomnia, backache, bloatedness and engorgements of the breast. Premenstrual tension and dysmenorrhea occur only preceding ovulation, never accompany unovulatory bleedings or when ovulation is depressed, thus proving that the disturbed interplay between estrogenic and luteal hormone gives the first stimulus toward the disturbance. The complaints can be relieved symptomatically by medication, but the role and extent of emotional disturbance cannot be evaluated with precision. Psychoanalytic experience indicates that the premenstrual tension may go along with a flare-up of neurotic traits, which in turn may exert influence on the hormonal balance. Following successful analysis, excessive premenstrual tension or dysmenorrhea, as one symptom of neurotic manifestations may disappear or decrease to a minimum. The response to the onset of menstruation will depend on what it means to the patient. Quite often the flow after the tension is experienced as relief. Several authors report that their patients compared the tension and following relief of menstruation to pregnancy, labor and delivery. On the other hand, if the patient, either consciously or unconsciously, hoped for pregnancy, the depression will continue throughout the menstruation.

There have been various theories elaborated and experimental investigations made on this problem in regard to the systemic and local tissue changes due to sodium and water retention. Estrogens are made responsible for the sodium and resulting fluid retention in the tissues. The high concentration of estrogen might act on the hypersensitive vegetative nervous system. "Congestion fibrosis syndrome" was described by Taylor[22] as a clinical entity, causing pelvic symptoms and premenstrual tension. Thirty per cent of his observed patients had obvious psychiatric manifestations and 60 per cent at least one significant extragenital complaint. Most authors agree that the hormonal and chemical changes are not necessarily the primary cause of the tension and accept the probability of emotional imbalance leading to interference with pituitary gonadotropic function.

Premenstrual tension seems to increase in frequency and intensity in the late thirties or approaching menopause. This, and the fact that it mostly responds favorably to physical treatment, seems to indicate that decrease of hormonal function gives rise in this age group to the symptoms under discussion.

Throughout this chapter the attempt has been to give a rather brief survey of the interplay between emotional and physical factors which may be causative in the disturbances of menstruation. The strength of emotional factors is further confirmed by the frequency with which the onset of psychosis, the committing of a crime or suicidal attempt, coincides with menstruation.

LEUCORRHEA

Leucorrhea without underlying physical evidence was recognized about the beginning of the century as having an emotional basis. Masturbation, or masturbation fantasies may initiate the discharge which easily may become secondarily infected. Pelvic hypermia caused by unreleased tension in cases of frigidity might be another underlying psychological cause for intermittent or persistent vaginal discharge.[22]

There are, however, women complaining about leucorrhea in whom on examination hardly any increased secretion can be found. These patients apparently are preoccupied with their genital region which either may cause some additional secretion or renders them more sensitive to the normal amount of secretion. Not infrequently, to such patients, the vaginal discharge seems to symbolize something dirty. They behave as if they still feel like children and differentiate little between the various body openings.

Their reactions of disgust to their vaginal secretion can best be understood as deriving from the disgust which some children are imbued with by the parents with regard to their bowel function, in the course of cleanliness training. To other patients, the secretion seems to be related to masturbatory habits which they do not even dare to mention to the doctor, and which they secretly and wrongly consider of potentially great harm.

Occasionally one may observe in neurotic individuals who suffered from trichomonas or moniliasis, that although the infection subsided the symptom of leucorrhea still persists. This too can be explained on the basis of preoccupation with the genital region, the more so, since the treatment of this condition mostly consists of application of vaginal inserts for a long period of time. The patient forms a habit of manual contact with the genitals and, therefore, retains either the symptom or the preoccupation with the genitals.

Generally it can be stated that complaints of leucorrhea without underlying cause are getting rather infrequent. This is probably due to the improvement of the diagnostic and therapeutic measures recently achieved in treatment of the symptom.

PREGNANCY

Attitude Towards Pregnancy

The wish for pregnancy and motherhood is a normal and appropriate desire in the course of feminine development. The wish, however, occupies the female mind long before it is physiologically and socially possible of fulfillment. Pregnancy fantasies fill the psychic life of many girls from their early childhood and play an important role in shaping their attitude towards pregnancy up to the time when it becomes feasible. The fantasies contain not only the wish for pregnancy but they also have components of fear. These conflicting elements may manifest themselves alternately.

Some of the fantasies are unconscious and have their origin in the conceptions of early childhood. The popular phrase that the baby grows in the stomach leads to the notion that it got into the stomach like food. The little girl who lacks factual information about sex tends to consider pregnancy and delivery as something dangerous and dirty. Not infrequently she thinks that the child is born by bursting the abdomen or that it emerges from the rectum. Infantile guilt feelings and anxieties in connection with sex contribute to the terrifying character of these fantasies.

Every woman wonders to what extent pregnancy will interfere with her personal freedom and the pursuit of her personal life.[3] If the child represents to her a promise for the future she will be happy to take the interference in her stride. Another decisive factor is her relationship toward her husband and his attitude toward pregnancy. The realistic fears of pregnancy will be easier to overcome if she feels confidence in her husband's protective role and if the husband does not object to pregnancy. There are numerous realistic reasons for postponing pregnancy to offset the genuine desire for it, such as financial insecurity or the wish in newly wed couples to take time for better adjustment or for the proper spacing of children. The role of social influence on the attitudes toward pregnancy is considerable. The woman's prestige is increased within the family and in the community when she has children.[16] The immature, childish woman who fears pregnancy because of the responsibilities of motherhood nevertheless often wants to have children merely to compete for such prestige. Frequently they express their wish by saying that all their friends are pregnant and that is why they would like to become pregnant too. The wish for pregnancy is expressed in such a manner that one is reminded of the little girl who wants to collect dolls.

Often, however, there may be an unconscious conflict about the problem, and women who express a conscious desire may have unconscious anxiety and frequently inner prohibitions against motherhood. Some may even consciously reject parenthood. In either of these cases, if pregnancy occurs, the conflict will present itself psychologically and physically. The mother may suffer from physical symptoms, emotional disturbances or she may suffer from both.

The competitive attitude may be directed toward one particular person as a continuation of sibling rivalry. One of my patients who was being treated for sterility once came to my office highly disturbed saying: "Something terrible happened, my younger sister is pregnant." She was in continual competition with her sister who was far more successful than she and could not cope with the blow that her sister had again achieved what she had not. Her rejection of pregnancy may be rooted in childhood fantasies when strong sexual wishes and a desire for children were not only unrealizable but were strongly condemned and repressed. Emotional immaturity in women who want to be taken care of by their husbands may be traced back to the same origin. They themselves want to be considered and loved as children and do not feel that they can give enough love and maternal care to a child. This immature type of women often can not give up the father-daughter relationship and merely replaces the father by the husband. Failure of acceptance of the feminine role or masculine identification is another reason for rejection of pregnancy.

An ardent overtly expressed wish for a child also is not necesarily the proof of true motherliness. The masculine woman may be unduly preoccupied with the desire to become pregnant as overcompensation for her masculinity by proving that she is able to fulfill her biologic function. If she does not become pregnant this type of woman will try to reach her goal with the greatest insistance. She will subject herself to all examinations and treatments, will frequently change physicians and will never be reconciled to her sterility. Neither will she be able to accept other ways of satisfying her desire for motherhood. For instance adoption of a child will not solve her problems. In cases of sterility the feminine motherly woman gratifies her wish for motherhood in her love for her husband or adjusts happily to the adoption of a child. If in spite of the conflicting inner situation, pregnancy occurs, its course and the delivery, as well as the attitude towards the child, will all reflect the mother's personality.[16]

Emotional Disturbances of Early Pregnancy

The earliest and most frequent disturbances of pregnancy are manifested in changes in appetite and eating habits. They may show themselves either as cravings and overeating, or in nausea, morning sickness and, often— the most serious manifestation, the vomiting of pregnancy.

For the last two decades it has been emphasized how important it is for the pregnant woman not to gain excessive weight. This often is felt as a severe deprivation since anxiety makes her crave food. Overeating also may be due to the other frustrations a pregnant woman may encounter in so many areas of her living, e. g., if she does not get enough sympathy from her husband or family. The need for this oral gratification may also become important because of reactivated childhood fantasies in which getting candy is the reward for being good. Frustrating the oral satisfaction may have a deeper effect on the patient than is apparent. Not only can the physician become a stern parental figure in the patient's mind, but if her need for oral satisfaction is too severely curbed, it may be reflected in her feelings about the baby who is the cause of her frustration. There is also the antiquated though still potent idea that she must eat for two. Moreover, the pregnant woman also has the feeling, albeit unconsciously, that the baby draws on her strength and reserves. Belief in this idea was the reason for the former overfeeding of pregnant women. Often women are proud of the fact that they can eat without nausea. In short, the pregnant woman is much concerned about food. Intellectually she accepts the dictum that weight increase must be controlled because it is better for her health and for the course of labor, but she has conflict in doing so. Mainly for emotional reasons, she often develops a ravenous appetite as pregnancy progresses and new and additional restrictions are being added. She wants to compensate for these restrictions by giving in to the pleasure of eating. Towards the end of the pregnancy, when she feels she looks "distorted," she feels it no longer matters, since she has lost her figure anyway and she might at least have the gratification of food.

The loss of figure plays a very important role in many women's minds since they invest pride and ambition in their bodily appearance. It cannot easily be determined how far this fact may counteract a woman's wish to become pregnant. During the second half of pregnancy the apprehension becomes quite evident and also the concern to regain her previous figure.

The other early (and often discouraging) symptom is "morning sickness." This symptom is still a controversial subject in gynecologic and psychiatric literature. There is the fact that no exact cause for it can be determined, that it does not occur in every woman, nor even always follow the same pattern in an individual from one pregnancy to the next. There is also the fact that there is no specific treatment for the condition to which it invariably responds, all of which contributes to the assumption that there is no organic basis for the condition. The fact is that in our cultural milieu morning sickness is generally accepted as a normal accompaniment of pregnancy which is often even expected; that it frequently occurs in nervous women and in those who reject the pregnancy; that it is often easily remedied by superficial psychotherapy and suggestion—all leads to the assumption that it has a wholly psychogenic etiology. In view of the fact that every woman's childhood fantasies once held the concept of oral impregnation, this psychogenetic mechanism is assumed to represent an attempt to rid herself of the fetus in the same way as it was acquired—according to that infantile concept.

Women who suffered in their childhood from gastrointestinal disturbances and frequent vomiting, nearly always suffer from nausea and pregnancy vomiting. It may express not only the unconscious wish to get rid of the fetus, but also disgust of the pregnancy or hostility to the husband.

The psychological factor may be causative for the majority of cases and there may also be a psychological component in those patients who have very severe physical manifestations and chemical changes. However, every obstetrician has had an opportunity of observing cases in whom a physical basis could not be ruled out. Neither can the pernicious and toxic vomiting leading to acidosis and severe liver damage be accepted on an emotional basis and merely as a continuation of nervous vomiting. Even in the less serious cases with whom psychotherapy and vitamin therapy fails, and the vomiting stops after the third month, the psychological explanation that the woman at that point no longer regards the fetus as a foreign body but rather as a separate entity does not answer the question.

Endocrinologic disturbance in the sense of sodium and water retention as a result of high estrogen level is being made responsible. According to another theory the condition may be due to deficiency of placental steroid hormones, since it usually clears up in the fourth month of pregnancy, when the placenta is taking over almost the entire production of steroids. Greenhill[8] compares early toxemia to premenstural tension since in both these conditions disturbance of water balance is present.

Older literature[16] referred to the fact that in "faked abortion" when women were given general anesthesia and told that the pregnancy was terminated, their vomiting stopped. This might hold true for many cases.

However, the author recently learned about a patient who was a severe cardiac, on which basis her pregnancy was terminated in its sixth week. The patient called the physician one week later complaining that her nausea and vomiting were getting increasingly worse. Because the curettage had brought out a rather small amount of tissue the physician was concerned lest the ovum had remained intact in the uterus although he felt the uterine cavity had been emptied. On re-examination of the patient an intact ectopic pregnancy was found. This, but one of the many cases, illustrates the fact that the symptoms are not always developed on an emotional basis.

Last Weeks of Pregnancy

Delivery must be considered as the ultimate goal of female biologic function and her greatest pleasure-pain experience. As in all biologic and physiologic functions a woman's emotional past plays a decisive role. The final attitude toward the delivery is shaped during the very last weeks of pregnancy. The woman feels increasingly uncomfortable because of the physical changes and this, in turn, may give rise to a variety of impulsive attitudes. In contrast to the early part of pregnancy during which the woman's interest is centered around her own bodily changes, as time progresses, she is increasingly preoccupied with the development and behavior of the baby. The mother's relationship toward the baby is already developing during pregnancy, and prepares the ground for her later maternal care and devotion. The fetal activity serves her as a proof of pregnancy. Many women who in the early part of pregnancy repeatedly say that they "just cannot believe it" display their concern from this point on in a different manner. The same anxieties which made them doubtful whether they would be able to become pregnant from now on will be expressed by asking the physician whether they will be able to have a normal baby. The reality of fetal activity may mobilize other and hitherto suppressed tendencies. For instance, one of my successfully treated sterility patients, who ardently wished for a child, was overwhelmed with happiness when she became pregnant, but developed such severe anxieties upon feeling the fetal activities that psychiatric intervention became imminent. She suddenly felt the reality of the baby as a separate individual who might interfere with her harmonious relationship with her husband.

The type of the fetal activity becomes a new concern. Worries about too little activity alternate with anxieties because of the baby's restlessness. There is usually great concern as to whether the child will be normal. The curiosity about the sex of the child also grows. If the sex of the first baby has great significance to the mother, it usually means that she wants the child to compensate for her own unfulfilled wishes. If she could not become a boy, at least she must be able to create one. If she is narcissistic, she wants her daughter to fulfil what she could not achieve. In a truly well-adjusted marriage, the woman wants to satisfy her husband's wish in giving him the child he was longing for.

Behind all this verbalized curiosity there is a conscious or unconscious fear of the delivery. Although delivery is a physiologic process, it is connected with pain and bleeding and therefore represents a danger situation and may be feared as a threat to life. In many cases, however, no matter how much reassurance and information are given, the patient accepts it only intellectually and it does not give her true relief. Even though explanation may be very helpful, and aid in building up reserves of composure, some women refuse information about the course of labor and delivery, possibly because it might precipitate elaborately suppressed fears. They say, "Don't tell me, I don't want to know." In an emotionally normal woman the joyful expectation, the wish for the child is not unduly disturbed by the fear. The fear is mitigated or exceeded by the feeling of happy anticipation of the baby.

Frequently, however, earlier fears and childhood fantasies are being reactivated and may mobilize unconscious anxieties. One of the sources for this may be the relationship of the pregnant woman to her own mother. Since every little girl is more attracted to her father and would like to take the mother's place, with her own approaching motherhood, she develops guilt feelings toward her mother and expects punishment if her relationship toward her own mother is unresolved. It is significant how much pregnant women talk about their mothers, chiefly about their mother's pregnancies and deliveries. Not only do they all know their own birth weight, but they claim to know all particulars of their own delivery. It is striking how often the latter event is related to a danger situation in which mother or baby "nearly died." Whether these are really facts learned from the mother or are the pregnant woman's fantasies due to guilt feelings, cannot always be decided. The complexity of this reactivated conflict between mother and daughter is confirmed by the frequent occurrence of peculiar apprehension over the grandmother's first visit to the hospital. This is only partly explained by the woman's justified motivation that she wants to be left alone with her husband after the strain of delivery.

She may feel too triumphant over being able to achieve the same status as her mother, or she may feel guilty because perhaps for a very long time she regarded motherhood as her mother's prerogative.

It is not only the mother from whom the pregnant woman learns about all possible complications of labor and delivery. It is very probable that with her watchfulness and reactivated fantasies she senses and suspects more than she actually is being told. However she may hear about all possible horror stories from all her friends which make her more anxious as she learns about the possibilities of abnormal labor.

Generally, there is a growing impatience to see the baby, to get relief from the physical discomforts and also impatience over the many restrictions of pregnancy. The sexual abstinence of the last weeks of pregnancy is often tolerated with great apprehension. Bodily disfigurements are experienced as troublesome toward the end of the pregnancy, even by women who throughout their pregnancy were placid and enjoyed it. The expectation of a more or less definite date, the threat of something inevitable, provokes fear, to which some women respond with overactivity. They create heavy schedules for themselves as though they were leaving no time for the delivery. The emotionally immature woman, who played the role of a child and let herself be taken care of, may now develop additional unconscious fears about giving up the exceptional position she had enjoyed in attracting her husband's and her family's attention. Instead she must now look forward to the responsibility of taking care of her child. As pregnancy advances, and under the impact of a growing fear of delivery, the relationship to the obstetrician becomes increasingly important. Sometimes the woman endows him with magic qualities. He is take over all responsibility and is expected to perform miracles, possibly without participation of the parturient. Even in more realistic women the relationship assumes increasingly infantile traits. The obstetrician is cast into the role of a parental figure and becomes the giver of the child. He is expected to make up for deprivations in childhood from mother or father. For those who have bad relationships with their mothers, the obstetrician (regardless of sex) is the substitute for a good, giving mother. A positive attitude toward the obstetrician is of great importance. There is, however, in every patient's mind some doubt as to his competence (because in fact he is not a magician) or to his understanding and patience. Sometimes by a casual, unimportant remark of the physician, her confidence is undermined and the basis for a good relationship disturbed. This is due to the revival of the patient's ambivalent feelings towards her parents, and the resulting hostility is turned against the person of the physician.

All pregnant women inquire at some time in their pregnancy about what analgesia they will be given. The main concern of most women is that they do not want to experience any pain. Frequently, however, they are afraid of general anesthesia. Some of them have had traumatizing experiences during previous surgery, or even without previous experience, they are still afraid they may never waken.

During the last years the pendulum has swung in the opposite direction. This trend was initiated by Grantly Dick Read's views in publications such as *Natural Childbirth* and *Childbirth without Fear*.[19] Read attributes pain during delivery to fear which he claims is due only to environmental influences, incorrect education and misconceptions about the course of labor—fear-tension-pain syndrome. He also claims that all this can be eliminated by education and relaxation achieved by exercises. Enlightenment does play an important but not an entirely decisive role in childbirth. It can eliminate a considerable amount of fear but there is often a more deeply rooted anxiety which cannot be approached by explanation alone. Previous indoctrination of the patient is important as a preparation. However, the good relationship to the obstetrician, his presence, watchfulness, reassurance and his understanding of the patient's need while she is in labor are prerequisites of the method.

There is the widest range of attitudes from complete success to the utmost lack of cooperation and intolerance to pain following training for "natural childbirth." It is obvious that there are other factors involved other than the woman's physical condition and her individual threshold to pain. It would seem that the parturient's suggestibility is an important factor. By indoctrination, mainly if it is given in a class which can be considered as group psychotherapy, ambition and a competitive spirit are induced, the conscious fear can be eliminated, and the unconscious fears further repressed. Most of the patients who had previous training are more relaxed and less fearful at the beginning of labor, require analgesia less soon and need less sedation than they would have without the training. However, as labor progresses and contractions become more frequent and intense, the use of analgesics still becomes necessary. The patient is, of course, quite dependent on the presence and attention of the physician and is supposed to be informed about the progress of labor and about changes she is to expect. However "natural childbirth" seems to have become a fad. It almost looks as if those for whom it is least suited insist upon it most. Those who are most disturbed and tense turn to it to prove that they are not. Those who are afraid not only of the delivery but also of the anesthesia feel that this will be the means of avoiding both. Many others expect the *method* to work like magic and keep away the pain without their participation. I think women should be encouraged to try it but they need some explanation as to its limitations. Otherwise they will be disappointed if they are unable to accomplish it and will feel too inferior or ineffective when medication is needed. Women who needed only a few whiffs of anesthesia are usually delighted by the experience of the actual delivery and the immediate sight of the baby. Those who are admittedly overanxious and afraid of pain should not be encouraged to use it since they would not be promising candidates for the method. Instead, they should be helped as much as possible toward painless delivery. Although there is a certain amnesia toward labor pain, many women cannot forget the "ordeal" of delivery. This may throw some shadow on the mother's relationship to the child and also occasionally gives rise to a very definite objection to subsequent pregnancies.

Delivery

Following the long expectation and preparation during this heavily charged period, it is usually a relief when the labor finally starts. Here again, as in all physiologic processes, the emotional influences play an extremely important role. The mechanism by which the actual process of the delivery is started is still unknown. Its progress, however, is dependent on the interplay of sympathetic as well as parasympathetic nerve fibers both of which respond to emotional stimuli. The first disturbance may start with untoward response to Braxton-Hicks contractions, which in nervous individuals can become not only painful but also regular and simulate true labor. The anxious woman overestimates the significance of these and rushes to the hospital without asking her physician for advice. The disappointment is great when she is sent home because of a false alarm.

That fright may induce labor is probably overestimated in popular belief but is nevertheless substantiated in the professional literature and in large scale observations, such as the bombardment of cities during the war The opposite reaction can also be provoked by fear, as is often observed when parturients stop having contractions after entering the hospital.

When true labor contractions start, the patient gets anxious and feels more protected in the hospital. How she tolerates labor pains depends, besides her physical condition, on her emotional status. The normal woman is willing to accept a certain amount of pain. The first stage of labor makes a great demand on the woman's patience, which, if she is capable of it, will be manifested in a certain placidity between contractions. The emotionally immature woman will not be willing to participate in the delivery and expects the physician to take over the entire procedure without her cooperation. The overactive, rather masculine type wants to prove her efficiency but although she tries to cooperate in the beginning soon lacks perseverance, usually has a very low pain threshold and easily becomes unmanageable. It is usually at the beginning of the first stage that the parturient talks about her husband. It depends on her personality and relationship to him how she responds to his departure from the hospital. Often she becomes anxious and would like her husband to stay. Sometimes the reason why women want to choose the method of "natural childbirth" is the wish to have the husband stay with them. Read considers the presence and participation of the husband in the delivery as very important. However, hardly any hospitals comply with this requirement at present.

There is considerable variation in behavior during the second stage of labor. Now the patient's cooperation has real values in the progress of delivery. Some, if not tired from the strain of the first stage, experience it as relief that they can finally cooperate, the more so since the contractions are less painful when supported by the abdominal muscles and relaxation between contractions may still be complete. When pressure of the presenting part upon the rectum manifests itself, it becomes clear that at this point the woman associates delivery with an excretory function. The pressure is perceived as a quasi urge for defecation. The encouragement they get for cooperation supports this concept when they are told to "bear down and push hard." Infantile anxieties about involunatry bowel movements are reactivated by the actual stimulation and there is fear of humiliation in this situation. Moreover, they may unconsciously be reluctant to part with the so long familiar and cherished content of their body.

Post Partum Period

Psychiatrists have become increasingly aware of the importance of the earliest possible reunion of the mother and child for the sake of the mother-child relationship. The less anesthesia given, the earlier this reunion can be effected. To follow this trend, the rooming-in method is more and more emphasized. It is a detour via scientific observations to the old and natural situation which not only has always existed in primitive cultures, but which was practiced all over the world up to the beginning of this century. What effect it has on the newborn to be separated for about one week from the mother is being observed and investigated and needs more comparative studies than could be obtained up to now.

Our knowledge about the mother's relationship to the child is more definite. Up to the delivery, the mother has more or less vivid fantasies about the child and her motherhood. These must now be transformed into reality. The first response of the mother to the delivery is great relief. The reaction which the obstetrician observes is not a pure psychological reaction, inasmuch as there is practically no delivery without anesthesia, and the chance to observe the immediate response of the mother to the baby is at first colored by its effects. Then a great pride in the achievement sets in, which gradually gives way to joy and love for the baby. What up to this point was fantasy and illusion now becomes reality.

Many women who were overanxious about the delivery, project their anxiety onto the baby. Those who want to nurse are worried whether they will be able to do so and whether the baby will be brought to them in time. Frequently, the new mother claims that she can hear and differentiate her baby's cry from the nursery. When the time of leaving the hospital approaches anxieties are expressed about handling the baby at home. Most of these anxieties can be prevented if the mother has the baby in her room and experiences the implications of motherhood at once and learns how to handle the baby while still in the hospital. However, women who have ambivalent feelings toward their pregnancy carry this over into their motherhood. Some display an immature attitude and want to be taken care of, admired and praised for their accomplishment and are unable to offer complete maternal devotion. A great number of women have many intellectual interests and ambitions and are afraid of the demands which motherhood may require of them.

At this point, the problem of breast-feeding must be mentioned, which is the optimal and appropriate situation for the development of a healthy mother-child relationship. It certainly should be welcomed and, where the potentialities for a good relationship prevail, there will be no difficulty. But here again, as with the wish for "natural childbirth," many unconscious factors are involved. Misgivings, doubts and intellectually enforced attitudes may give rise to complications which may result in greater disappointment than if the seemingly so natural plan to nurse is not even attempted. How largely the milk production is dependent on emotional factors has long been common knowledge. The mechanism of this influence is apparently via hypothalamus, pituitary-to-prolactin release.

It is known to every clinician that at about the fifth or sixth day of the lying-in period, many women get nervous, irritable, depressed and demanding. This mood is somewhat similar to premenstrual tension. What the physiologic implications of these manifestations are, is unknown. Usually this mood subsides within a few days; however, it is helpful to explain to the mother and the husband that these symptoms are rather common.

Pregnancy and its termination in the delivery are the greatest events in a woman's physical and emotional life and may provoke a tremendous upheaval and lead to far-reaching changes in the mother's personality. In rare cases, a post partum psychosis may occur—which is beyond the scope of this chapter. To the motherly woman, childbirth means the fulfilment of her deepest wish, but even the neurotic woman's personality often makes considerable strides toward normal maturity and acceptance of her feminine role.

STERILITY

If pregnancy does not occur when it is wanted this fact creates a very great problem. This is true regardless of the underlying reason for wishing to have a child—be it genuine motherliness, competition with the environment or overcompensation for a rejection of the feminine role.

The last three decades have made great progress in our knowledge of physiology, endocrinology and pathology of the reproductive function. The new investigations have brought us much closer to an understanding of hormonal functions and their disorders. The utero-tubal insufflation has great merit as a diagnostic and sometimes therapeutic procedure. There are, however, a great number of sterility cases in which in spite of all investigative studies no physical reason for the sterility can be established. There is increasing acceptance of the idea that sterility can occur on emotional basis. A great variety of theories were elaborated about this problem, though they cannot be proven. The mechanism of such emotionally caused sterility is not known. Sellheim,[21] for instance, claimed that the desire for pregnancy may lead to a pathologic growth of the ovaries and discharge of ova not yet ready for fertilization. Ovulation may be early or delayed because of changes in abdominal circulation.

Peculiar cases of a first pregnancy, after many years of trial, may be ascribed to the fact that the woman becomes gradually reconciled to her sterility and the disturbing emotional influence on the ovarian function subsides. Helene Deutsch[3] states that difficulties of conception which result from disturbing factors can appear directly in the mechanism of coitus and spasmodic expulsions may be responsible for a failure of conception or may lead to premature labor or spontaneous abortion.

A site of spasticity in the female genital tract which can be demonstrated and recorded are the fallopian tubes. Utero-tubal insufflation illuminates many of these problems. Rubin[20] attributes great importance to the character of the tubal peristalsis which can be recorded on insufflation. Spasms which are often present may be consistent or transitory. Since spasm of the smooth muscle is a common visceral response to emotional tension it seems probable that functional sterilities exist on this basis. Sedatives are of no clinical value in overcoming spastic closure. Morphine, demerol and nembutal stimulate rather than depress contraction.[2] Kroger and Fried[12] mention that the tubal spasm is not necessarily relieved by anesthesia. I had occasion to observe the following patient:

Thirty-four-year-old woman with a history of five years' sterility. Menarche at the age of 13. Normal 28 day cycle of 4 days duration, no dysmenorrhea. No medical or surgical history. BMR +6, CBC normal. Pelvic finding: normal size, anteflexed, freely movable uterus, no adnexa pathology, cervix clean. Sex life satisfactory, normal orgasm. The husband's seminal fluid as to quantity, sperm count, motility and morphology satisfactory. Patient ardently wished a child and although medically quite well informed (laboratory technician) was extremely disappointed at not becoming pregnant at the first exposure. Her disappointment developed into anxiety and depressive states during the course of time. There were three insufflations performed at six-month intervals, with no patency. The probability of spastic closure was repeatedly discussed because of the negative findings. Following the third in-sufflation, patient requested insufflation under general anesthesia on the assumption that if the closure was caused by spasm it should be relieved by the anesthesia. The insufflation was repeated under intravenous sodium pentothal. There was no patency. One year later in a radically changed and extremely unfavorable life situation she became pregnant. Although she was overwhelmed with happiness, felt physically very well, she had a spontaneous miscarriage in the third month of pregnancy. She did not become pregnant again.

The above-mentioned case, although not psychoanalytically investigated, gives the impression that if unconscious difficulties in accepting mother-hood prevail, even if conception takes place, there is an inability to carry it to normal termination. Friedgood[6] believes that there is a functional pathway from the cerebral cortex through the diencephalon and the anterior hypophysis to the ovaries and the uterus.

Pregnancy following adoption has become proverbial among the laity to such an extent that many sterile women want to adopt children in order to become pregnant following adoption. Orr's[18] publication of one such example throws more light on the problem. He reported that analysis of both the woman and her husband made it clear how the decision to adopt a child gave the woman a legitimate reason to quit her job and helped her to accept the feminine role. Even more impressive is Jacobson's[10] publica-tion. In this case, the endocrinologic disturbance of the patient started in adolescence, in connection with a secret love affair between a Jewish girl and a gentile boy whom she was not allowed to marry. The amenorrhea set in when the patient had conscious fantasies of being pregnant by him. I had occasion to examine the patient at the beginning of her analysis in order to evaluate the prognosis of her amenorrhea. She had been previously treated by a physician who published her case as a very probable Sim-mon's cachexia, but who, nevertheless, maintained a very optimistic atti-tude toward the patient. The treatment consisted of high doses of stilbes-terol, following which during the course of several years, she had a few withdrawal bleedings.

At the time I saw her she was at the beginning of her analysis and was 35 years old. Her menarche had been at the age of 14, 28 day cycle of 3–4 days' duration. The last menstrual period was at the age of 18. She was underweight, boyish-looking and seemed younger than her age. The secondary sex characteristics showed small breasts with inverted nipples, pubic and axillary hair normally distributed but scant. On pelvic examination: narrow introitus and vagina, the uterus very small, firm, atrophic upon probing 2½ inches. Blood count normal, weight 97 pounds, height 63 inches, pulse 66, thyroid not enlarged, BMR—21, endometrial biopsy revealed a non-func-tioning atrophic endometrium. I advised thyroid therapy and considered pituitary stimulation by x-ray. The radiologist, however, was not optimistic as to the effective-ness of the treatment considering the severe atrophy of the endometrium. I left it up to the patient whether or not she wished to undergo this trial with the possibility of a new disappointment. She decided on no treatment. Fifteen months later during analysis the patient became pregnant. She conceived during her amenorrhea apparently at her first ovulation and was not aware of her pregnancy up to the fourth month, when she noticed the change in her figure. She had an uneventful spontaneous delivery, was menstruating regularly afterwards and became pregnant six months later again.

Cases of women who became pregnant after prolonged amenorrheas are reported in the literature although they are rare. R. T. Frank[5] reports the case of a woman who started to menstruate without treatment and bore two children after an amenorrhea of 17 years. This woman was under observation for hormone level determination when she started to menstruate. In the latter case we do not know what psychological factors were at work, although it may be that the initiation of investigation itself acted as psychological influence.

In spite of all the information which ample clinical material has yielded the fact remains that women in spite of great conscious and unconscious resistance still become pregnant and carry the pregnancy to term, even if the psychological material would indicate the contrary.

CONTRACEPTION

The need for contraception has been increasingly recognized both by women and by society, although there are many conflicting views about the problem. Its advocators consider it a great social achievement, while certain religious believers are opposed to it.

The gynecologist is only concerned with contraception as a psychosocial hygenic problem of his patient. He is aware, however, that there are conscious and unconscious reasons for practicing or resisting birth control and that the patient's attitude toward its use will be greatly influenced by her sexual adjustment.

Apart from reasons for physical illness, the motivations for the use of birth control are manifold. Often newly wed couples want time to become adjusted to each other and to married life. Sometimes they are apprehensive about the lasting character of the marriage; some women do not want to give up their freedom or others want to pursue their career and therefore postpone pregnancy. There are the unmarried women who feel entitled to sexual gratification but for social reasons cannot afford to bear children. Many women feel mature enough for sexual intercourse but are not emotionally mature enough to have children. They fear pregnancy and delivery as well as the responsibilities of motherhood. The most rational reason is the one of spacing of children. The fear of a pregnancy, which for inner or external reasons is not permissible, may greatly interfere with normal sexual gratification and may be a contributory factor to dyspareunia. To avoid unwanted pregnancy is important, not only for the welfare of the parents, but also for that of the child. But most parents become reconciled to a pregnancy which they did not want and forget their resentment by the time the child is born.[15] However, a repressed rejection still may break through and it can be the most traumatizing experience for the child to learn that he was unwanted. The extent to which opposition and fear may block a rational decision is often revealed by patients when they admit that they had been advised, or had considered the use of contraceptives for months or years without being able to come to a decision. It is striking how frequently girls who had been having sex relations for many months or years do not seek contraceptive advice up to the time of their marriage. Sometimes they rationalize that their attitude was the fear that the contraceptive device might be discovered by their mothers. This may be true in some cases. However, the real explanation is that they feel guilty about premarital sex relations and cannot face the responsibility of assuming previous preparation. They can accept intercourse only as an unexpected situation in which they are unwillingly seduced. They want the man to take the responsibility for the "sinful" action. Again, the fears and objections against birth control may be on the unconscious level. The most powerful objection is religious. In solving this problem the physician cannot be helpful. However, where the religious prohibition is not strong enough to prevent the use of contraception, the feeling of sinfulness is frequently present and expresses itself as a fear that birth control may lead to sterility as a punishment for having previously rejected pregnancy. This feeling of immorality may again reactivate the fears of masturbation or the recollection of previous forbidden sexual activities.

Many patients are afraid of the physician's attitude and are embarrassed to ask for advice. Frequently, they go to see the physician under another pretext and only after they have gained confidence do they admit their original purpose. The most common objections to contraceptives are fear and disgust of handling their own body which is expressed as an anxiety of doing harm to the genitals. This might bring fear of masturbation, or recollection of previous forbidden sexual activities, to the fore. The reason for this is partly lack of anatomic knowledge and probably also a repressed fear of early masturbation. There is an aversion against the messy preparation which, they feel, deprives sexual gratification of its spontaneity, making it a planned act. There is also anxiety about failure of the method. There is a surprising ignorance about the anatomy and a fear that the diaphragm might get lost inside the body. If all these fears do not originate from a deeper disturbance they can be eliminated by proper explanation of the anatomy and physiology involved and this may play an important role in improving sex relations.

In case of serious psychosexual disturbances neither the contraceptive advice nor the information about anatomy will be sufficient in order to adjust the patient to the practice of the method. The well adjusted woman with a satisfactory sex life does not create major problems about the use of contraceptives and accepts the diaphragm and jelly method as the safest and the one which least interferes with sexual gratification. Following the postnatal period, for the sake of spacing pregnancies, most women want to practice birth control even if they did not do so before.

Those who do not want to use contraception postnatally are usually the sexually disturbed, who do not experience sexual gratification, and who consider intercourse merely a marital duty. The gynecologist is often asked by women approaching menopause how long to use contraception. Probably originating from wishful thinking, there is a popular belief that women approaching menopause are particularly fertile. It does happen, though rarely, that a woman becomes pregnant at this age and attributes her amenorrhea to menopause. Since irregularities and delayed menstruation at this age create anxieties for both reasons, namely fear of pregnancy as well as dread of the menopause—some conflicts can be avoided if the woman practices birth control until the final menopause is established.

With proper indoctrination and exact technique, birth control rarely fails. The failure, however, can sometimes also be traced to emotional reasons.

One of my patients who practiced birth control for four years with good results, became pregnant as soon as she planned to. Unfortunately she developed placenta previa and because of severe hemorrhage had to be delivered by cesarean section in the seventh month of an unviable baby. Afterwards she was advised not to become pregnant for at least one year. The pregnancy, which because of bleeding kept her in bed for many weeks, and its unfortunate outcome, were so traumatizing to her that she claimed she did not want to attempt it for quite some time. Three months later she returned stating that one day, in removing her diaphragm, she noticed it was not properly placed and she also missed her following menstrual period. After I told her she was pregnant, she commented: "Is this how my unconscious works?" This time she was delivered of a normal full-term baby and has been practicing the same kind of birth control for the last seven years without failure. Another patient who was using birth control with no failure for eight years, became pregnant the very month her husband told her he was in love with another woman and wanted to divorce her.

FRIGIDITY

Frigidity is not a distinct clinical entity. True frigidity is but one manifestation of usually deep-seated emotional disturbances, which reach back to early psychosexual development. Due to the configuration of female anatomy, the most easily discovered part of the genitals is the clitoris. This part yields pleasure on stimulation and is the site of early masturbatory activities at a time when the girl has not yet conscious awareness of the existence of her vagina. Concentration on the clitoris may block the path of development leading to normal vaginal sensitivity.

However, there are many cases of what one might call pseudo-frigidity in which the disturbance is not so deeply seated. This pseudo-frigidity is produced by the inhibitory influence of certain social and cultural factors such as the restrictions, warnings and moral disciplining to which the female sex is subjected to a much greater extent than the male.

Premarital sex relations are rigorously condemned as far as many girls are concerned. The first intercourse is often anticipated as a painful bodily injury by the male organ when it pierces the hymen. In their fantasies, this may lead to excessive bleeding. There are also fantasies about rape and fear of impregnation.

Although most women know that no gratification may be derived from the first intercourse, they still hope otherwise and thus feel disappointed if not cheated. This first experience of intercourse tends to perpetuate the girl's potential frigidity. The criterion of frigidity is the absence of vaginal orgasm. There is, however, a great variation as to different manifestations and various degrees of gratification. Many women suffer from dyspareunia and submit only painfully to intercourse. There are some who do not respond at all and do not even realize that coitus can culminate in orgasm. They accept intercourse as marital duty to which they submit to please the man. (Deutsch[3] differentiates a type of benevolent frigidity of the woman who is deeply gratified by giving the man satisfaction by tender motherly love without feeling the need for sexual excitement.) Others can be aroused and may experience weak or strong excitement without orgasm or may have clitoral orgasm but vaginal hypo- or anesthesia.

Those who can be aroused but do not reach the point of culmination constitute the group of women who suffer from frigidity and seek relief. The lack of genital release leads to more or less severe tension, to disappointment, with a feeling of inadequacy or inferiority which the woman turns against herself. As a further consequence, she may become apprehensive toward her partner and, according to her personality make up, develop anger and hostility which finally shape her behavior—not only toward her husband as a result of her dissatisfaction—but may also be projected onto the outside world in generalized hostility or anger. As to the symptoms: the frustrated excitation also has its physical manifestations in pelvic hyperemia which causes somatic tension, vague abdominal or lower backache, leucorrhea, and pruritus. Usually, *these* symptoms as such, or sometimes as a pretext, induce the patient to seek gynecologic examination or advice.

Many women are convinced that the cause of their frigidity is anatomic or an abnormality. Those who sense that this is not the case still would welcome the discovery of an organic basis as the cause of their symptoms. They very seldom present their frigidity as their chief complaint but usually bring it up only after they have been reassured that no pathology has been found. If the examination does not reveal physical abnormalities one has to determine the degree of the disturbance. If true frigidity is one symptom of a deep-seated disturbance, psychoanalytic treatment is indicated. If the symptom is due to inhibition, an explanation of the anatomy and physiology involved, and the information that many women have difficulty in reaching an orgasm, sometimes gives more than superficial relief. There are strikingly large numbers of patients who, because of very superficial inhibitions, as, perhaps, the location of the bedroom or lack of good sexual technique or other different external reasons, are prevented from experiencing orgasm. In such cases, of course, the physician will have the easiest response to his explanation.

THE MENOPAUSE

Menopause represents, more or less, a threat to every woman long before it reveals any kind of manifestation. Frequently, because of a delayed menstruation, women in their late thirties develop anxieties as to whether the delay is not an indication of the menopause. Many women, however, have no special discomfort during this period. They take the slight physical and emotional disturbances in their stride without seeking medical help. They accept their aging and the cessation of their reproductivity sometimes with placidity, sometimes with the feeling of relief and, if their emotional instability or discomfort is not too severe, do not even attribute it to the menopause. Many others who were absorbed with their reproductivity, may turn their energy and libido into other directions and return to activities in which they were interested before marriage or before having had children. This attitude can be considered as an active struggle against aging, which is sometimes consciously planned but accomplished more successfully by those who intuitively reach out for new or former activities. Yet women who suffered from severe premenstrual tension or dysmenorrhea and who claim to look forward to the termination of their "misery," still feel greatly disappointed when the menstruation actually ceases. Although their maladjustment caused a constant struggle for them, they cannot give it up without protest since they are still waiting for some feminine gratification. Occasionally, the active struggle against becoming "useless" creates the wish for a new pregnancy even in women who had children before. Most women no longer want to become pregnant but are unwilling to acknowledge its impossibility.

Women who have had no children nor even sex relations feel cheated by life. To many the menopause is a great blow to their feminine pride which is difficult to overcome. How she will be able to cope with the problem depends not only on a woman's actual past, but much more on her personality. The first stage of the climacterium may be characterized by an increase of sexual excitation and a yearning for approval, admiration and new sexual experiences. They display an exaggerated interest in their bodily appearance and compensate for aging by youthful clothing and behavior. The well adjusted woman may turn her energy toward more constructive activities and sometimes engage in further studies, or turn her interest towards art and literature or concentrate, with an increased intensity, on her professional work.

Since this age, more or less, coincides with the time of her children's growing up, the task of adjustment is more difficult although more necessary to achieve. Near the age of menopause many women reach the status of grandmotherhood which is usually a very satisfactory continuation of their own motherhood. However, the proverbial good grandmother is not as ubiquitous as might be expected. Some women have difficulties in accepting this status.

There are various physical as well as emotional changes which characterize this period. There may be a rapid onset of the signs of aging, such as tendency to increase in weight, and changes in fat distribution which alter the figure. There are the well known vasomotor symptoms of hot flushes. There may be emotional symptoms such as irritability, insomnia and depression. But all of these signs and symptoms show individual variations in intensity.

The majority of women are ignorant about the fact that with the cessation of menstruation, sexual desire and the possibility for gratification do not cease. The decrease of libido and orgasm is gradual and may exceed the menopause by many years. The duration of physical and emotional symptoms of the menopause varies greatly. The emotional disturbances often outlast the physical symptoms. On the basis of predisposition, involutional depression may occasionally develop.

Surgery for preexisting or newly arising pathology becomes necessary with increasing frequency. Hysterectomy is dreaded as a mutilating operation and has a greater emotional impact than any other operation. Postoperative psychosis is more frequent following hysterectomy than any other surgery. To lose the capacity for reproduction means more to the women than the function itself. It also represents the loss of femininity. Often they imagine that sexual intercourse is no longer possible and they are always afraid of loss of libido and orgasm. Most women do not know that removal of the uterus, if the ovaries are left in does not lead to hormonal disturbances. Intellectual acceptance of this fact does not always help to relieve the fear of losing the womb.

Surgery is always connected with the fear of malignancy. This fear, however, is not even verbalized and thus does not give the physician a chance to reassure the patient in this respect.

The medical management of the menopause is quite clearly indicated. Hormone therapy and mild sedation have beneficial results not only on the vasomotor changes but also on the emotional condition. Substitutional ovarian therapy was started at the beginning of this century for treatment of ovarian deficiency. Excellent results were reported by patients and physicians. Now that the exact composition of the two ovarian hormones is known and their potency experimentally established, it is also known that in the earliest ovarian extract there was only a very little or a negligible amount of estrogen. Nevertheless, the therapeutic results were satisfactory. This gives rise to the question of how much the symptoms are functional and for how many of the patients did the ovarian extract medication serve as a substitute for psychotherapy? There are clinical observations in regard to the administration of estrogenic hormones as compared with placebos. While there are many patients who respond only to estrogens, there also are some women who have not only the same but even better results from placebos, proving that not all the symptoms are due to real hormonal deficiency, nor if so, do they continue on this basis throughout the entire duration of the menopause. Often the symptoms and the need for medical help develop into a habit which is difficult to give up.

The content of the apprehension and emotional instability is clearer in the menopause than in many other psychosexual disorders, and, therefore, the gynecologist can achieve good results with explanation and reassurance.

The menopause is often compared to adolescence in terms of being a vulnerable period of the female life. As in puberty, the hormonal upheaval easily creates lack of balance before instinctual impulses can be channelized. Through hormonal imbalance and deficiency, the emotional status of the individual during the menopause is also in a continuous state of unpredictability and oversensitivity. There are different physical manifestations, such as the gastrointestinal disturbances, hyper- or hypothyroidism, which likewise occur frequently in puberty, and which in the same individual may reoccur in the climacterium. However, the prohibitive social and cultural influences which added to the conflicts of youth, do not exist in the climacterium. The social and cultural development of the last decades are to the benefit of this period of life. They give opportunities for a new release of the creative forces of the personality, so that, today, women in their fifties may find wider areas of self-expression and satisfying activity than ever before.

BIBLIOGRAPHY

1. Benedek, T. and Rubenstein, B. B.: Sexual cycle in women. Psychosomatic Medicine Monographs. *III:* No. 1 and 2.
2. Davids, A. M. and Weiner, I.: The Effects of Sedation on Fallopian Tube Motility. Am. J. Obst. & Gynec. *59:* 673–678, 1950.
3. Deutsch, Helene: Psychology of Women. New York, Grune & Stratton, 1944 (Vol. I) pp. 158; 1945 (Vol. II) pp. 121.
4. Dunbar, F.: Emotions and Bodily Changes. New York, Columbia University Press, 1946.
5. Frank, R. T., Goldberger, M. A., Salmon, U. J. and Felshin G.: Amenorrhea; it's causation and treatment.
6. Freedgood, H. B.: J. A. M. A. *109:* 1863, 1937.: *In:* Kroger and Freed. Psychosomatic Gynecology. Phila., W. B. Saunders, 1951.
7. Fremont-Smith, M. and Meigs, J. V.: Menstrual Dysfunction Due to Emotional Factors. Am. J. Obstet. & Gynec. *55: 1040,* 1948.
8. Greenhill, J. P. and Freed, S. C.: The mechanism and treatment of premenstrual distress with ammon. chloride. Endocrinology. *26:* 529–531, 1940.
9. Halban and Seitz: Biologie und Pathologie des Weibes Berlin, Springer Verlag, 1926, Vol. II.
10. Jacobson E.: Case of sterility (with cure following psychoanalysis). Psychoanalytic Quart. *15:* 330–350, 1946.
11. Knight, R. P.: Functional disturbance in the sexual life of women. Bull. Menninger Clinic. *7:* 1943.
12. Kroger, W. S. and Freed, S. C.: Psychosomatic Gynecology. Philadelphia, W. B. Saunders Co., 1951.
13. Loeser, A. A.: *In:* Fremont-Smith, M. and Meigs, J. V.: Menstrual dysfunction due to emotional factors. Am. J. Obstet. & Gyn. *55:* 1037, 1948.
14. Markee, J. E.: *In:* Fremont-Smith, M. and Meigs, J. V.: Menstrual dysfunction due to emotional factors. Am. J. Obstet. & Gynec. *55:* 1037, 1948.
15. Menninger, K.: Psychiatric Aspects of Contraception. Bull. of the Menninger Clinic Vol. 7, No. 1, 1943.
16. Menninger, W. C.: Emotional factors in pregnancy. Bull. Menninger Clinic. *7:* 1943.
17. Novak, Emil: Textbook of Gynecology. Baltimore, The Williams & Wilkins Co., 1944.
18. Orr, D. W.: Pregnancy following decision to adoption. Psychosom. Med. *3:* 441–446, 1941.
19. Read, G. D.: Childbirth Without Fear. New York, Harpers, 1944.
20. Rubin, I. C.: Diagnostic and therapeutic aspects of kymographic and uterotubal insufflation with comparative observation on hysterosalpingography. Obstet. & Gyn. Brit. Empire. *54:* 733–745, 1947.
21. Sellheim, H.: *In:* Dunbar, F.: Emotion and Bodily Changes. New York, Columbia University Press, 1946.
22. Taylor, H. C.: Vascular congestion hyperemia. Am. J. Obstet. & Gyn. *57:* 654, 1949.

CHAPTER 8

Psychiatric Aspects of Diseases of the Genitourinary System

JOSEPH M. SILAGY, M.D.

Dr. Silagy received his Medical degree from New York University Medical School and had four years of in-hospital training in urology at Mount Sinai Hospital, as well as one year's residency in urology at Bayonne Hospital, New Jersey. He has taken a number of courses in psychoanalysis at the William A. White Institute of Psychiatry.

He was formerly Chief of Urologic Section of a number of General Hospitals in the United States Army; Adjunct Urologist at Montefiore Hospital and Bronx Hospital and is at present Adjunct Urologist at Mount Sinai Hospital and Associate Urologist at Beth David Hospital.

Dr. Silagy is a member of the New York Urological Society, a member of the Academy of Medicine, and AOA, as well as a Diplomate of the American Board of Urology.

THE DIAGNOSTIC TECHNIQUES available to specialists in genitourinary disorders have reached so high a level of accuracy and objectivity that these physicians, probably more than any other group, have become confirmed organicists. They have all but rejected the psychic and somatic interrelationships that have been so widely and enthusiastically accepted in other fields of medicine. Yet, it is highly probable that psychogenic causation and emotional factors play as important a role in the production of morphologic changes and functional disorders of the genital and urinary organs as they do in any other organ system. It is certainly true that the personality and the conscious and unconscious attitudes and biases of the urologist are important factors in determining his relationship with his patients. These are also factors in determining the choice among different diagnostic methods and forms of treatment, and often, their ultimate therapeutic effectiveness.

This chapter will concern itself with commonly seen genitourinary problems that are of particular interest from the somatopsychic standpoint. An attempt will be made to show how a deeper interest in, and understanding of, the patient's emotional life and psychosexual development will lead to a more rational and etiologic treatment, as well as improved results.

THE GENITOURINARY EXAMINATION

It is usually with more than the ordinary amount of apprehension that the patient with genitourinary complaints comes to the doctor. The patient cannot discuss his sexual difficulties as easily as he might a defect of vision. So many inhibitions have been generated in our society in relation to the genital area, and so important has our *stereotype* of the "he-man" and the "rugged individualist" become, that symptoms of genital and urinary dysfunction are usually bound up in the patient's mind with feelings of shame, guilt, inadequacy and fear. The body-image of masculinity is often threatened. The presence of an urethral discharge often elicits the disproportionate reaction of feeling stained and unclean.

The patient is also under great emotional strain because of the imagined terrors of the anticipated examination. There is a great psychic investment in the penis and the other genital organs (see chapter on Obstetrics for a discussion of the female problems). From earliest childhood on, the little boy associates his genitals with vaguely pleasant sensations which are often actively forbidden by parental injunction. Anybody who has ever watched children, can observe the pride and curiosity that they invest in the penis—showing it off and comparing. We know from clinical psychoanalysis that the little boy also compares himself with his father, not so favorably, and that a number of circumstances make him afraid he might lose the penis. To these circumstances belongs the fact that he observes that little girls do not have penises at all (and he concludes that they, too, must have had one and lost it somehow). He is often threatened with illness if he plays with his penis, and he entertains a number of vague fears that he might lose the penis for forbidden desires and fantasies.

Thus it happens that the genitals are the center of particular fears. If the patient comes to the urologist with some concern over a disorder, these fears have already been increased over the quite sizeable normal complement of fears. In addition now, he wonders what painful procedures and fearful pronouncements the doctor will make. Vaguely in his mind are thoughts of operation—of precisely *that* loss, or trauma, of genitals that he has dreaded (consciously or unconsciously) all his life. No wonder urological patients are tense!

Add to this the fact that among other things, the urologist may very well ask him about his sexual habits. Hardly a person will not have some guilt feelings or embarrassment over past or present sexual activities of one kind or another, and secretly will feel that his present disorder might possibly be the result of them—however irrational such a thought might be.

Further, add the fact that the mere exposing of his genitals, not to mention the handling of them, may cause him severe emotional upset. The touching of one man's genital by another is highly taboo in our society.

All the dread that the ordinary man harbors about homosexuality is aroused.

Instrumentation, such as cystoscopy or even catheterization, has been widely discussed among lay people as being unbearably painful. Having an instrument inserted into a body opening may well make the patient feel unconsciously as if he were being entered—like a woman—and will arouse the worst anxieties man knows.

The rectal examination, again, will produce anxieties ranging from those of homosexuality to the feeling of embarrassment usually connected with the ano-genital area in our society. The whole area of investigation, including the kidneys, is one which probably is even more unknown to most people than the rest of their anatomy. With lack of knowledge comes fear—fear of the hidden illness which is beyond comprehension. Thus, it is probably time well spent if a urologist will take a few minutes to let the patient talk freely; if the doctor will establish a feeling of confidence, and if he will use simple explanations of the proposed examination.

Giving the patient false reassurance will not work well for future contacts. Simply taking the bogeyman factor out of the proceedings will be appreciated by the patient and will be rewarded by better cooperation. A simple explanation of some of the anatomic and pathologic conditions found may give the patient the frame of reference he needs to be able to better control irrational anxieties.

The Meaning of Illness in the Genitourinary Tract

As has already been mentioned, the urologist's domain is one of special significance for every person. It is the area of first concern in human development and socialization in connection with toilet training. Erections can be observed in early infancy, and so can self-stimulation.

Much fear and pride is invested in the genitals even before puberty. One of the most widespread early forms of competition and exhibitionism takes place when boys try to see who can eject the urinary stream higher and farther, and hardly any boy does not compare himself, with trepidation, in gymnasium or swimming pool dressing rooms.

With puberty, concern over the genitals becomes conscious. This is in connection with masturbation and possible harm the boys expect from it, goaded on by more or less irrational ideas about it from parents or, often, even by the family doctor. Early sexual experimentation arouses fears of venereal disease; the less one actually knows about it, the more dreadful the fantasies. Potency later becomes a matter of pride and concern.

All these feelings are involved when illness strikes anywhere in the genitourinary system. The most widespread fear in case of any affliction is the one that the illness may be a venereal one. To this concept are tied all the guilt feelings and unconscious expectations of punishment for the various forms of sexual activity the patient may feel guilty about. The disease now seems to the patient as punishment for his supposed earlier misdeeds. And thus he expects mutilation, impotence and rotting away of his body. He feels dirty, immoral and ashamed.

Surgery in this area probably evokes more fear than anywhere else (see chapter on Surgery). It brings the fear of castration and the fear of loss of masculinity most violently. Even after successful surgery, the patient may be greatly concerned over minimal or nonexistent changes in his anatomy, and depressions and anxiety may take on major proportions.

Based on mistaken physiologic notions, one man who had one testicle removed because of tuberculosis of that organ, became impotent and remained so for years despite later reassurance that the operation did not in any way interfere with any function related to potency.

Another man had deep concern over his masculinity because he recalled the incompletely descended testicles of his youth—despite the fact that the later development was perfectly normal.

Having a relatively small penis is prevalently incorrectly associated with feelings of sexual inadequacy. Clinical experience indicates that the size of the penis bears no relationship to the degree of satisfaction to either partner. And, of course, innumerable cases come to clinical attention where normal sized organs or even unusually large ones do not prevent the patient from suffering from all forms of impotence.

The sexual afflictions of potency have, of course, the most pronounced traumatic meanings for men—and are, therefore, discussed separately as part of the discussion of sexual dysfunction.

At the same time, much that is presented to the urologist as seemingly non-sexual afflictions of the system, is—in fact—but a disguised and emotionally and somatically displaced sexual problem; such as a certain proportion of cases of so called chronic prostatitis.

CHRONIC NON-SPECIFIC PROSTATO-URETHRITIS

A very large number of men come to the physician complaining of a symptoms complex involving most or all of the following: abnormal sensations in the urethral canal, testes, perineum and anus, urinary frequency, occasional urethral discharge or prostatorrhea, diminished sexual desire, premature ejaculation, poor erections, easy fatigability and low back pain.

The onset of symptoms may date to adolescence but most often first appear in the third or fourth decade of life. A history of enuresis in childhood and/or excessive masturbation in youth is not infrequently elicited. Physical findings in this group are variable but disproportionately minor in relation to the degree of disease produced. The prostate is rarely appreciably enlarged and is firm and elastic in consistency. The expressed secretions may vary from a few to numerous detrital and white blood cells. Bacteriologic examination shows a variety of organisms of indeterminate pathogenicity. The panendoscopic examination yields findings that do not significantly vary from those of a group of similar age who are free from the above listed symptoms and who are examined because of organic urologic disease such as stones or tumor. Minor congestion of the posterior urethra with some enlargement of the veru and irritative changes about it, are sometimes found. No evidence of hypogonadism or other endocrine imbalance is ordinarily present.

In urologic texts this syndrome is described as caused by a chronic nonspecific infection of the prostate. Treatment is accordingly directed to the area in the form of prostatic massages, urethral sounding and instillations, antibiotics and foreign protein therapy.

It is the author's belief, based on complete histories and thorough urologic investigation of a large group of patients, that a strictly organic orientation towards this syndrome is in need of revision. A careful history in these cases, usually requiring several sessions for its completion, will regularly reveal many disturbed elements in the patient's psychosexual development and numerous emotional conflicts. While no common personality type is specific for this syndrome as compared to normal persons, or those suffering from other conditions, nonetheless, a real similarity of personality structure has been evident in patients under my care.

These men are on the surface rather diffident and withdrawn, but harbor large ambitions that they recoil from attempting to realize. They are immature in their interpersonal relations and frequently remain bachelors. There is less than the usual masculine aggressiveness evident, with more emphasis on the passive "feminine" characteristics. The masturbatory activity of adolescence is not succeeded by the normal progression toward heterosexual love. These patients seem fixed, or have regressed to a level of preoccupation with sensations about the scrotal-perineal-anal area and have not attained the full genital primacy of the healthy male.

A study of the embryology of the cloaca and urogenital sinus may throw some light upon this matter. The primitive cloaca early splits into rectum and urogenital sinus. The nervous innervation, however, of both areas by the internal pudendal nerve is retained in the adult. The verumontanum (uterus masculinus) is of Müllerian derivation and is homologous to the uterus in the female as is the perineum and scrotal sacs of the man to the vulval area of the woman. The abnormal sensations complained of by these patients, seem selectively localized to the more "feminine" areas of their genital anatomy, in keeping with the greater prominence of the feminine characteristics in their personality structure.

The symptoms these patients complain of in the urethral, sexual and rectal spheres, may be interpreted as the effects of inadequate psychosexual integration mediated via disturbed internal pudendal innervation. Local pathologic tissue alterations follow as a consequence.

It is important to understand the secondary gains which the aformentioned symptoms have for the patient, but of which he is unaware on a conscious level. The development of pathologic changes in his "prostate" corporealizes all his anxieties in relation to sexual and other inadequacies into the sexual organ itself. He now has a culturally acceptable excuse for avoiding or minimizing heterosexual activities and for explaining his poor sexual performance. His sickness also furnishes an out for not competing in the world at large on the accepted aggressive "cocksure" masculine level.

However, the unconscious conflicts and tensions of the patient which are the true etiologic background of his symptoms, are not resolved by these maneuvers (which are what is meant by "secondary gains"). In fantasies and dreams he still indulges in aggressive, destructive, and socially highly forbidden acts, thus generating deep feelings of guilt, shame and unatoned sin, and with them, a need for punishment. The urologist, by performing painful instrumentations and treatments, provides this punishment there by relieving the patient of much of his anxiety. Clinical improvement sometimes follows.

If one is aware of the reason for the success of such treatment, one will also appreciate its weaknesses. In some cases, local therapy may relieve anxiety and may ameliorate pathologic changes in the posterior urethra which would tend to aggravate the condition.

In other cases, local treatment only serves to fix the "prostatic" nature of the disease in the patient's mind. In all cases, however, the local treatment leaves the total personality of the patient unaltered. To make it possible for the patient to achieve a higher and healthier psychosexual organization free from urinary and sexual difficulties and symptoms, we must treat the whole patient and not merely his posterior urethra. This implies, first of all, an understanding of the psychodynamic principles involved and then an orientation of therapeutic endeavors.

Some urologists have doubtless understood this more or less intuitively. It now becomes imperative for all urologists and other physicians who may be called upon to help such patients, to deepen their interest and skill in this type of psychosomatic medicine. A careful, thorough, and probing anamnesis designed to elicit informations concerning all facets of the patient's psychosexual development and personality, is the first essential. The type of local treatment, if any, and the extent of the psychotherapy which the urologist himself can administer must be highly individualized. A large majority of patients can probably be handled on this basis alone, with considerable success. However, when the occasion demands it, the urologist should prepare the patient for, and suggest, more thoroughgoing and experienced psychiatric care.

SEXUAL DYSFUNCTIONS IN THE MALE

Sexual dysfunctions in men are a most frequent complaint in clinical practice varying from the mildest form of occasional premature ejaculation to total permanent impotence. Not infrequently, as noted before, there are urinary and other associated symptoms.

Thorough urologic, endocrinologic and neurologic examinations rarely uncover an organic cause. There are, to be sure, important aspects of the problem that are evident on a conscious physiologic level. The wife who openly shows her repugnance to the sex act, or who frigidly submits to what she regards as her "wifely duties" will eventually induce at least a facultative impotence in her husband. Chronic ill-health, obesity in one or both partners, or gynecologic disease such as marked cystorectocoele or senile vaginal changes also militate against normal potency. However, premature ejaculation and impotence, in the overwhelming percentage of cases, are truly functional in the most literal sense. They are definitely not to be regarded as disease entities but rather as manifestations of an underlying neurotic disorder.

The physical union of the sexes is the most intimate of interpersonal relationships and is probably the most easily disturbed. The operative factors are often subtle, complicated, and vary from case to case. In both ejaculatio praecox, and impotentia, there is a conscious wish oriented toward the female, but at the moment of the sexual act, unconscious counter-impulses prevent fulfillment. Menninger[4] has summarized the etiologically important unconscious factors somewhat as follows:

Fear of Punishment:

Most of the important influences upon the growing child in our society, e.g., parental guidance, religious training, supervision of nurses and teachers, etc., inculcate the idea that sexual activities are evil. The formulation—that which is pleasurable is sexual, that which is sexual is bad, that which is bad is to be punished—may unconsciously dominate an individual's behavior for the rest of his life and may be powerful enough to inhibit any sexual effort. If punishment is forthcoming, however, the forbidden act may then be carried out. This may explain the favorable results sometimes obtained by painful treatments administered to the genital organs by the urologist.

Conflicting Loves:

A man cannot be potent with a woman because he loves another, without consciously being aware of this. Many men are still so attached to their mothers that they cannot love any other woman. To respond to another woman would be disloyal.

Homosexual elements do not disappear in some men with the result that they are unconsciously deeply attached to homosexual love objects and cannot perform normally on a heterosexual plane.

Inordinate unconscious love of self, a persisting narcissistic factor, can interfere with normal sexuality. His overvaluing of himself leads to an overvaluing of his own penis with excessive fear of loss or damage ot it. There is thus the "unmanly retreat" lest the organ be "lost or damaged" in the vagina. If infantile stages of sexuality have not been superseded, there is an overvaluation of the penis as an organ of micturition leading to later impairment of its sexual function. Abraham[1] has pointed out that premature ejaculation is like normal ejaculation only as to substance (semen) but is like the involuntary micturition of childhood as to the manner of it.

Conflicting Hates:

Aversion or actual hate for the very person consciously desired, may be responsible for inhibiting the sexual functions. The usual reasons for this unconscious hatred are fear or a desire for revenge. The revenge may be for things that happened to him in childhood. Hatred of the mother engendered by unhappy relationships may be repressed, only to emerge in later years as an unconscious hatred for all women. This motivation is evident in premature ejaculation where the aroused sexual feelings of the partner are completely frustrated. The ejaculate is symbolically "a soiling," "spitting upon," revenge and defiance. Consciously, however, the male often exhibits great shame and anxiety.

Another form of sexual dysfunction is that of a need for too frequent sexual activity. In these cases, a specious impression of hypersexuality may be created by the same factors that produce hyposexuality. These individuals strive again and again (but always in vain) to discharge through genital activity the sexuality they are unable to satisfy. They rarely achieve true satisfaction in orgasm or postcoital relaxation, and are, in fact, "orgastically impotent." The figures of Don Juan and the nymphomanic woman flitting from lover to lover fall into this category.

The foregoing brief survey of sexual dysfunctions in the male is more readily understood when related to the concept of the attainment of normal healthy masculine sexuality as a process beginning in infancy and continuing through adulthood. The psychosexual development is a continuum in which successive phases of sexual character are integrated. No phase wholly disappears but is merged into the total structure. Thus the pregenital, oral and anal level (incestuous, sadistic) of the child yields at age five or six to the phallic stage with its greater emphasis on urethral functions. Later, the pubescent boy evidences his sexuality in muscular activity involving the entire body. "Necking" and "dating" are pursued on a competitive level to prove masculinity by conquering as many women as possible. Full heterosexual genital primacy is attained at the adult level with tender, marital, protective aspects of sexuality coming to the fore. Competition here is no longer muscular, but intellectual.

Disturbances in relatedness to the significant persons of his formative years, complex unconscious instinctual conflicts and irrational motivations may interfere with an individual's normal psychosexual development.

This results in fixations at, or regressions to, immature levels. The specific forms of impaired potency are seen to correspond to these levels.

A young veteran who had received disabling bodily injuries in the war which necessitated a great limitation of his physical activities (especially athletic), returned home and adjusted well to his family life until he was turned down for an advanced professional course because of his physical limitations. He reacted to this by developing a great increase in his sexual drive. This consisted of persistent nagging of his wife to have sexual relations with him several times a night which produced resentment and withdrawal on his wife's part. The wife felt intuitively that she was being used as an outlet for some frustration and not as an adult love object. Investigation of the patient's symptom showed clearly that his physical limitations were not felt as a barrier to continued masculine competition as long as he was able to feel that his educational development was not obstructed. When this occurred (for valid reasons), he was forced back upon this more infantile mode of competitive sexual activity.

A forty-five-year-old man who worked in a doll factory came to the clinic complaining of loss of libido and inability to have an erection. He was in a third marriage. His first two wives had been quite openly unfaithful to him and although these marriages were unhappy and full of strife his potency had never failed him in sexual relations in either of these marriages. As a young man he had worked in a circus strong man act where he played the part of an "anvil." While lying suspended across two chairs, another man with a sledge hammer would break rocks upon his chest. He prided himself greatly upon his apparent strength but confided in the interviewer that it doesn't require as much strength as it appears to. In his third marriage he chose a devoted housewife who was entirely faithful to him. Shortly after this marriage, he lost his interest in sexual activity and his potency with his wife. Investigation revealed that although the impotence was a complex psychological phenomenon, one component of it was the loss of rival males with whom the sex act was an implied competition and challenge for supremacy.

This second case illustrates that part of many men's genital activity is unconsciously based—to a greater or lesser extent—upon the immature game of phallic competition. When this competitive aspect is withdrawn for some reason, there is not enough adult genital drive left for potency to be sustained.

In this formulation, the sexual dysfunctions are but symptoms of a disorder of the total personality; "the penis behaves like the man." Treatment, accordingly, must begin with an attempt at understanding the man. It is evident that no sovereign remedy or injection exists which will be uniformly successful. A complete examination and a comprehensive general and sexual history is the first step in treatment. In connection with the sexual history it is necessary to ask a series of probing, provocative questions in order to elicit the important data within a reasonable time period. Bergler[2] has elaborated on this point. The patient should be asked why he consulted a physician at this particular time? Does he have sexual intercourse because of a sexual need or because of a sense of duty? What partner or partners does he choose? What is the strength and duration of erection? What is the usual manner of performing intercourse? How long does it last? What is the manner of ejaculation? To what degree does he experience participation and excitement during the act? Does he have have fantasies during intercourse? Can he sleep after coitus? Are there dreams related to it? What are his moods the day after? Does he spend much time worrying about himself and his health? Do external difficulties influence his sexual desire? Why did he marry (or remain a bachelor)?*

The discussion involved in taking such a history may itself be of therapeutic value. General and local treatment must be particularized for each patient. Reassurance and suggestive therapy may be helpful by permitting a degree of identification by the patient with his "omnipotent" doctor from whom he can receive a measure of masculinity to supplement his own. Long continued local treatments, on the contrary, increase the patient's dependence upon the doctor and frustrate really masculine identification. Because other aspects of the patient, not only the sexual, often require treatment, intensive psychotherapy may frequently be necessary.

URINARY FREQUENCY

Urinary frequency with clear, sterile urine but without any remarkable lesion evident in the urethra or bladder, is a common syndrome in women. These patients will often remark that the frequency is worse when they are under any "emotional tension." That the urinary bladder responds to anxiety with increased tonus has been demonstrated by Straub, Ripley and Wolf,[6] who determined intravesical pressures in subjects and noted an abrupt rise in pressure when emotionally charged material was discussed with them. The increased frequency of the usual clinical case is evidently produced by this mechanism. However, when emotional disturbances, usually of an unconscious nature, continue over a protracted period, it is probable that the persisting vesical hypertonus leads to morphologic changes within the bladder wall. This may very likely be the pathogenesis of so-called interstitial cystitis or "Hunner's ulcer" where there is little change in the bladder as viewed cystoscopically, but where the capacity of the organ is so reduced as to require frequent voiding day and night. These patients are "highly nervous" and "neurasthenic," and when they are only seen in the end stage, their nervousness does not seem disproportionate to the actual difficulties of their life situation. However, the younger female patients, seen before substantial diminution of bladder capacity has set in, give the impression of being the female counterparts of the male with "chronic prostatitis" as described in a prior section.

* It must be borne in mind that such questions may be most traumatic to some patients. Therefore, the questions should be gentle and casual; one must take one's cue from the patient and sooner cease than persist.

It seems, in this context, that the urge to urinate may substitute for a sexual urge. It is, in some patients, as though the excitement were simply displaced from the clitoris and the vagina to the urethral orifice and the bladder, and that the vesical sphincter experience the orgastic contractions which ordinarily belong to the genitals. The micturition, then, can practically attain the equivalent of the orgasm.

Such aspects of urinary frequency are not restricted to females, but probably occur in them more often than in males. As already mentioned, some forms of premature ejaculation of the male must be considered equivalents of urination, in terms of the emotional stage of the patient and the aggressive content of his fantasies about intercourse. In children of either sex, enuresis and other forms of urinary incontinence, may at times be related to sexual excitement with or without definite relationship to masturbation. (See discussion of enuresis in the chapter on Pediatrics.)

CONCLUSION

That there is a definite relationship between abnormalities of psychosexual development, life stress, emotions and the production of diseases of the genitourinary organs, has become increasingly evident. Further elucidation and understanding of the mechanisms whereby these disorders become manifest is necessary. It will be forthcoming when more urologists and other physicians concerned will interest themselves in these problems and, by controlled observation, planned experimentation, and statistical interpretation, will make their contributions to this important area of medicine.

BIBLIOGRAPHY

1. Abraham, Karl: Ejaculatio Praecox; Selected Papers. London, Hogarth Press, 1927.
2. Bergler, Edmund: Neurotic Counterfeit Sex. New York, Grune & Stratton, 1951.
3. Cone, Robert E.: Psychosomatic problems in urology. J. Urol. 56: 146, 1946.
4. Menninger, Karl A.: Impotence or frigidity from the standpoint of psychoanalysis. J. Urol. 34: 166, 1935.
5. Shapiro, Bernard: Premature ejaculation. J. Urol. 50: 374, 1943.
6. Straub, Ripley and Wolf: Experimental approach to psychosomatic bladder disorders. New York M. J. 49: 435, 1949.

CHAPTER 9

Rehabilitation, Orthopedics and Psychiatry

MORRIS GRAYSON, M.D.
ALLEN S. RUSSEK, M.D.

Dr. Grayson received his M.D. from the University of Lausanne, Switzerland, and, after internship, took psychiatric training at the Salpetière Hospital, Paris and Bellevue Hospital, N. Y. He took his psychoanalytic training at the New York Psychoanalytic Institute.

He is at present, Director of Psychiatric Research in Rehabilitation at the Institute of Physical Medicine and Rehabilitation, New York University, Bellevue Medical Center. He is also an Instructor in Psychiatry, New York University Medical College, New York University Post Graduate Medical School as well as Assistant Attending Neuropsychiatrist, Bellevue Hospital and University Hospital. He served with the MTO as Flight Surgeon and Psychiatrist.

Dr. Grayson just completed a three year study of "Psychiatric Aspects of Rehabilitation" under the auspices of the Commonwealth Fund. He is a Fellow of the American Psychiatric Association.

Dr. Russek received his medical degree from the Royal College of Physicians and Surgeons, Edinburgh, Scotland. He interned at the Rockaway Beach Hospital, Rockaway Beach, Long Island. He received orthopedic training at the Veterans Administration Hospital, Hines, Illinois and at U. S. Marine Hospital, Staten Island, N. Y. He trained in physical medicine at the Mayo Clinic.

He is now Assistant Professor of Physical Medicine and Rehabilitation, New York University College of Medicine; Attending in Physical Medicine and Rehabilitation, New York University–Bellevue Medical Center; Director of Physical Medicine, Roosevelt Hospital, New York; and Attending Orthopedic Surgeon and Director of Rehabilitation, Willowbrook State School, Staten Island, New York.

REHABILITATION

R EHABILITATION IS THE RESTORATION of the individual to the fullest physical, mental, social and economic usefulness of which he is capable. This latter qualifying phrase, "of which he is capable," implies a certain responsibility upon the medical profession which they have not heretofore been called upon to assume; namely, to recognize and utilize the abilities of the patient. A good deal of the opinions in this regard (until recently) have been based upon tangential evidence and, to a great extent, upon the physical components of the disability. This latter overweighting of the neuro-muscular and skeletal structure has been apparent to orthopedists as well as to all clinicians in the field of physical medicine.

To repair the mechanical defect in a dropped foot or a broken leg or arm, for example, never assures the orthopedist that the patient will walk. And if the patient does walk, what assurance do we have that the patient will again take his place on the job and in society? The orthopedist can well say that such is not his job; that he has done his surgery within the limits of his capacities. However, the modern orthopedist feels a responsibility not only toward the arm or the leg, but to the human being.

The orthopedist can point to innumerable examples in which he finds that repair of the mechanical difficulty is just the pivot point around which he practices his specialty. Some of the other problems encountered in ortho-pedic rehabilitation are: (1) chronic invalidism; (2) chronic back pain; (3) compensation neuroses; (4) fracture rehabilitation; and (5) plaster cast problems.

While these general problems do not cover every psychological problem encountered in orthopedics, they serve in a general way as an introduction to a psychodynamic understanding of the total individual.

Chronic invalidism is the ghost that stalks every specialty and ortho-pedics is no exception. The number of patients upon whom excellent surgery is performed and who nevertheless become bedridden are innumerable. Obviously, something went wrong. The degree of invalidism is quite vari-able. It may be the extreme of being completely bedridden and not engaging in any vocation or avocation. Or the invalidism may reach the point of extreme withdrawal. Invalidism in this sense means that the individual has become unproductive.

Incrimination of the psychic apparatus in this withdrawal is justified. However, the psychic apparatus does not suddenly come into play when the injury takes place, during the operation, or after the operation. The psychic apparatus is constantly at work in relationship to the physical being. To separate the mechanical function of the skeletal structure from its psychic function is a very arbitrary separation as can readily be seen from the emotional chaos that can result from a relatively minor injury to the hand or to the leg. In psychiatry, we refer to the investment of a particular part of the body with psychic energy as "cathexis." We do not know exactly what cathexis is, we cannot really measure it; but we do know that parts of our body have *special meaning* to us beyond their mechanical structure. For example, to the orthopedist, a hand may mean that particular structure which is composed of a certain number of bones, muscles, blood vessels, etc., and has a certain physical configuration. It is used for work and the fingers and wrist can be flexed, pronated, supinated, etc. However, to the patient, beyond its mechanical structure, the hand may be an object of which he is proud because it is handsome or because he can do his particular work with it. It has accessory meaning for him because he can caress his own body with it or he can caress a loved object with it. He may have guilt feelings about the hand because it is used in masturbation or as a means of striking someone. Therefore, to each individual, each part of the body has a different meaning, and it is just this individualized meaning that accounts for the differing reactions to orthopedic correction.

Another psychic mechanism that should be understood, is the mechanism of regression. *Regression is the unconscious act of reverting to emotional mechanisms which were used in early childhood.* In any injury or disease, the psyche tries to defend itself and uses every mechanism it has experienced in the past to ward off danger. One of the easiest it can use is to withdraw, and withdrawal means going back to the comforts of being taken care of, of having the body caressed, of being fed and, in a larger sense, of having no responsibilities except eating, sleeping and defecation. This, of course, is not always accepted by the individual, and the individual makes efforts at restitution toward the adult stage of psychic development.

The efforts at restitution made by the individual are frequently hampered by:

1. The overwhelming nature of the physical disability.
2. Tendencies on the part of the environment to encourage infantilism.
3. The limitations of the individual's psychic resources.
4. Unconscious motivation.
5. Depression.

1. *The Overwhelming Nature of the Physical Disability.* Despite the psychic drive of the individual to take his or her place in society as an adult, the physical disability may be so overwhelming that the individual may make many attempts at psychic restitution but may find the physical disability just too much and will have to lapse in a regressed state despite himself. This may frequently be seen in severe quadriplegics, the arthritides and fractures of the hip in the older age group.

However, such is not necessarily the case. We have seen, and many cases have been reported, in which—on their own initiative or with the help of concentrated efforts—individuals have been able to gain their place in adult society on an equal level (and occasionally on a superior level) in spite of severe crippling disabilities. The recent results in rehabilitation have indicated that if the disease process is not in itself progressive, concerted efforts in a team approach can prevent regressive phenomena in many cases and prevent invalidism.

2. *Tendencies on the Part of the Environment to Encourage Infantilism.* One cannot think of the patient as an isolated individual. Psychologically,

in a disability, environment plays an important role. The patient has parents, a husband or wife, children, an employer, friends, and last but not least, a physician, nurses, attendants, etc. They all play a role in the patient's willingness or unwillingness to hold on to the psychic "benefits" of regression.

The psychic benefits of regressive behavior are many. In fact, it is frequently easier for the environment to encourage regression. The actual work expended on the part of the individual, the family, friends and physician to make a disabled individual adult and productive is great. It is for that reason that rehabilitative measures may fail. It is frequently in response to the family's neurotic need that the individual is not encouraged to become independent. Despite protestations to the contrary, some mothers will prefer to have their "baby" back again; some wives will go out to work and support their disabled husbands and encourage the dependency of the mate. Nurses often discourage efforts at independence. Physicians, themselves, psychologically overwhelmed by the crippling of the patient, may resort to more futile surgery or may give up. The author has been a witness to frequent depressive bouts in physicians who wonder out loud "why the patient does not give up."

The neurotic needs of the environment to encourage withdrawal on the part of the patient is a subject worthy of a text in itself. This subject will not be discussed in this paper. Suffice to say that crippling sets up anxieties in the environment which are defended by rationalizations. While we are making great strides in getting jobs for the handicapped, their employment is always beset by technical objections which essentially reflect society's basic anxieties about crippling.

3. *The Limitations of the Patient's Psychic Resources.* Some form of regression always takes place in physical disability. Naturally, one has to ask oneself, what level of psychic maturity had the patient reached before the injury. Was this individual always a child? Psychic invalidism may have been present before the physical insult. This factor must be known before any efforts at rehabilitation are made. It would be somewhat ambitious to expect a basically immature, passive-dependent individual to suddenly blossom out with a different personality because of a physical disability.

However, the basic psychic resources are frequently used as an excuse by physicians to avoid the work necessary in rehabilitation. Intellectual endowment is a poor indicator in rehabilitation. Emotional maturity and good interpersonal relations are better indicators. The author and his co-workers have found that the ability to relate to people* is an excellent index for

---

* "The ability to relate" is a condensed phrase for the concept of primary and secondary narcissism. Readers interested in a highly technical but excellent discussion and elaboration on the subject are referred to Freud's original papers on the subject.[6]

prognosis in rehabilitation. Such an index naturally cannot be put in numerical terms. It requires careful qualitative examination and can readily be obtained by the good clinician whose interest is directed beyond the mechanics of the affected part.

4. *Unconscious Motivation.* In the opening paragraphs of this chapter, it was pointed out that each part of the body has a special meaning for each individual. This meaning is based not only on recent experiences in the life of the individual but to a great extent on very early experiences when the child was beginning to experience the meaning of his bodily functions in relation to the outside world. These experiences are supposedly forgotten but in reality become part of one's unconscious self (repressed). These unconscious formulations invest our behavior and play a great role in the restitutive efforts of the disabled.

Unfortunately, when the unconscious self begins "to show," it creates problems for the individual and for the environment.

A thirty-year-old married woman sustained a left hemiplegia following childbirth. Although physical methods helped this patient considerably, she became withdrawn, refusing to leave the house except at night "when people couldn't see me." She became a problem to herself, to her husband and above all, to physicians. She kept consulting physicians constantly insisting that she needed more physical exercises. Careful psychiatric examination and periodic interviews revealed that the patient was blaming the disability on a premarital abortion and unconsciously felt that by looking at her paralyzed arm, people could know all about her "sin." She thus avoided contact with other people.

In another instance a young man with a flaccid upper extremity insisted that "people hate cripples" and became "a problem" at the hospital because of his objectionable attitude toward other patients and the family. Working with this patient revealed that some of his early memories related to threats by his mother that if he imitated cripples, he would become like them.

Unconscious material never presents itself in the simple fashion outlined above. Some knowledge of psychodynamic formulations is necessary to bridge the gap between the symptomatology as it presents itself and the apparent unrelatedness to logical reasoning.

Some of the statements which reflect deeper psychological problems are the following: "People stare at cripples," "Nobody wants to marry cripples," "I am useless to anybody," "Without the use of my arm I am useless," and "Nobody wants to employ cripples."

All the above statements have strong elements of truth in them, yet they always reflect individual dynamic problems which form part of the unconscious formulations within the individual. The incontrovertible fact remains that severely physically handicapped individuals do get married, do lead useful lives, do get jobs, and get along very well with their fellow men. The individuality of the patient's formulations must be stressed.

5. *Depression.* Hostility as an active component in the unconscious of a patient (who is angry at the world which "let me down") can give the examiner some working basis for understanding the patient's problems. Hostility in its conscious manifestations may be "free-floating" so that the patient will express it indiscriminately. When the patient is depressed and is contemplating suicide, it means that the hostility has been turned toward himself. "Killing" which is what the patient feels like doing when he contemplates suicide, is turned from the outside world on to himself. In simple depressions, one can say that the patient does not like himself. When he is disabled, he has to blame somebody. When he directs it to the outside world, one sees aggressiveness, free-floating hostility, and even paranoid projections. When he directs it toward himself, one sees depression (and the two can be present simultaneously and alternatingly).

This relatively simple formulation has therapeutic implication. A depression is readily recognized. However, when the patient attempts to relieve his own depression, one will observe the movement of aggression and hostility outwardly. It is then that the physician, family and attendants may be the unwelcome recipients of this hostility and it is then that the environment must recognize it as a means of restitution and treat it as such. Treating hostility with hostility may reproduce the depression and further psychological (and physical) invalidism.

Specific Orthopedic Problems

Chronic Back Pain. Chronic back pain constitutes one of the many unsolved problems of orthopedic practice. Psychosomatic medicine is making many contributions to the understanding of chronic back pain, yet complete scientific formulations remain elusive. The answer to this elusiveness can probably be explained on the basis of the multiplicity of the causation. Just as in the organic approach wherein chronic back pain may be due to the involvement of any of the systems (gastrointestinal, genitourinary, neuromusculoskeletal) or a combination of all of them, the psychological structure may be just as diffusely involved.

Efforts at isolating the psychic mechanism of low back pain have been relatively unsuccessful. The particular meaning of this particular symptom is an individual one. In some cases it may mean repressed hostility, in others it may be a combination of hostility and passivity. In others it may mean an unconscious identification with the opposite sex (identification of the male with premenstrual pains in the female). In some patients the posture that the patient assumes as a protective mechanism has unconscious meaning (camptocormia*). "Tension," as a well recognized musculoskeletal

* This is a static deformity consisting of a forward flexion of the trunk. It is an hysterical condition.

finding, has as much meaning to the patient in the psychic sphere as it does in the musculoskeletal sphere and it is unscientific to separate them. Low back pain frequently acts as a good "excuse" in the avoidance of sexual relations. An observation which the author has made and which requires further study is that the greater the functional element in low back pain, the less there is of sexual intercourse. Severe back pain does not usually interfere with sexual intercourse.

The approach to low back pain by the orthopedist will be most rewarding, if he thinks in terms of "what is the patient trying to tell me by the low back pain." In order to approach this question, it is necessary to obtain as good a psychological history as one does a medical history and to see if one can parallel some of the findings in the organic sphere with the psycho-social events as related by the patient. If at first, parallelism is unrewarding, frequent interviews will often make the situation clearer. The either/or approach to causation should be avoided and the physician should manifest as much interest in the patient's interpersonal relationships as he does in the physical examination.

The frequent objections on the part of the orthopedist to deviation from the pure physical examination and physical prescription is that any other approach is time consuming. *This objection is invalid since the "low back pain" patient is a chronic returner and frustration is actually seen first in the physician and secondarily in the patient.* It is suggested that physical examination can be alternated with a psychosocial approach to the problem.

A basic orientation in rehabilitation is toward the abilities of the patient rather than his disabilities. As such, the abilities have to be explored. After a good relationship is made with the patient and he has an awareness of the effect of psychological conflict as an activating force in the disability, the patient should be encouraged toward a utilization of his abilities which do not effect the low back pain. It can be thought of as "adjustment therapy."

Needless to say, such an approach requires the complete confidence of the patient. When the patient begins to assume his modified role socially, vocationally and psychologically, he needs continued support. Such support should be only in part physical and a good part should be devoted to his psychological conflicts. It the orthopedist feels himself incompetent in the latter approach it may best be accompanied by a working relationship between an orthopedist and psychiatrist.

FRACTURES

To understand the meaning of a fracture to an individual, one should recognize that legs and arms have special meaning to each individual beyond their physical function. One should again be reminded that sexual and aggressive drives may be expressed through the appendages. As such, a fracture of the physical structure also means an involvement of those particular drives. The patient reacts to them according to his previous experience with those drives and according to his previous personality structure.

An aspect more conscious and well observable by the physician is the reaction of the family to the fracture and to the operative procedures. The patient and his family usually want to know at the earliest possible moment whether he will be a "cripple," and after reduction of the fracture the question frequently arises "is it healing all right?" It is difficult to give positive answers to these questions without benefit of the time factor; and on the basis of x-ray findings, an over-optimistic viewpoint is often held by the surgeon. Few major fractures heal with no disability. The patient and his family must understand that in most instances during the healing period of the fracture there is an unavoidable development of functional deterioration relating to the adjacent joints and muscles. Much of the worry and unnecessary anxiety following the removal of plaster casts can be avoided if some hint of the anticipated disability in the joints and muscles is given in advance. This serves to establish confidence in the surgeon by implying a familiarity with the condition, and avoids having the patient face an unexpected development in the course of the injury.

In the convalescent stage of fracture treatment, the patient should be an important member of the rehabilitation team and should be invited to carry his full responsibility as a member. He must have definite instructions with regard to the necessary exercises for those parts which can be exercised. X-rays of the injured part should be taken during the course of the healing of any major fracture, at appropriate intervals. While it is true that many patients "cannot afford x-rays," it is equally apparent that few patients cannot afford a lawyer. The time spent in the early phases of treatment in explaining the nature and sequelae of the particular fracture dealt with will always be rewarding to the physician, patient and the family.

In cases where injuries to the body have been frequent, it is most important to look into the question of accident-proneness. When an individual has been injured more than once or twice, we can postulate a desire to hurt himself. Sometimes it is conscious, but more frequently it is unknown or unconscious.

PLASTER CASTS

The long history of the use of the plaster cast in the treatment of fractures and postoperative fixation for orthopedic operations has established a certain familiarity in the lay mind with the waiting period following such procedures. Most people, however, do not realize that the plaster cast itself is a method of fixation of the bones and contributes nothing to the healing process. In addition, the cast also immobilizes joints and muscles. For this reason, it is necessary to dispel the idea that in the cast, nature takes its course and all will be well. The disappointment often seen when a cast is removed is evidence enough that the patient must be given some insight into what has been taking place. Some advance knowledge of the stiffness in joints, the weakness of muscles and the visible atrophy as anticipated complications of prolonged immobilization must be conveyed to the patient in time to prevent his complete dissatisfaction with what may have been perfectly adequate treatment.

The patient's responsibility for using the disabled part after the cast has been removed must be impressed upon him so that he does not "wait" to get well passively. The need for his cooperation in carrying out specific orders provides an important objective during the period of immobilization and continues on a tangible basis in the convalescent stage when active movement is permitted.

It is difficult to explain to many persons the reason for not using a cast in the treatment of certain fractures because of the long association of plaster of Paris with the treatment of fractures. A physician must be constantly prepared to ask himself some very serious questions with regard to the continued use of a plaster case. Prolongation of the period of immobilization may fix the disability physically as well as psychologically since the functional disabilities attendant to fractures hardly ever are related to the fractured bones. It is more often the stiff joints, weakness of muscles, and pain which are disturbing to the patient and ultimately constitute the physical disability. This disability may be quite serious even in the course of a fracture which by x-ray has healed according to schedule, and it appears somewhat unfair to the patient and his family to be kept completely ignorant of this possiblity while being told that the fracture is "doing fine." Successful treatment is ultimately measured by succesful function and not by x-ray findings.

Again, the special meaning of the plaster cast must be emphasized and only with careful attention to the mood, attitude and verbalizations of the patient will the physician be rewarded. The illogical, fantastic notions that the adult patient may have about the cast will affect his mood, pain reactions and attitudes toward the present and future. Such notions may be entirely "childish," but if we remember that regressive thinking is always prominent in the sick, we will not be caught unaware. In a recent report from the Mayo Clinic, some interesting observations were made about phantom limb pain (see chapter on Neurology, and chapter on Surgery). The authors found that in three separate cases, disturbed fantastic notions as to the disposition of the severed limb affected the sensory complaints about the phantom. While these fantasies are not necessarily the same in all phantoms, it points up the necessity for the exploration of the patient's psyche in order to explain what appears to be physical complaints. That which is going on under the cast and what the patient believes is going on, may be two different things. Rational or irrational, bizarre symptoms usually are explained on the basis of the irrational, since the unconscious has a rationale of its own.

Compensation Neurosis. This term is used as a catch-all for the psychological problems encountered in dealing with a patient who has a delayed recovery and at the same time is receiving monetary remuneration as long as he is incapacitated. This parallel situation is another apparently insurmountable marriage which is giving rise to a great deal of loose thinking on the part of the medical profession.

The whole system of putting a monetary value on the loss of a limb, an eye, a toe, etc., creates a working basis between the physician, attorneys, insurance companies, and compensation agencies, and the whole economic structure which is as complex to the psyche of the individual as it is to physician. Although monetary values pervade medical thinking, there is a strong tendency to incriminate this relationship in many forms of invalidism.

There is no question but such is the case in many instances of psychological invalidism. However, one must be aware of the number of cases in which the pre-morbid earning capacity was far in excess of the financial remuneration. As such, the gain cannot be purely financial and one must seek for it elsewhere.

Psychologically, we refer to this type of gain as "secondary." Money may be the "secondary gain." However, other factors within the compensation may also be the secondary gain, such as: hostility toward the wife and children, hostility toward an employer, physician or insurance company. Patients say: "I will show that insurance company that they can't push me around," or "The first doctor that treated me said I was a faker." The gain may be in the form of attention-seeking mechanisms.

Primary gain refers essentially to unconscious gain in which the meaning of the disability is vested in the childhood experiences of the individual. Primary gain can be recognized only by intensive psychological examination. It is most conspicuous in the conversion symptoms. One frequently sees instances in which the physical disability will produce a reversal of roles between a man and his wife. The man will stay home and take care of the household while the wife goes out to work. We consider this a gain which cannot be accounted for on the basis of the financial compensation. Although the patient protests that it is not what he wants, other inner forces are holding him to this reversal.

In either primary or secondary gain, therapy must be directed at offering the patient "something better." One is frequently hard put to find such substitutes. In such instances, the physician must avoid projecting his own ideas of "something better" upon the patient. If, however, one "knows" the patient in the true sense of the word, then real needs can be worked with, within the framework of gratification to the patient. Accomplishment is usually a source of gratification to the anxiety-ridden patient and if he can see that he can really do things in a vocational setting, and if some arrangements can be made for therapeutic vocational placement, then some of his needs may be met.

There is a current top level misunderstanding as to insurance liability in the employment of the physically disabled. It is not true (as frequently stated) that insurance premiums rise in the employment of the physically handicapped.* As such, vocational therapeutic trials can be arranged with the agreement of compensation carriers.

In the rehabilitation of "the compensation case," a great deal of attention must be focused on his interpersonal relations, familial setting and social needs. Such a focus will be most rewarding provided the treating physician can get the real confidence of the patient and that he does not treat the patient as a malingerer. Slips of the tongue, casual remarks, hostile attitudes are readily picked up by the patient (as a child does), and such may negate any other so-called "frank" discussions.

In orthopedics, as in all other medical practice, the whole patient, and not just an ailment, needs be understood and treated.

BIBLIOGRAPHY

1. Barker, R. S., Wright, B. A. and Gonick, M. R.: Adjustment to Physical Handicap and Illness: A Survey of the Social Psychology of Physique and Disability. Bull. No. 55, Soc. Sci. Research Council, New York, 1946.
2. Blazer, A.: Backache as a Psychosomatic problem. Am. J. Psychotherapy. 2: 441, 1948.
3. Boland, E. W. and Carr, W. P.: Psychogenic rheumatism. J.A.M.A. 123: 805, 1943.
4. Buchwald, E.: Physical Rehabilitation for Daily Living. New York, McGraw-Hill, 1952.
5. Fetterman, J. L.: Vertebral neurosis. Psychosom. Med. 2: 265, 1940.
6. Freud, S.: On Narcissism, Collected Papers, London, Hogarth Press, 1946. Vol. IV.
7. Grayson, M.: Concept of "acceptance" in physical rehabilitation. J.A.M.A. 145: 893–896, 1951.
8. Jones, W. L.: Backache in industrial injuries. Wisconsin M. J. 44: 1069, 1945.
8a. Kolb, F. W.: Treatment of the acute painful phantom, Proc. Staff Meet. Mayo Clin. 25: 1952.

* From "The Report to the Chairman Manpower Policy Committee—Office of Defense Mobilization," by the Task Force on the Handicapped, Washington, D. C., January 26, 1952.

9. Luck, J. V.: Low back pain. J. Indiana M. A. *37:* 452, 1944.
10. Menninger, W. C.: Psychosomatic medicine, somatization reaction. Psychosom. Med. *9:* 92, 1947.
11. ——: Emotional Adjustments of the Handicapped. Read before the National Society for Crippled Children and Adults, Nov. 7, 1948.
12. Maloney, J. C.: The effort syndrome and low back pain. J. Nerv. & Ment. Dis. *108:* 10, 1948.
13. Paul L.: Psychosomatic aspects of low back pain. Psychosom. Med. *12:* 116–124, 1950.
14. Paulette, J. D.: Low back pain. Lancet. *2:* 272, 1947.
15. Ruesch, J.: Chronic Disease and psychological invalidism. Psychosom. Monogr. No. 9, 1946.
16. Rusk, H. A.: New Hope for the Handicapped. New York, Harpers, 1946.
17. Smith, A. DeF.: Causes of low back pain. Tr. A. Life Insur. M. Dir. America. *33:* 23–34, 1949.
18. Solomon, A. P.: Low back pain, the psychosomatic viewpoint. Indust. Med. *18:* 6, 1949.
19. Weiss, E.: Psychogenic rheumatism. Ann. Int. Med. *26:* 890, 1947.

CHAPTER 10

Ear, Nose and Throat Diseases and Psychiatry

ADOLF ZECKEL, M.D.

Dr. Zeckel received his M.D. at the Medical School of the University of Groningen, Netherlands. He also received psychiatric and neurologic training there and was made Chef de Clinique of the Department of Neuropsychiatry.

He was in private practice in Rotterdam and received his psychoanalytic training in the Netherlands and at the New York Psychoanalytic Institute. Dr. Zeckel was Director of the Psychological Laboratory at the Institute for the Deaf in Rotterdam and worked particularly on aphasias, speech disorders, and deafness. He is an Associate in Psychiatry at Columbia University and is at present collaborating with Dr. Edmund P. Fowler, Jr. (Chairman of Department of Otolaryngology, College of Physicians and Surgeons, Columbia University), on psychosomatic problems of deafness and Ménière's disease.

He is a Member of the New York Psychoanalytic Society, Fellow of the American Psychiatric Association, Member of the New York Academy of Sciences and the American Psychosomatic Society.

THE GENERAL PRACTITIONER and the specialist encounter a vast amount of emotional problems in this branch of medicine. The majority of these problems are connected with an important function that is disturbed in these disorders, namely *communication*. Communication with the outside world, either by hearing and by understanding speech of others or by conveying one's thoughts to others by means of phonation and articulation, is impeded or not possible at all in diseases of the ear or of the larynx and nearby organs. This disturbance as a rule leads to a great deal of conflict with the environment and also to considerable inner problems. Our whole society is based on an intricate system of communication, which is continuously becoming more complex.[13] The more specialized such a system becomes the more vulnerable it will be at the same time when certain vital elements of which it is composed are failing. If important functions like hearing or speech break down, the psychological structure of the person who is dependent on well-functioning organs is endangered.

Another function that can be the cause of similar psychological issues is *respiration*. When free breathing is seriously hindered, an immediate threat to the patient's life exists, of course. Sometimes, however, fear of choking occurs in neurotic individuals without sufficient local pathology. The emergency character of acute inflammatory or mildly obstructing conditions in pharynx or larynx may not infrequently cause a great amount of anxiety, even when the situation is basically entirely harmless. (See also chapter on Internal Medicine and the section or chest surgery in chapter on Surgery.)

Other factors that have emotional implications will be mentioned only briefly, as they will be found in various other chapters.

In the following paragraphs, the realistic as well as the symbolic meaning of each organ will precede the discussion of emotional attitudes of the patient and the problems that his surroundings and his physicians have to cope with.

THE EAR

The Real Meaning of the Ear

Not only hearing, but also orientation in space can become disturbed in diseases of the ear. Of these two, however, hearing loss is by far the more important cause of psychiatric problems. Hearing loss is often a chronic problem, occurring both in healthy and in sick people. It is an annoying disturbance, because the hard-of-hearing person usually has every reason to believe that, except for the deafness, he could have functioned just as well as others. Deafness, especially if it is congenital or acquired in early life, will isolate the patient to such an extent that education in public schools is impossible. In almost all cases admission to special schools for the deaf is desirable at a very early age. In all these cases deafness will limit the child's contact with the hearing world and it will be of decisive importance for his whole development.

The Symbolic Meaning of the Ear

The symbolic meaning which the organ itself and its functions have in the patient's unconscious plays a role in his unrealistic attitudes towards the ear and hearing. In other chapters of this book the manner in which the body and performance of its organs are unconsciously understood has been repeatedly stressed. Here we shall see the significance of symbolism again.

The ear is an apparatus that in the first place receives sounds. The emphasis should be on the act of receiving; it is mostly seen as a passive happening. Sound waves pass the outer auditory meatus to finally reach the inner ear, the organ of Corti, from where they are conducted to the central organ of perception, the brain.

As in the unconscious, one opening can stand for any other one, the ear-opening may become equated with female genitals, mouth, anus, etc. The penetration of the sound waves through the outer opening of the ear makes an unconscious equation with any other opening possible.

The function of hearing may unconsciously be conceived as passive or active, or both at the same time. Listening requires active direction of the attention. In the case of sounds of low intensity an excellent acuity of hearing is needed. We can readily see that in eavesdropping, hearing and listening easily acquire forbidden active qualities. Since hearing can be an active process, impairment or loss of hearing can be felt as a weakness, which means a deficiency, a lack of power. Good hearing then means to the individual the same as being clever, powerful, potent; whereas loss of hearing may become equated with stupidity, impotence, frigidity, doom. Loss of hearing can deprive the individual of background sounds (rain, wind, street noises) that usually are unconsciously perceived. When this faculty is lost, the unconscious perception of sounds cannot be coupled with the individual's organic rhythmic activities (respiration, heartbeat, etc.). The result can be that the deaf person feels no contact with a living world and feels like dead.

Ramsdell explains the depression often seen in the beginning of deafness as loss of the outside world because disappearance of sounds at the primitive level, as explained above, makes the person no longer part of a living world.[12]

This may be very true; yet conscious loss of hearing probably means primarily a loss of relationship with other people. Such a loss, more than that of background sound, is annihilation, and this type of unrelatedness causes depression. This, more than anything else, means "nobody cares for me."

Whatever the predominant symbolic meaning of ear and of hearing for a patient will be depends, of course, on history, personality, environment, etc. All these factors will finally decide what kind of attitudes we should expect.[10] Aside from unrealistic, neurotic attitudes, we can learn the symbolic meaning of the ear in everyday life and from myth and legend.

Erotic meaning. Certain types of erotic kissing in which the outer meatus of the ear is touched and tickled can with some women lead to orgasm. Mutual stimulation of the external canal is practiced as erotic foreplay. In legend and myth, conception through the ear is described. In such cases the level of thinking is so primitive that the ear is more equated with a cloacal concept than with a vagina. Such symbolism seems to be probable in the legend of the Madonna's conception through the ear according to Jones.[8]

Anal meaning. That the ear is equated with the anus can be seen often in children who consider the yellow cerumen a form of fecal matter. Adults in whom cerumen is removed sometimes react to this procedure with shame. They believe that the physician must think that they did not clean themselves well. Unless the physician explains the mechanism of cerumen formation and removal, they may feel guilty and dirty and may be too embarrassed to appear again for another treatment. In some diseases of the ear that are accompanied by a bad-smelling discharge, early emotional patterns that once belonged to childhood problems around toilet-training can be revived.

The Attitudes of the Patient in Relation to the Ear

As was briefly mentioned before, the patient's problem is dependent on the age at which hearing loss started. The child who was born deaf or who lost hearing early in life has problems entirely different from those of the child who became deaf when speech was already firmly established. Again, the adolescent and the young person have a different problem to deal with than the middle aged person or the patient who turns deaf at an advanced age.

Deaf-born children or those who become deaf early in life, called the adventitiously deaf, sometimes have insurmountable difficulties if they grow up with hearing children. In that case they are totally inadequate, become very early frustrated and depressed and finally make no attempt to establish any contact with the others. Some of them are regarded as mentally deficient, until their deafness is diagnosed. The remedy of this situation was formerly to place the children early in institutions where they could communicate with other children who were handicapped similarly; in recent times, however, it has been felt more desirable that the children go to day schools for the deaf and that the parents participate intensely in their education and that they are encouraged to devote considerable time and effort with the guide of home courses to establish a meaningful and affectionate contact between the family and the deaf child.

Sometimes a child comes to the institute for the deaf already so depressed that he is considered of very low intelligence due to his awkward behavior. In the following paragraph an example to illustrate such a case is given:

A boy of about 14 years of age was seen in an institute for the deaf where I was doing intelligence testing. The teacher sent this boy with the remark that he seemed to be intellectually very retarded and that he would probably lack the basic understanding required to do the performance test. To our surprise this boy belonged to the highest group of IQ's that I have seen among the deaf. In the conversation that followed it became evident that the depression was caused by his frustration and isolation while living for a long time with hearing children and adults. He withdrew completely and due to his apathy, which was in reality depression, gave the impression of being backward. His skill in the performance test, which was also unusual with a depression, gave us insight which led eventually to a better type of adjustment.

Aside from depressions or from real organic defects, a deaf child is apt to be intellectually underestimated by the hearing environment, because the deaf and the hearing speak an entirely different language for a long time.[1, 11, 14]

It is not until the deaf child has acquired a sufficient grasp of the symbolic expression that we call speech that he gets a chance to be accepted by the hearing world.

Deafness in Child in Whom Speech is Established. When the child becomes deaf at the age at which full possession of speech has already been acquired, he often behaves for a long time as though he hears fully well, denying any difficulty in hearing. This leads again often to a diagnosis by teachers of mental dullness, or by others is explained as obstinacy, apathy, hostility, whatever the situation may be. Once the hearing loss has been found out, another danger looms, and that is the over-protection by the environment, especially by the mother. At this stage a parent may basically feel that the disabled child has to be protected in all ways. He may not play with others, the streets are so dangerous for the hard-of-hearing that it is better for him to be always accompanied, he must stay home when it is slightly windy, etc., etc. We know from psychoanalysis that such attitudes are really based on hostility, an unconscious desire that the child should remain handicapped (see chapter by Grayson) and be controlled. The hostility is often derived from the fact that parents may feel hurt in their pride of the child who is crippled. This hurt leads to hostility which can find no other acceptable outlet than in over-protective attitudes. Needless to say, the deaf child as well as the deaf adult are here exposed to serious dangers that may eventually lead to an enforced passivity in the personality structure or to continuous rebellion, depending upon the age, severity of the loss, basic character structure, etc.

Deafness in Puberty and Adolescence. The problems of a hearing loss in puberty and adolescence are similar, but special circumstances make for a few characteristic attitudes. The girl who is losing her hearing easily feels herself unattractive. She keeps à conversation artificially going, but fears always the moment her deceit is found out. Even when she uses a hearing aid she feels insecure in most cases. It is always possible that the battery will go dead. In school, in jobs and especially on dates the insecurity is evident. Often the girl feels that she is to be rejected and unattractive because of discharge due to inflammatory conditions. The smell of the pus from the ear has to be camouflaged, feelings of inferiority increase while symptoms are being masked. The boy too feels shy about asking girls for dates.

The situations described here easily lead to regressive patterns. As explained elsewhere in this book, a regressive pattern of behavior develops when a person cannot successfully deal with the behavior patterns that fit his present age; he goes back to behavior patterns that go with earlier ages: masturbation, day-dreaming and pleasures of earlier years may be resorted to again. With this pattern developing, psychoneurosis has already set in.

Deafness in mature life is often marked by loneliness, difficulty in establishing social contacts with others and also in problems of a vocation. The hard-of-hearing music teacher or pianist has to give up the job. They have all to face the fact that they really do not hear and that they have to wear an instrument that will help them to hear.

In most cases one would expect that a hearing aid would be gladly accepted. This, however, is not true in many cases. Patients frequently delay getting such a device or do not want one at all.

It apparently means to many people that their hearing will not really come back with usual methods, with medicine, diets or with injections. The loss is now definitely established. They are disabled—and for good. It is not to be compared with glasses for poor vision. To many deaf patients the device means that the outer world now knows that they are handicapped. Rationalizing this attitude, they say that it looks bad, that deafness means to other people that one is simply stupid. We know that unconscious reasons have to do with this attitude. It was pointed out before that the symbolic meaning of the function of hearing could be that hearing was a sign of strength and that the loss of this faculty was comparable to a deficiency in power of the personality, the loss signifying weakness, lack of intelligence, etc.

A *therapy* which is sometimes acceptable to the patient seems to be a fenestration operation. The operation is the magic which restores the inferior person to a position of superiority that was not even achieved before the deafness set in. Another aspect is that normal hearing without the use of devices would be the same as good health. Some people are very proud of their fine hearing as others are proud of their good looking automobile, their children, their intelligence or their sexual potency. Unfortunately, a great deal of disappointment is seen when the magic effect of restoration of hearing or of establishing superiority due to normal hearing is not established. Sometimes dramatic psychic manifestations, more serious than before, come into the open. Fortunately, in other cases, where not such an unrealistic desire existed before, the patient is given a chance with the operation to develop more normally.

Relation Between Deafness, Neurosis and Psychosis. We often wonder whether the patients do not unconsciously prefer withdrawal into a world of silence and isolation. The suspicious personality of the deaf has often been observed. Questions as to whether deafness would be related to paranoid conditions or even paranoia have been considered. At the present time, we have to hold this viewpoint obsolete. A normal amount of suspicion is to be expected as a healthy defense when people do no longer hear. This has nothing to do with a neurotic or psychotic mechanism. Whenever we meet truly paranoid patients, we have to assume that their pre-deaf personality pattern was predisposed to such symptom-formation.[15] In general, most strong reactions to deafness are indicative of pre-existing psychoneurosis or psychosis. It may very well be that these conditions are in some causal psychosomatic relation to many forms of deafness.

The following case of otosclerosis shows the existence of a depression which was not strongly related to the deafness which started at about the same time:

This patient is a 49 year old lady who has a very marked deafness. She noticed the beginning of hearing loss about 20 years ago. Before that time her husband had been hard of hearing and she had admittedly been impatient with him because of it. When she had to accept her own deafness she at first was disturbed and tried to avoid using a hearing device. Finally, she accepted it reluctantly. About 10 years ago she got severely depressed and went into psychoanalysis. The treatment lasted a little over four years and was terminated because patient had improved considerably. At the time when I interviewed her, patient seemed to be rather serene and resigned to her deafness. She regretted having to miss beautiful music but had come to accept a situation that could not be changed. She did not in any way remember ever having felt that deafness could be an asset. When asked later about her childhood, she remembered that her parents had always quarreled. She recalled holding her hands to both her ears in the morning when she heard the to-and-fro arguing of her father and the shrill voice of her mother. A great disgust for arguments developed and she began to develop a character trait which was more or less passive, accepting insult or aggression, if possible avoiding it, rather than having any disagreeable discussion. She related her depression later in life to her mother's psychosis. Her mother, in a depressed condition, was for many years in a state hospital for the insane, where she later died.

In this case, about which I know very little as to the psychodynamics, we see a depression that developed 10 years after she had become deaf and that was related to her mother's depression. The reaction to hearing the arguments between her parents in her youth is an interesting element that may be connected with a tendency to withdraw from auditory stimulation that could be threatening. It is a factor that can possibly play a psychogenic role in certain cases of deafness.

How sometimes the patient prefers to fall back on the deafness and use it as an asset may be illustrated from the following example:

A married woman of 38 years had been deaf since childhood from chronic otitis media. At the time she was seen by me, she was contemplating a divorce from her husband, whose constant nagging she could not stand. Her active shutting out of auditory stimuli came clearly out when she said: "When my husband nags at me and I do not want to hear him, I turn the knob of my hearing aid and tune him out."

From this example of a patient with organic deafness we can learn that not hearing is not necessarily a passive state; actively hindering the passive reception and perception of sounds is practiced too. "Nobody is as deaf as those who do not want to hear," is certainly a correct statement in many cases.

More important is this factor of auditory withdrawal in cases where it is unconsciously practiced.[5] Those cases of deafness where either no organic basis can be established or where there is a strong psychogenic overlay have probably confused or deceived observing otologists for a long time. After the Second World War many patients were seen who, after explosion of shrapnel or due to the noise of the battlefield, showed signs of deafness that looked inappropriate with the present physical damage. A considerable number of these patients when in battle were, without becoming aware of it, reminded of earlier times in their life when hearing was very disagreeable.[9] In most of these cases psychotherapy in which earlier conflicts were discussed and compared to the present onset of deafness, full restoration of hearing was accomplished or the basic organic hearing defect remained, not aggravated by psychogenic deafness.

Other Ear Disorders and Their Psychological Implications. In adulthood and also at an advanced age another symptom that can be tantalizing to the patient is *tinnitus.* In some patients the tinnitus is a remnant of fading auditory hallucinations or a sign of beginning psychosis. Occasionally, especially when tinnitus is very irritating, the sounds in the ears represent sentences, words of a compromising, obscene or noxious nature and the more the patient wants to get rid of it, the more it haunts him. In such cases we are reminded of obsessive thoughts that are replaced by vague sounds; the emotion originally belonging to the conflict that is present in the obsessive thought or fantasy is then shown as a hyperemotionality and great intolerance to tinnitus. Sometimes instead of painful thoughts, the patient, in cases bordering psychosis, hears arias of operas and other beautiful music. However, the listening cannot be enjoyed; it becomes obsessive and drives the patient into despair. Psychiatric treatment of various nature depending upon the diagnosis and severity of the symptoms is indicated in such cases.

The other important function of the ear, maintenance of the *equilibrium,* is more disturbed in later adult life and advancing age than in earlier years. Ménière's disease, which is marked by increasing nerve deafness and tinnitus, has as its most dramatic symptom severe attacks of vertigo. Vertigo is an emergency situation, mostly accompanied by severe vomiting. After the attack the patient is severely handicapped by the fear of a following attack. He feels unsafe and afraid that he may lose his equilibrium at any time. Sometimes an operation, consisting of destruction of the labyrinth, has to be resorted to. In a very large percentage of these cases we have noted that the attacks of this syndrome were preceded by very severe emotional upsets that were related to the onset of the symptoms.[3, 4] Certainly it is important that the otologist be aware of the very brittle psychic equilibrium of these patients or of the severe psychic traumata that they may be exposed to. Delay of operation or operation on one side in unilateral cases followed by psychotherapy seems to be indicated. Here are a few brief examples: One young woman got her first attack of the Ménière triad following a row with her lover. He had kicked her and bruised her. Hospitalization for the bruises was needed. The vertigo attack followed. Another patient got his first attack when he threw his two sons with their two mistresses out of his house with the help of the police. A woman got an attack on the street when she left court where bankruptcy proceedings against her husband had started.

Certainly not all cases are equally dramatic; in many it is difficult to find a psychic trauma. However, in some cases we learn that a great deal of patience is required to get insight into the psychology of the patient.

The more we see deaf patients or patients with Ménière's disease, the more we see individuals who were previously neurotic but who more or less successfully use their existing disease to tag all their previous symptoms too.

A neurotic man of 20 years of age has nerve-deafness following viral meningomyelitis. He got deaf at the age of 13. He began to feel very insecure due to the deafness and felt that money and women could help him to make up for his insecurity. Jobs were undertaken that were much too hard for his bad physique. The first marriage ended after six days, the second after a few years in which separation and reunion alternated continuously. The third wife was worse than all the others combined and scratched him, but he could overcome her always. This man needed overcompensation and got a certain amount of pseudo-security from acquisition of money and from sex. He ascribed his insecurity to his deafness.

Before his deafness, however, we learned that he hated his father who was impatient and strict, and that he always had a fear of losing his mother, who was his main source of security. That she should not die before he was 20 was remembered as having been a constant thought before he got deaf. The insecurity definitely could be traced back to the earlier times when he had so much reason to dislike his father. In the poverty-stricken family of 16 children, this boy had grown neurotic and pondering about his future long before his deafness interfered with his life and made contact more difficult. A certain amount of psychogenic deafness was present and diagnosed correctly by the otologist.

The *outer ear* is sometimes the seat of *eczema* and *itching*. In a number of cases it could be found that itching of the ear replaced masturbation. In one patient this came out clearly in orgiastic feelings and erotic fantasies whenever the physician put elongated instruments into her ear. This patient, a sexually dissatisfied person suffering from hysteria, could get her satisfaction via scratching of the ear.

Malformations of the concha may mean genital mutilation and plastic operations are often sought by the patients to satisfy an additional unrealistic aim. In these cases we deal with mechanisms that are analogous to those described in Linn's chapter about rhinoplasty.

THE NOSE

The Real Meaning of the Nose

The nose has two main functions; namely, it is the passageway for inhaled and exhaled air and it serves the sense of smell. When the nasal meatus are closed, we have to breathe through the mouth. Dryness of mouth and pharynx is the result. As soon as normal nasal respiration is interfered with, we see in some people disagreeable sensations which cause fears of choking. In neurotics, we notice, for example, that in examinations of basal metabolism, in which a clamp is applied to the nose, the changed mode of respiration through the opened mouth contributes to phobic sensations.

The sense of smell, though in human beings of a more rudimentary character than in animals, undoubtedly is an important function, i.e., being used as a warning signal and with modifications still playing a role in sexual attraction. In nasal disorders, smell is often disturbed or lost, with all its subtle consequences. The gustatory component of smell in addition often lost in common colds may in depressively inclined patients contribute to a feeling of drabness of life. "Everything tastes like straw" may be in depressions or in some forms of neurosis an additional loss of vital external stimulation.

The Symbolic Meaning of the Nose

The symbolic meaning of the nose is, as we know from psychoanalysis, like that of most organs, of a bisexual nature. As any protruding organ, the nose can represent a phallus. Deformities of such an organ are often related to or equated with sexual inadequacy. The inside of the nose can stand for the vagina. Patients may find the outer meatus too wide or too narrow. Disorders will be reacted to according to what they mean for the special type of person. Then the turbinates, covered with spongious tissue, may with varying excitation of the autonomic nervous system become hyperemic like the cavernous tissue of the penis when it gets erect.

Connection of the turbinates with the internal female genitalia has been assumed, so that operations on the turbinates during early pregnancy have been avoided so as not to provoke an abortion. Vicarious bleeding from the nose, replacing menstrual flow, has also been observed. Autonomic nervous control of both the inside of the nose and the internal female genitalia seems to account for these occurrences. Like the ear, the nose can also represent the anal opening. Discharge from the nose is often referred to in a similar way as feces.

The Attitudes of the Patient in Relation to the Nose

Nose poking, correctly considered a masturbatory equivalent, is a very common pastime of many people. It can be a form of anal masturbation and may also occasionally replace genital masturbation. This practice can lead to severe hemorrhages, sometimes to infections which endanger the patient's life, because of the proximity of the intracranial sinuses. In nose-bleeds patients often are afraid that it may not stop at all and that they may die. In this case we have to be aware of the possibility that the patient may consider the hemorrhage and its results the punishment for forbidden erotic pleasure, in this case masturbation. The filling up of the nose with foreign bodies, as some children do, is connected with the enjoyment of passive, anal pleasures.

Sneezing, caused by an irritation of the nasal lining, can come close to orgiastic sensations. The use of snuffboxes a few centuries ago gave a generally permitted autoerotic pleasure that has become obsolete. It is quite probable that frequent sneezing in allergic disorders is, like itching of the skin, a substitute for orgiastic inadequacy. Cocaine is often used by drug addicts as a nasal spray, giving a refreshing feeling in the nose with free breathing and a simultaneous euphoric sensation due to the absorption of the drug itself. Like the abuse of other vasoconstricting drugs that temporarily give a free passageway for the air, it leads to subsequent hyperemia of the membranes. It is certainly to be considered that in some cases this alternating swelling and shrinking of the nasal pathways has, aside from the inherent pathology, a psychological significance as pointed out above. Some patients in whom no rhinological treatment led to any result were finally helped by psychoanalytic treatment for swelling of nasal membranes with unknown etiology.

In cases of allergy, too, a combination of psychological and organic factors has been observed. Attacks of hay fever could be produced experimentally in which both these factors were present.[7] Frequent colds are in many cases either due to unnecessary exposure or to insufficient protection from noxious stimuli after the cold has started already. "Diplomatic colds" are, like headaches, not always pretended but nevertheless can come in very handy. The psychiatrist has not infrequently an opportunity to see how the patient exposes himself to a cold or after it starts reveals signs of unconscious needs for illness, resulting in extra attention. Sometimes, however, we see colds developing without any exposure, coinciding with rather important traumatic situations.

An unmarried woman of 42, born in France, had been unable to make a living, to establish a successful social life or sexual adjustment in America. From a trip to Europe, undertaken to find out how living possibilities would be over there, she returned to New York. On the pier she began to feel the beginning of a cold which developed to a classical severe cold in the next few days. Nobody was at the pier to meet her and life seemed drab and to hold no future. On several occasions of a similar nature in the course of her psychiatric treatment, colds were observed.

Another patient, a man of 37, in analytic treatment, developed colds that were coinciding with frustrating life situations, sometimes related to rejection by his girl friend, sometimes to depressive feelings connected with conflicts with his parents. The colds developed often with a sudden diarrhea and not seldom were preceded by headaches of a migrainous nature.

The patient seen in all medical specialties who has insignificant pathology but needs continuous medical attention is the compulsive perfectionist who cannot tolerate any temporary dysfunction or who always needs physical perfection. Consulting the ear-nose specialist for a minor inconvenience in breathing freely, a deviated septum may have been diagnosed or a slight thickening of the turbinates. If the physician tells this to the patient, and reassuringly adds that the symptom is unimportant or is due to a lingering virus infection, he has not counted on the patient's fear of something worse. Our specialist is suddenly confronted with the patient's need that something be done to straighten out the septum or whatever is the case. Anxiety is caused by the awareness that something is imperfect. The patient wants an operation and if the bonafide specialist refuses, he will shop around till he finds somebody who will satisfy his needs—until he finds something else that is wrong.

THE THROAT

The Real Meaning of the Throat

For our purpose, only some diseases of the pharynx and larynx will be considered. As an extension of the respiratory tract, the pharynx and larynx are the organs which for the patient are easily related with fears of lack of air or choking. The pharynx has an additional function in the act of deglutition (swallowing). The larynx is the organ for communication, in this case for active expression of one's thoughts, in other words of one's verbally relating to other people. Of all the functions here mentioned, the respiratory function is probably emotionally the most significant one.

The Symbolic Meaning of the Throat

The symbolic meaning of the throat is related to its shape and its function. The tube again has an opening through which one can fill up, stuff and also choke the patient. The filling up here is much more connected with overt anxiety than in the case of the nose, as the throat is the only passage-way for air, and death would be the result of closure. The hysterical "globus" sensations are due to spasms of the esophageal musculature. The patient feels a lump stuck in his throat. A variety of fantasies has been found in these cases. One of these fantasies is that impregnation has taken place through the mouth and that pregnancy exists in the oral-pharyngeal tract. (See chapter on Obstetrics.) A remnant of such a fantasy exists in the folk tale that a piece of the apple got stuck in Adam's throat, hence the term "Adam's apple." The fruit was forbidden and the punishment is the lump that got stuck, altogether a primitive coitus-pregnancy fantasy.[2] Other fantasies deal with fellatio, cunnilingus, etc. In physical illness of the oral-pharyngeal-laryngeal region, fantasies of this kind, related to the organ symbolism, are frequently reactivated and contribute to the amount of real anxiety with an extra amount of neurotic anxiety. Especially in surgical procedures these problems can become manifest.

Attitudes of the Patient in Relation to the Throat

   Tonsillectomy. In tonsillectomy of children we see that the neurotic child, already anxiety-ridden, reacts to the throat surgery with great anxiety. Attitudes of the parents, at times unconsciously sadistic, may increase the child's anxiety. (See chapter on Pediatrics.) The former procedure in which tonsils were removed without anesthesia was often the immediate cause of an anxiety hysteria in children, as it means for some children a severe mutilation of the body by a cruel person. In many cases of later neurosis one can often find the adeno- and tonsillectomy as a severe traumatic incident of childhood. On the other hand in some children and adults a general anesthesia activates fears of death and can be similarly traumatic. Keeping these facts in mind, surgeon and anesthetist can find out with some patience what the best technique in individual cases will be, without undue neglect of the patient's mental structure. (See chapter on Surgery.)

   These children with hypertrophic adenoid tissue, not being able to breathe through the nose, make a mentally dull impression due to their keeping their mouths open; concomitant disturbances in hearing and, therefore, often a lack of attention may contribute to the impression of their back-wardness. This may cause worries in the environment which are frequently cleared up when free breathing through the nose and hearing are restored. The physician should be aware, however, that it is not always brightness that goes together with this syndrome and that even when all of these symptoms are removed, dullness still may persist.

Disorders of the Larynx and the Pharynx

   Changes of or loss of voice for somatic reasons may pose a considerable emotional problem for the afflicted. A change of voice occurs in the adolescent boy: he may welcome it as a sign of maturity but at the same time feels a bit ridiculous every time his voice is derailed. To him as to every one with a voice change, the loss of control over an organ which otherwise functions automatically or according to conscious regulation is frightening (see discussion of loss of control in chapter on Medicine and chapter on Neurology). To the adolescent for whom the voice was either a source of social or family acclaim (singing in the choir) or even of professional importance, the mutation may have nearly catastrophic significance; it may mean to him a loss of distinction.

Such a loss of singing voice or of speaking voice may be particularly traumatic emotionally because the voice can be heavily invested with meaningfulness. People are often proud of their voice—be it volume or timbre, socially or professionally. In many situations he who can shout loudest wins, and loss of voice means loss of communication or decreased social significance and often lessened self esteem.

Hysterical aphonias are not difficult for the laryngologist to detect. A little bit more complex are those inflammations of the pharynx and larynx which follow compulsive clearing of the throat. Undoubtedly treatment of an organ will not change an attitude. An attitude is not so simply given up without the individual having discovered and understood the underlying psychogenic factors. Sometimes complaints remain present after the patient has recovered from the physical manifestations of the disease. The following case history of a patient who had recovered from tuberculosis of the larynx may shed some light on possible psychogenic factors.[6]

The patient is a woman of 36; she is married and has a boy of 16. Four years ago patient had tubercular ulcerations in the larynx for which she was treated in and out of hospitals. She was ordered not to speak during this time. She recovered a few times, but got relapses. Reason for psychiatric referral was that during observation of half a year, although patient went on complaining of severe pain in the laryngeal region and scarcely dared to speak lest she would get a relapse, the laryngologist at Vanderbilt Clinic could not detect any pathology locally or in laboratory findings. In her history we see that she had a very strict father; her mother and the children used to go out of his way when he came home. She was deeply attached to her mother. At the age of 11, patient had diphtheria and was extremely ill. When the physician came he yelled at mother and said, "Why did you wait so long to call me? This girl is deathly sick."

Before her larynx tuberculosis developed, patient had anxiety and obsessive fantasies of killing her son. A psychiatrist recommended shock treatment at the time. When she was in the hospital for her tuberculosis, her mother suddenly died of a heart attack. In connection with a dream, patient tells that she still cannot overcome her emotions related to the death of a friend of her son. This friend died of tonsillitis two years ago. Many of patient's dreams have to do with serious diseases of the throat.

Psychotherapy has made her less anxious, but there is still a very great fear of speaking. As soon as she feels a slight pain she is afraid her ulcerations will return.

She never talked a lot, but she did not completely refrain from showing her resentments when she felt them.

Discussing this case we can see that this is a neurotic woman with a great deal of anxiety. She was a shy child, fearful of her father who was very strict. Resentment in her youth could certainly not be expressed. In later years and at the present, too, conflicts with the family are avoided; when she got into conflicts with her father, who remarried three years after her mother's death, she did not discuss anything with him, but simply did not want to see him any more. In the same way difficulties with the whole in-law family are treated by avoiding meeting them. Several episodes happening in a previous hospitalization and at present indicate her avoidance of arguments or discussion that may be felt as agressive by the opponent.

A case which illustrates a few points also relating to the function of communication of the larynx is the following:

Patient is a woman of 43 who at the age of 26 underwent a partial laryngectomy for a squamous cell carcinoma. Her history is as follows:

She never liked to talk. When she was seven, she visited a young aunt of 12 in another town who had a laryngitis and could only whisper. Patient recalls that she admired the aunt because she had no voice and was different from the other children. She clearly remembers that she wished also to lose her voice. At the age of nine she complained of a toothache to her mother. The latter did not believe her and patient pledged to herself that she would never complain to her mother again. From the age of 12 she had almost uninterrupted spells of tonsillitis. At high school she was an excellent student, especially in mathematics. Rhetorics and written composition, however, were a torture for her. She remembers how she disliked conversation and used to look out of the car, bus or train instead of participating in small talk.

She married at 17 and went to live in another town, where she acquired a laryngitis. She was hoarse, could only whisper for approximately two weeks and was better then. For the next five years she had a severe attack of laryngitis for two weeks every year. When she was 23 she got hoarse and her voice never did get better; always remained a whisper. She went to several clinics; tonsilectomy was done at age 25, and finally at the age of 26 a cancer was diagnosed in Presbyterian Hospital, New York City and partial laryngectomy followed. From that time she has been treated continuously for stenosis in the operated region. There has been no recurrence of the cancer, however.

She admits that she often falls back on her inability to speak clearly. It is especially easy for her that she cannot talk with her mother who phones her occasionally.

She was referred to the psychiatrist in 1949, because she had homicidal fantasies regarding her husband. The latter had, after a marriage which she described as ideal, for quite some time been unfaithful. Patient, an idealistic woman with very high standards, was so disturbed that she needed help. She wanted to kill him instead of working it out, but finally psychotherapy led to a better adjusted situation.

If we look at both these cases with serious larynx disease, we see two very masochistic women. Undoubtedly, in both cases, the organ of speech, the most important peripheral tool for communication, was physically disturbed and had been from earlier years on a so-called "accentuated organ", i.e., that organ which seemed more predisposed to dysfunction and illness. Interference with the function of communication, that is a materially enforced silence, could keep the energies bound which would otherwise have to lead to verbal expression. I do not imply that such findings are the rule in larynx diseases, but I find the psychogenic implications striking enough to relate here.

It is in this connection interesting to note that laryngologists have observed that, following extirpation of the larynx, many times patients who are requested to converse by writing on a pad can for unknown reasons hardly succeed well in this; communication remains very poor. We may have to think of the possibility that psychological obstacles to oral and even written modes of communication may be present. So far we know very little about the psychosomatic factors in larynx diseases.

BIBLIOGRAPHY

1. Barker, R. G., Wright, B. A. and Gonick, M. R.: Adjustment to physical handicap and illness: A survey of the social psychology of physique and disability. Bull. #55, Soc. Sci. Research Council, New York, 1946.
2. Bellak, L.: A note about the adams apple. Psychoanalyt. Rev. *29:* 1942.
3. Fowler, E. P., Jr. and Zeckel, A.: Psychosomatic aspects of Ménière's disease. J.A.M.A. *148:* 1265, 1952.
4. —— and ——: Psychophysiological factors in Ménière's disease. Psychosomat. Med. (In press.)
5. Foxe, A. N.: Psychoanalysis of a case of deafness. Psychiatric. Quart. *15:* 438, 1941.
6. Froeschels, E. and Jellinek, A.: Practice of Voice and Speech Therapy: New Contributions to Voice and Speech Pathology. Boston, Expression Company, 1941.
7. Holmes, T. H., Goodell, H., Wolf, S. and Wolff, H. G.: The Nose: An Experimental Study of Reactions Within the Nose in Human Subjects during Varying Life Experiences. Springfield, Thomas, 1949.
8. Jones, E.: The Madonna's conception through the ear. *In:* Essays in Applied Psycho-Analysis. London, The International Psycho-Analytical Press, 1923.
9. Knapp, P. H.: Emotional aspects of hearing loss. Psychosom. Med. *10:* 203, 1948.
10. Menninger, K.: Mental effects of deafness. Psychoanalyt. Rev. *11:* 144, 1924.
11. Pintner, R., Eisenson, J. and Stanton, M.: The Psychology of the Physically Handicapped. New York, Appleton-Century-Crofts, 1944.
12. Ramsdell, D. A.: The psychology of the hard-of-hearing and the deafened adult. *In:* Davis, H. (ed.) Hearing and Deafness. New York, Murray Hill Books, 1947.
13. Ruesch, J. and Bateson, G.: Communication, The Social Matrix of Psychiatry. New York, W. W. Norton, 1951.
14. Zeckel, A. and Van der Kolk, J. J.: A comparative intelligence test of groups of children born deaf and of good hearing, by means of the Porteus test. Am. Ann. Deaf. *84:* 114, 1939.
15. ——: Psychopathological aspects of deafness. J. Nerv. & Ment. Dis. *112:* 322, 1950.

CHAPTER 11

Psychiatric and Psychoanalytic Aspects of Neurologic Disease

ALBERT ROSNER, M.D.

Dr. Rosner received his M.D. from the Medical School of the University of Pennsylvania and after internship took residencies successively in Psychiatry and Neurology at the New York State Psychiatric Institute and at Neurological Institute, graduating from the New York Psychoanalytic Institute thereafter.

Dr. Rosner was a Research Assistant with the Matheson Commission for Research in Encephalitis and was Chief of Neuropsychiatric Department, Army Airforce Hospital, Greensboro, North Carolina, among other posts. He is Instructor in Neurology, College of Physicians and Surgeons, Columbia University; Associate Attending Neurologist, Neurological Institute, New York; Attending Neuropsychiatrist, Dean's Committee, Bronx Veterans Hospital and Consulting Neuropsychiatrist to the American Red Cross, New York.

He is a Diplomate of the American Board of Neurology and Psychiatry; Fellow of the American Academy of Neurology, of the American Psychiatric Association and is Associate Member of the New York Psychoanalytic Institute.

THE MEANING OF NEUROLOGIC ILLNESS

THE TRADITION THAT THE BRAIN is sacred and untouchable derives from a common fear of the particular variety of signs and symptoms that accompany a disturbance in its function. The bizarre and eccentric behavior of the mentally ill patient has been regarded since earliest times with the awe and reverence that is always accorded the feared and unknown. The eccentricity of symptoms and the odd blend of familiar as well as unfamiliar modes of behavior, speech, and thought provided a stimulus for the imagination and an excuse for indulging in magical speculation as to their cause.

The anxiety that was aroused by these mysterious symptoms found ample means of expression in the violence of the treatment methods invented to control them. In lieu of any attempt to explore real causes, no distinction could be made between functional disorders and organic diseases of the nervous system. The neurologic patient and his odd retinue of symptoms—convulsions, tics, choreas, tremors, paralyses, pains, paraesthesias and anaesthesias—was as much an object of suspicion and mystery as the patient who was mentally ill. The epileptic and the insane were equally possessed by spirits and treated accordingly. The fear that attends disease of the nervous system is often in evidence in persons who observe its peculiarities as well as in those who suffer with them, and probably stems from the same unconscious roots that, common to mankind, resisted for so many years a rational understanding of brain disease and its effects. To a certain extent, these fears have elements in common with those of patients ill with diseases of other functional systems, but at the same time, they are characterized by certain special affects and prejudices. These are likely to be manifested either in the form of strong attitudes, neuroses or possibly psychoses deriving from the neurologic symptom that is manifested, and the special significance that this symptom possesses for the patient's conscious as well as unconscious mind.

A patient with a chronic progressive neurologic disease like multiple sclerosis, aside from problems arising from inability to earn a living, hardship imposed on his family, and dependence on others, has to face the unpleasant realities of the physical manifestations of his disease. To the hypochondriacal preoccupations that illness frequently brings with it are added the additional problems that this typical neurologic disease imposes— for instance, the loss of motor control and loss of sphincteric function. The loss of these functions, both having been acquired in early life at the expense of great expenditure of effort and sacrifice and repression of natural instincts, revives old conflicts having to do with mastery, submission, and compromise, and burdens the ego with the necessity of solving them again. The outcome of this conflict depends upon the success with which the ego, in the past, has been able to accomplish its task. Ferenczi[6] and Beres and Brenner[2] noted in a recent study that in each patient, it was the pre-morbid "weak points" in his personality which determined which of his disabilities caused unconscious conflict and which did not. It was not so much the physical symptom itself, but the unconscious meaning of the particular disability that set off the danger signal, which in turn brought out the defenses and thus set the stage for conflict. A typical neurotic reaction-pattern may result as illustrated by the following example.*[2]

Loss of Sphincter Control. A 23-year-old single man with multiple sclerosis developed severe neurotic stammering. The disease began suddenly at the age of 12 and resulted in paralysis of lower extremities, weakness of upper extremities, and incontinence of urine and feces. A gradual remission enabled him to get around with crutches, but a second attack at 22 brought a return of neurologic symptoms, with total paralysis of the lower extremities and loss of urinary and sphincter control.

Patient was the oldest of four siblings, breast-fed, and weaned without difficulty. Toilet training was accomplished early, but at the age of three, there were several

---

* Permission to quote details of this case was obtained from the authors.

episodes of soiling. At that time, he developed acute rheumatic fever, and as he recovered, he manifested a striking change in behavior, becoming disobedient and stubborn. Following the sudden death of his father, he became a well-behaved, conscientious, serious child, and assumed the role of the male head of the family.

Stammering appeared first at the age of 10, became worse, but improved as the neurologic symptoms improved. With the second attack, it recurred in a severe form which persisted and was intensified in the presence of anyone in a position of authority.

Observations of the patient's behavior, analysis of his verbal productions under sodium amytal, and analysis of his dreams revealed that the stammering was closely associated in his unconscious with conflict about his sphincteric dysfunction. Thus, the "weak point" that was threatened by this symptom was the incomplete mastery of anal function in childhood and the aggressive impulses that were associated with it. The stubborn and aggressive behavior that prevailed at one period represented one indication of this important struggle against strong, undisciplined wishes to soil. The following dream revealed his unconscious preoccupation with and anxiety about anal drives.

"I am in the Museum of Art with my brother. I have an urgent desire to move my bowels. I rush to the toilet. The doors are too low. I have to crawl under the door. It is too late. I move my bowels in my pants."

In the early part of his illness, he was in a constant state of anxiety that he would be scolded for soiling himself. In the course of the next three years, as his anxiety about soiling himself disappeared, the stammer appeared.

Under sodium amytal in response to a suggestion that he talk about the onset of this symptom, the stammer disappeared, and there followed a flood of associations dealing with bowel control and with aggressive impulses directed against a nurse who once refused him a laxative which he required to regulate his bowel function. An uncompromising and aggressive demand for a woman's attention as his "right" was also revealed in a former love relationship. Once when his girl refused to share her mail with him, he became very angry and wanted to "let loose," but his stammer became so severe that he could not articulate. It was concluded, in accordance with the observations of most investigations of stammering, that the patient's speech difficulties were the expression of neurotic conflict over anal and oral instinctual drives. Concern about anal function was transferred to the oral zone.

After the death of his father, he became well-behaved, conscientious and disciplined, an indication that this important event had brought about a repression of sadistic and anal drives. The character change represented a manifestation of defense that was strong enough to control the unconscious drives satisfactorily until the onset of his neurologic illness. With the reappearance of anal disturbance, as a physical consequence of disease, the patient was confronted not only with the conscious realities attending his illness but with an unexpected consequence of it—a struggle against the unconscious reverberations, touched off by one of its symptoms.

Ferenczi[6] coined the term pathoneurosis to designate mental symptoms that occur from physical illness, in contrast to physical symptoms consequent to mental disturbances. He showed that the choice of symptoms of this disturbance is related to fixation points and that in each patient, it was the pre-morbid "weak points" which determined which of his disabilities were traumatic and which were not. Such "weak points" may not be at all apparent in the form of symptoms in the well individual. However, they are very frequently apparent in the form of attitudes that the individual adopts toward anything in the outside world that touches upon them. For example in the patient quoted above his attitude toward soiling was strongly antipathetic. As revealed by his history the patient's prejudices about soiling were a consequence of his own unconscious inclinations toward the very thing he consciously felt was so distasteful. But soiling represents only one aspect of the universal prejudice and antipathy toward characteristic manifestations of neurologic disease.

The Patient's Concept of Neurologic Deficit. In neurologic practice, one is confronted with many examples of highly charged feelings and antipathies directed against particular symptom complexes that characterize the specialty. It is at this point that the neurologist's understanding of his patient's concepts of his disease—both conscious and unconscious—can effect his patient's ability to bear the illness. Epilepsy is feared beyond reason as is the sudden paralysis or anesthesia of a limb. Hyperkinetic involuntary movements are likewise looked upon as something particularly uncanny. A common element of many of these symptoms is the "involuntary" aspect of the symptom; the prospect of anything happening to one's body beyond the influence of conscious control seems calculated to arouse the greatest fears and apprehensions. The brain is unconsciously conceived as an omnipotent organ that will brook no contradiction in exercising its prerogative of total body control. Closely allied are similar feelings regarding its need to control all manifestations of thinking: loss of control on this level is correlated with fear of insanity. The universal concern about these aspects of brain function is best understood in terms of defense, which takes the form of protecting the brain against change. The common apprehension that the nervous system is very sensitive to pain represents one manifestation of this over solicitous attitude toward its structural and functional integrity.

Pain. The brain, aside from other functions, the great receptor for painful and other sensations coming from the periphery, is in fact, insensitive to pain. Sensations experienced during the course of surgical procedures dealing with it, for example, originate at peripheral points in the skin, periosteum, blood vessels and dura, and are localized to these areas by the discriminating function of the parietal lobe. The matrix and ganglionic elements are generally not responsive to surgical manipulations. Similarly, with regard to pain elsewhere in the body, the tendency is to blame a disease of the peripheral nerve for pain that has nothing at all to do with the nerve. The term "neuritis" carries with it the implication that the nerve is "sensitive" and that it is easily aroused to pain by minor influences affecting it. In most types of peripheral neuropathy, the neuropathologic changes are such that even where the sensory conducting unit is affected, pain does not necessarily result. As often as not, the opposite is true; that is, loss of peripheral sensibility, as in infectious polyneuroradiculitis or in the neuropathies associated with syphilis or leprosy. In the same way that the patient anticipates pain where it does not exist, he will deny it or overlook it where it does. In these cases the denial deals not so much with the primary modalities of pain sensation as such, but with its psychological representations in the brain—for example the "painful" realization of a loss of a limb by amputation, or the loss of function of this limb by paralysis.

The Phantom Limb. The proposition that "nature abhors a vacuum" finds interesting corroboration, in a figurative sense, in many neurologic situations. S. Weir Mitchell[9] was the first to note that the sudden loss of a limb by accident or surgical amputation may be followed by the phantom of its continued existence. Most observers have noted that the phantom is chiefly represented by tactile and kinesthetic sensations, and that its persistence is attributable to peripheral excitations arising in the stump. Cocainization of the area and surgical removal of neuromata has met with some success as a means of dealing with strongly persistent symptoms, but in a surprising number of patients, such sensible and logical methods have failed to bring any relief. These patients will state that in their opinion no amount of manipulation of the stump will succeed in making them forget the phantom limb: they will report that they not only feel sensations of pain or touch or movement, but are also able to visualize it. They will report, moreover that it appears to them in various postures, not all of them comfortable, or even anatomically correct. In the course of time, familiar parts of the limb may disappear. In an amputation at the shoulder, for example, the hand may appear at the elbow either small or larger than the original.[12] The phantom, according to Schilder, follows its own laws. It not only departs from the standard structural model but also disobeys the laws of matter—though often immobile it may move, and in moving, may pass through inanimate objects with apparent ease. Such phenomena occur in apparent conformity to forces that are beyond the influence of the conscious will of the patient. But the phantom limb is not altogether beyond control. It can be influenced, according to Betlheim[3] by hypnosis—that is, by suggestion or other psychological mechanisms. Its behavior is not altogether capricious and unpredictable, but conforms to the laws of the unconscious as described by Freud.

The patient who is suddenly confronted with a limb that does not respond to his will, as in paralysis, or seemingly moves under its own power, as in the hyperkinetic disturbances, or who finds himself unable to elicit familiar sensations from it, is confronted with a paradoxical situation. He knows the limb belongs to him, but no effort of will can fully reassure him of this knowledge unless he can test it by reality—that is, by moving and feeling with it in the familiar way. The situation is likely to frighten him because it is novel to his conscious recollection, and altogether foreign to his standard of behavior. There are manifestations in the situation reminiscent of those accompanying phantom limb phenomena. Not infrequently a patient with a paralyzed limb will behave as though it were still normal and functioning.

Schilder[12] records several instances of hemiplegic patients who behaved as though they were not paralyzed, "who asserted that their paralyzed arm is as good as their other arm, and who insist they walk as well as they did before. When ordered to raise both arms, they of course move only the healthy one, but insist they have raised the paralyzed one too . . . some of them do not consider their paralyzed limb as their own." Some patients with left-sided hemiparesis refuse to look at the paralyzed side, and one such patient when confronted with it declared that it belonged to someone else.

Schilder considered the tendency to avoid the tormenting perception of a physical defect a result of the influence of unconscious as well as conscious factors, as though the ego cannot accept the loss without some protective measure that serves even in fantasy, to preserve the unity of the body image. Patients who are so threatened may strive with great perseverance to maintain a position of status quo with regard to this ideal of strength, good health, and physical perfection, and the reality of an amputation or a neurologic defect may force the ego to achieve a compromise between the unpleasant fact and the wish to remain unchanged. The price paid for such a compromise which aims to minimize painful perception, is the obligatory acceptance of a certain degree of falsification of reality. As pointed out by Ferenczi in the pathoneuroses,[6] this is the neurotic device that occurs as defense against symptoms of physical disease.* From the observations of both Ferenczi and Schilder, taken from different sources, are thus derived the same conclusion as to the importance of unconscious rather than conscious determinants of these mental reactions.

Hollos and Ferenczi[8] were able to show that many of the symptoms of general paresis, where brain damage actually existed, was not due to brain damage exclusively, but to the inner perception of cerebral impairment, to which the patient reacted with compensatory delusions that magnified his sense of importance.

Beres and Brenner[2] describe a 30-year-old male patient with multiple sclerosis whose neurotic reaction to the "disgrace" of his urinary incontinence resulted in self-mutilation of his penis as well as a defensive character change. The patient associated the humiliation attached to his incontinence with earlier embarrassment with his small penis. He attempted to control his incontinence by a series of mechanical devices culminating in the use of a clamp which he applied so tightly to his penis that it became cyanotic and swollen. When bleeding occurred from the irritated penis

---

*See discussion of "denial" in surgical problems, Chapter 5.

he remarked, "I am like a woman who has a constant period." Upon gaining weight in the hospital, he complained that his "belly was growing like a pregnant woman's." The threat of identification with women he met by adopting a hostile, defensive attitude toward doctors and other men on the ward who he thought were picking on him and making fun of him.

In the unconscious, there is a need to conceive well-structured configurations. The tendency to preserve intact the totality of the body image is implemented by the instinctive need to defend against loss or damage to important body parts. The exaggeration of the importance of these parts, in turn, is influenced by sexual instincts, which largely unconscious, interpret any threat of damage or loss of function of the body part as a threat to the fulfillment of their sexual aims. The unity that the ego tries to effect within itself represents the need for unity with a sexual object in the outside world, the ultimate unity that aims to guarantee the preservation of the race.

The Hyperkinetic Disorders. The quality of the esthetic experience that accompanies phantom limb, paralysis and anesthesia occur also in connection with some of the hyperkinetic disturbances met with in neurology like tic, oculogyric crises of chronic encephalitis and some of the choreiform disturbances like dystonia musculorum deformans. The psychological reaction is quite characteristic and does not, in my experience, occur in diseases of other functional systems. The encephalitic patient, for example, is capable of a great deal of detachment with respect to his involuntary movements, and will often address his limb as though it were not part of him, but under the influence of forces outside his body. Nevertheless, a characteristic feature of the encephalitic patient is the fact that he is forced to acknowledge at the same time a certain degree of volition with respect to his tic or tremor. He is capable of shifting from the position of the patient with Jacksonian seizures who says: "I have a twitch in my arm," to one in which he says: "I have an urge to move my arm."[14] The neurologic fact of this observation is represented on a psychological level in the characteristic incapacity of many mentally-ill encephalitic patients to maintain an attitude of indifference and irresponsibility toward their own irrational thoughts and modes of behavior.

Von Economo[14] observed that in the early febrile stage of so-called epidemic encephalitis it is possible to arouse a patient from a seemingly profound depth of coma to full mental alertness sufficient to permit feeding, elimination and even rational conversation. The capacity to dissociate what is alien to the ego from an observing and judging part of it is one of the striking phenomena in chronic encephalitic psychosis. Wilson[13] notes that the patient can lift himself to a "practically normal level" even at a moment when conduct and reactions seem altogether insane, and Schilder states that these patients "maintain a surprisingly critical attitude" regarding their delusions.

An encephalitic child I observed,[10] driven by overwhelming impulses to commit petty thievery, to accost and assault strangers, was conscious during every misdeed that she was struggling with forces that impelled her to commit these acts despite the persistance of her own critical attitude toward them. Another patient from time to time became overpowered with an intense desire to lie down; in fulfilling this compelling impulse, he was fully aware that he was not in the least tired and had no desire to sleep; lying down on a daybed with his eyes wide open provided the only means of ridding himself of great anxiety. The historical record on another patient read: "He complained of a tendency to grin and smile spontaneously. This condition is quite embarrassing, as at a wake or at a board meeting."*

The simultaneous awareness in encephalitic patients of the source as well as the instrument of their acts, both familiar to the patient's ego, provides the setting for the sensation of "double consciousness" that similarly characterize déjà-vue phenomena, where the subject feels that the situation of the moment, though obviously new, seems oddly familiar, has happened before, and may proceed in a manner that he feels he can almost predict. The sensation is due to the subject's incomplete perception of memories related by association from the present to the past; the "familiar" aspect of the sensation arises from the partial awareness that these memories are his own, and stem from actual experiences of early life. In some encephalitic patients and in some hyperkinetic disturbances due to other neurologic causes, the state of partial awareness of the source of their unconscious impulses provides cause for great alarm, especially if the unconscious wishes they seek to avoid are agressive or destructive ones.[10, 11] Under the circumstances one can appreciate the readiness of these patients to revive superstitious beliefs in "possession" by evil spirits for whose impulses or deeds the subject need not acknowledge responsibility.

Loss of Motor Control. A 26-year-old married woman with chronic encephalitis who developed oculogyric crises six years after the initial onset of her disease, became progressively depressed after the appearance of this symptom. She prided herself on her attentiveness to household duties and rarely failed to emphasize her love for her children and husband. The only signs of outward aggressiveness were numerous quarrels with her mother occasioned by the latter's determination to dominate her daughter's life and family. A noticeable association between the occurrence of the oculogyric crises and the menstrual periods enabled the patient to predict them with surprising accuracy. When the oculogyric crises first became established, they were individually accompanied by great anxiety, fear of impending death, and a feeling of acute panic and desperation. During the course of one of her early spells, she attempted to kill her two children and herself by gas asphyxiation. She became panic stricken when her youngest girl became unconscious and she called for the police. The patient was ill but not unconscious for two days thereafter. After the episode had run its course, she looked back upon the incident with great horror, and

---

* These patients were observed under the auspices of the Matheson Commission for Research in Encephalitis.

could never understand how she could have taken such a course of action which she insisted was contrary to any conscious wish or desire.

Nevertheless, on a few occasions thereafter, independent of oculogyric attacks, ideas of an obsessive-compulsive nature obtruded themselves upon her consciousness. The first came about one year later, when on the occasion of bathing her two children, "I suddenly felt that I wanted to kill them, to do away with them, by drowning them in water. It was an idea that came into my head, but only an idea. I was terribly frightened. I knew I could never do such a thing, but I was afraid. . . ." Ideas of this nature later became a prominent feature of her oculogyric crises.

In the course of time the oculogyric spells came to be associated with a wide variety of psychological and symbolic representations in which highly charged emotional elements, ideas of reference, paranoid ideas, compulsions and a curious sense of timelessness became outstanding features. These bore an exclusive temporal relationship to the orbital crises, though in other respects, the patient's personality between spells remained remarkably intact.

(a) Compulsive ideas: "When I get the attack I feel the urge to kill my children. I actually want to kill them. Ordinarily, I would be afraid of such a terrible thought."

(b) Ideas of reference: She feels she is bewitched when she gets the spells. She is certain that "unknown methods" are being used to cause her eyes to turn up, and that "people who wish to harm me are the cause." Because of an associated increase in rigidity coming on with her attacks, the patient is almost totally incapable of movement. This, too, she attributes to outside influences.

(c) Voices: During spells voices "coming from inside . . . my conscience . . . accuse me of doing bad things." She is uncertain to the exact origin of these voices. They disappear when the attack is over.

(d) Aberration in the sense of time: During her spells, during which she remains fully conscious, she loses completely her sense of time. Unless so informed after the attack is over, she never knows their duration, though she recalls other details with remarkable clarity. The sense of timelessness is very apparent to her during the spells and is very disturbing to her, so that in order to keep herself correctly orientated with regard to the time element, she is compelled repeatedly to scan her clock, attempting to concentrate on each passing minute in order to appreciate more fully its significance.

Observations on this patient led to the following conclusions:

1. She was in conflict over murderous wishes which, like all such wishes, seek an outlet through motor activity. This wish, inacceptable to consciousness and under repression, was partly responsible for her character, her apologetic and ingratiating manner presenting a reverse picture of the unconscious intent. This impulse was largely responsible for feelings of guilt and depression.

2. The oculogyric attacks were feared because they threatened release of the aggressive impulses.

3. These impulses, during one spell, succeeded in overwhelming the patient's defenses and, in control of the motor apparatus, almost succeeded in their aim. The obsessive thoughts that followed were passively-perceived

ideational representations of her impulses to take aggressive action against her children.

4. After the near-death of one of her children, she was not only aware of the obsessive *idea* of killing them, but was able, though with great anxiety, to acknowledge the wish to act out the impulse.

5. The obsessive preoccupation with time was related to her concern about the periodicity of her attacks and the danger that attended their monthly appearance.

6. At a later date, she was able to build up defenses against the acknowledgment of her forbidden impulses by recourse to projection, during which the evil forces previously acknowledged to be her own were now attributed to a mysterious outside agency. It may be noted that even during this period of apparent capitulation to a defense, she was able to identify the origin of accusing voices. They were the expression of her own conscience.*

7. The failure of the projection to succeed in disassociating the patient from perception of her aggressive impulses was responsible for her great anxiety during her spell.

The consequence of the failure of a defense to protect against unconscious impulses coming from within is not only in an imperfect perception of these inner wishes, but an imperfect perception of the outside world of reality that is accompanied by a sense of strangeness so characteristic of states of depersonalization. This sense of strangeness is reminiscent of phantom limb, where again a protective mechanism is only partially successful—where the projection of the corporeal phantom of the lost limb only partially succeeds in overcoming the recognition cn the part of the ego of the reality of its loss. Similar emotional states may occur in other organic diseases of the nervous system like alcoholism or traumatic encephalopathy, in the so-called "para-cortical disturbances,"[1] in temporal lobe tumors, and in the convulsive disorders.

Convulsive Disorders. The fact that most of the so-called convulsive disorders are caused by either a known epileptogenic cortical focus, or by physiologic disturbances in cortical function due to toxic or organic influences upon it, or are influenced by hereditary factors yet unknown, in no way contradict the fact that psychological factors are an important component of them. There are many evidences of this, aside from psychoanalytic considerations. Students of epilepsy, even before the time of Jackson knew that mental and emotional states could precede, replace or follow ordinary epileptic fits. In 1850, Morel designated these well-documented conditions as "epilepsie larvee"; others have called them "masked epi-

---

* I recently had occasion to observe a psychotic encephalitic patient with oculogyric crises who exhibited marked palilalia. The voices he heard, especially during oculogyric crises, were voices of people who also suffered from the same symptom.

lepsy," "psychic equivalents," "voluminous states," and "affective epilepsy." Appearing suddenly, the attacks may bear no relationship to a known stimulus, or they may be related to quite specific situations in the patient's surroundings. The state of consciousness associated with spells varies from case to case and from spell to spell. There are cases reported in which not only is full consciousness preserved, but also the memories associated with the attack, the so-called "epilepsie consciente et mnesique." A common observation is the tendency of patients in some types of spells to express feelings and thoughts that otherwise are rarely expressed. These thoughts and feelings may be revived representations, often in distorted form, of actual experiences in the patient's past.[4, 5]

A 32-year-old patient under observation for convulsive disorder at the Neurological Institute of New York,* was noted, following each convulsive episode, to swallow repeatedly, making sucking noises with his tongue and producing a peculiar grunting noise produced by forcing air through the nasopharynx. The process was repeated every few seconds for about five minutes. When asked the reason for the action, he stated, "I can't help myself—I just have to swallow." When he attempted to resist the impulse to repeat this behavior, he became extremely anxious. When pressed further for his associations, he was able to recall that 19 years before when he was 13 years old, he had been given to this same compulsive habit, a source of great concern to him and his family at the time. The symptom gradually disappeared as he grew older.

The recollection of this early difficulty was disturbing to the patient and he insisted that the matter be dropped. When seen a few hours later, upon being re-interrogated concerning the compulsive symptom, he denied any recollection of the previous conversation. However, when reminded in detail of what had transpired during the post-convulsive state, he gradually recalled the events as they had occurred. He was surprised at his amnesia and became very much interested in the swallowing episode. He stated it was the first time since boyhood that he had thought of his former habit, and now found that the recollection brought with it a profusion of similarly lost memory records and vivid feeling tones concerned with that immediate age-period, which for him was a particularly unhappy and painful time in his life.

There are certain points of similarity between the periodic psychiatric manifestations that occur in epilepsy and encephalitis. In both, the reaction-pattern tends to retain its identity from spell to spell, to trace stereotyped configurations, and to stand apart from the usual behavior pattern in sharp relief.[11] At the time they are observed, these dissociated states may approximate classical neurotic or psychotic syndromes.[5, 11]

An 11-year-old white girl was admitted to Dr. I. S. Wechsler's service at the Mt. Sinai Hospital because of episodes of motor restlessness and "peculiar behavior" of three to four years duration.

When seven years of age she developed episodic attacks during which she became

* Service of Dr. Henry A. Riley.

dazed, stubborn and retarded in speech and markedly restless. She jumped about in bed, bit her fingernails, varied in obedience to commands. She had complete amnesia for the episodes. During periods between spells, she was considered a normal, intelligent girl with a happy disposition.

Upon admission to the hospital, she was noted to be negativistic, answered in monosyllables, stared at the examiner, and exhibited much facial grimacing and silly pointless giggling. She picked constantly at her toes and feet. Appropriate affective reactions were absent. She admitted she was hearing voices, particularly that of her uncle "who was saying nice things" to her. There was evidence of clouding of consciousness and sensorial deficiency.

When seen several hours later, she was discovered to be pleasant, well-mannered, intelligent and cooperative. She was completely alert, orientated and displayed normal spontaneity of thought and speech. There was no evidence of behavior disorder. She professed complete amnesia with respect to her earlier conduct.

The neurologic examination was entirely negative. The electroencephalogram revealed occasional slow 4 to 6 per second waves in all leads. These were accentuated by hyperventilation and approached a 3 per second pattern. The interpretation of the record (courtesy of Dr. Hans Strauss) was that of a convulsive disorder. Pneumoencephalogram was normal.

The Return of the Repressed. Epileptic patients fear their seizures, and their concern about how they behaved during their spells reflects a deeper concern about what they might do under any circumstance when provoked enough to lose control over their actions. The basic pattern of conflict is similar in this respect to those described in oculogyric crises and other hyperkinetic disorders where the motor symptoms become a threat as a potential outlet for aggressive impulses. In the encephalitic and epileptic patient the attacks may be accompanied by dramatic consequences in terms of violence and destructiveness. In both, especially during the paroxysmal episodes, revivification of memories which have been forgotten often bring with them a sense of the uncanny. These visitations from the past are not welcome ones and are likely to be greeted with feelings of distaste or even horror. They are "manifestations," that, to quote Shelling, cited by Freud in his paper on "The 'Uncanny,' "[7] ought to have remained hidden and secret and have become visible. There is a return of the world of infancy when the child's thoughts and feelings coming from within were also conceived at the time as coming from without. It is a particularly dangerous time, because of the child's vulnerability as the object of its own aggression, which, as in the nightmare, may later return in the form of revenant visitations. Due to the incomplete awareness of body-boundaries, it is also a time of doubt and uncertainty regarding ownership and responsibility for the actions of limbs and body-parts. It is a time in which the child conceived itself as a mechanical instrument under the influence of powerful forces that controlled its movements and feelings, the exact origin of which remained vague and indistinct.

The psychological reactions that accompany encephalitis or epilepsy demonstrate, as in all pathoneuroses, that the return of repressed unconscious fantasies depends upon a specific symptom and the degree to which, because of the patient's susceptibilities, he will respond with a greater or lesser degree of regression. Observation of these mental reactions reveal not only genital or anal components, but, in certain patients, even more primitive and archaic representations characteristic of the oral-projective phase of ego development.

The perception of neurologic phenomena revives the archaic phenomenology of this early period of life, the concept of the "phantom" limb and the "evil" eye, for example, representing unconsciously determined psychic elaborations of purely physical manifestations like paralysis or strabismus. This is also true of the physical "stigmata" of hysteria. These neurologic or hysterical stigmata, consistent with the laws of the unconscious, may portend evil for the observer as well as the observed; by these laws, a source of danger may be perceived with a shock of recognition that the demon that "possesses" the epileptic, the paralyzed, or the mentally afflicted may also possess those in contact with him. But excommunication does not succeed in putting a distance between the two, since the barrier that is erected does not divide the known from the unknown, but only the known from what is already recognized as a common possession.

BIBLIOGRAPHY

1. Bender, L. and Schilder, P.: Mannerisms as organic motility syndrome. Confinia neurol. *3:* 6, 1941.
2. Beres, D. and Brenner, C.: Mental reactions in patients with neurological disease. Psychoanalyt. Quart. *19:* 170–191, 1950.
3. Betlheim, S.: quoted by Schilder, P.: The Image and Appearance of the Human Body. New York, International Universities Press, Inc., 1950.
4. Brickner, R. M., Rosner, A. A. and Munro, R.: Physiological aspects of the obsessive state. Psychosom. Med. *2:* 369–383, 1940.
5. ——, —— and Yaskin, H.: Evidences concerning the neural groundwork underlying certain behavior patterns. Psychosom. Med. *5:* 20–26, 1943.
6. Ferenczi, S.: Disease—or pathoneuroses. *In:* Further Contributions to the Theory and Technique of Psychoanalysis. London, Hogarth Press, 1926.
7. Freud, S.: The 'uncanny.' *In:* Collected Papers. London, Hogarth Press, 1946, vol. IV.
8. Hollos, S. and Ferenczi, S.: Psychoanalysis and the Psychic Disorder of General Paresis. Nervous and Mental Disease Monograph Series No. 42. New York and Washington, Nervous and Mental Disease Publishing Co., 1925.
9. Mitchell, S. W.: quoted by Schilder, P.: The Image and Appearance of the Human Body. New York, International Universities Press, Inc., 1950.
10. Rosner, A. A.: The Psychiatric Sequelae of Epidemic Encephalitis. Chap. VII. Encephalitis—A Clinical Study, Josephine B. Neal and others. For the Mathe-

son Commission for Research in Encephalitis. New York, Grune & Stratton, 1942.

11. ——: Unit reaction states in oculogyric crises. Am. J. Psychiat. *99:* 224–228, 1942.

12. Schilder, P.: The Image and Appearance of the Human Body. New York, International Universities Press, Inc., 1950.

13. Wilson, S. A. K.: Neurology. Baltimore, Williams & Wilkins, 1950, Chap. VIII.

14. Von Economo, C.: Encephalitis Lethargica: Its Sequelae and Treatment. Trans. by K. O. Newman. London, 1931. See also: Psychiat. Quart., *4:* 142, 1930.

CHAPTER 12

Psychiatric Aspects of Pediatric Practice

_____MILTON I. LEVINE, M.D.

Dr. Levine received his M.D. from Cornell University Medical College. He is now Assistant Professor of Pediatrics, Cornell University Medical College; Associate Attending Pediatrician, New York Hospital, Cornell Medical Center, and Consulting Pediatrician to the New York City Department of Health.

Dr. Levine is a Fellow of the American Academy of Pediatrics, a Fellow of the American College of Chest Physicians and a Fellow of the American Public Health Association.

Aside from having been Pediatrician to the Bank Street Nursery Schools, etc., he has had a long-standing interest and background in psychiatry and psychoanalysis.

THIS CHAPTER HAS TO DIFFER—of necessity—in some principal ways from the basic structure of the other papers. While one could speak (in the others) of the meaning of illness, of surgery, and of invalidism for the patient afflicted, in the care of at least the smaller children and infants, the person afflicted and the person to be taken into consideration is not only the child but is also—and is often primarily—the parent. Most often the child can be favorably influenced only via the parents.

The relationship of an adult patient to his physician is distinctly different from that of a child to a physician. An adult who is ill will usually look to, and trust the physician as a symbolic father and will generally place his full dependence upon him, looking upon him and leaning upon him as a maker and performer of miracles. The child, however, as a general rule, still has his complete faith and trust in his _real_ parents and is not willing to accept a substitute even during times (possibly especially during times) of illness. This is one of the reasons why the physician must work _through_ the parents by reassurance and understanding. Another reason, of course, is that the child, _per se_, is helpless and to a large extent is directly dependent upon the parents. If the parents are tense and anxious the child is nearly certain to have to be tense, too, as a function of the parents' effect upon him.

Another way in which this chapter has to differ from the others is that to the field of pediatrics belongs not only the occurrence of illness (and thus the meaning of such disease), but also the emergence of a series of developmental events which, by themselves, lead to psychological effects upon parent and child comparable to that of illness. An understanding of these factors may help the physician to foster those factors which lead to optimal — development of the child and to avoid and reject those situations which would prove detrimental. In this sense, the doctor who counsels the care and development of children can have a more direct influence upon the future generation than anyone else.

It is for this reason—and particularly because many parents will habitually turn to him for plain educational attitudes, too—that the pediatrician ought to know a great deal about psychological facts and this is why we present some of these basic aspects even without specific reference to illness.

HELPLESSNESS

Of all the observations made of an infant during his first year of life, by far the most dramatic is his complete helplessness. Unable to keep warm by himself, to move from place to place, to seek food and obtain food, the newborn is entirely dependent for its life upon its mother or some other person who takes her place. Without this attention and care the infant could survive only a short time.

All of the numerous activities which a mother performs for her child repeatedly every day tend toward two important results—the baby expects and looks to its mother for the satisfaction of his every need, and if generally satisfied, gains trust in his mother.

This complete dependence of the child covers most of the first two years of life. Then, with the increase in physical coordination, with the ability to walk and run, to talk and fight, and with gradual development of understanding, this dependence is somewhat diminished. But until approximately six years of age a child is still largely dependent, fearing any loss of affection and even more, fearing separation.

Also during the early years of life certain activities are easily observed which seem to be of deep significance for not only are they noted in a great majority of all children, but the occurrence of these activities is more or less concentrated in certain specific age periods. Among such are finger sucking, resistance to weaning, resistance to toilet training and masturbation.

Primarily the sucking instinct is a necessity for the survival of the helpless infant. This is true of all mammals. But if one closely observes infants he will come across several most interesting facts. First, that sucking does not seem to be entirely related to the taking of food, some babies even suck their fingers or other objects when they have taken all the milk they desire. Secondly, that the amount of sucking varies greatly with different babies.

Apparently the infant has some deep need for sucking other than the securing of milk. There must be some real and pleasurable satisfaction for the infant in lip sensation and lip stimulation. In fact, there seems to be such a deep need for this stimulation that infants who receive inadequate lip satisfaction from the bottle will often suck their fingers or even suck on a protruding tongue. Young infants who cannot find their fingers or any substitute on which to suck, and who are deprived of an adequate amount of sucking pleasure, are usually very unhappy and cry a great deal, and often the blame for this crying is placed wrongfully on colic or improper formula.[15, 16]

It seems almost unnecessary and superfluous to review the above or to describe the frequency with which weaning and toilet training problems as well as masturbation are encountered for these are certainly observations of all physicians who have followed the development of children.

SEPARATION AND HOSPITALIZATION

A great deal has been written in recent years describing the detrimental and even disastrous effects of separation of young children from their parents. In view of what has been said above about the child's helplessness this fact can hardly be surprising. The response of infants to this lack of mothering has been described and well documented by Ribble,[21] Bender[1] Goldfarb[9] and Spitz.[22] The psychological harm in children over the age of infancy has been clearly demonstrated by Freud and Burlingham.[7]

But the results of such separation are frequently discernible to the physician who follows and observes his patients closely. Habit spasms, enuresis, sleep problems, stammering, stuttering, digestive disturbances and extreme separation anxieties are often found to be the sequellae of an experience or a number of experiences when a child has undergone separation from his parents. Numerous case histories could be presented to illustrate this point.

Every physician is familiar with the five year old, who, in the face of his first real separation from his mother, vomits each morning on the way to school. Just as familiar were the facial tics, stammering, stuttering and bedwetting of the children, during the past war, who saw their fathers leave for duty in the armed forces.

And all of the symptoms previously mentioned are also found with great frequency following hospitalization of young children where there is complete or almost complete separation from their parents.

At times, the symptoms may not appear until considerable time has passed, and parents are unaware of the connection between the various signs and the hospitalization. However, a careful history will usually reveal this connection and this history may, as a rule, be obtained by the physician, without recourse to psychologists or other outside sources.

The physician who realizes that parents represent survival to a child and that separation may cause deep emotional impact, will always try to project himself to the child—to attempt to set himself in the child's place. With this approach, hospitalization would be advised only under extreme circumstances when further studies, more intricate treatment or surgical intervention is imperative.

Only too often children are referred to the hospital for the convenience of the physician with little or no thought as to the effect on the children. One could safely say that over 50 per cent of children hospitalized could have been studied and treated at home.

A physician discovered sugar in a child's urine and immediately hospitalized the child for blood sugars, glucose tolerance tests and other diagnostic work-up, all of which could easily have been performed in the physician's office or in clinical laboratories. In much the same way, children are often hospitalized when a diagnosis of pneumonia is made, although there is no cyanosis or dyspnoea. Infectious mononucleosis, celiac disease, angioneurotic edema, asthma, chronic constipation, eczema, hypothyroidism and pyuria are among conditions for which children are often hospitalized without need.

But there are many instances where hospitalization is a necessity and where a physician can do a great deal to relieve the anxiety of the child. In such cases every effort should be made to arrange for the mother to remain in the hospital with the child as long as the child needs her support. In situations where an operation is to be undertaken, rectal anesthesia or some sedation should be give in the room so that the child will fall off to sleep with the mother nearby. When he wakes up postoperatively, he should find his mother still at his side, or, if this cannot be arranged, the physician whom the child knows should accompany the child from his room to the operating room. This avoids the separation from the parent during a time of great anxiety, in addition to the other concomitant experiences such as being wheeled through long and unfamiliar corridors by strange people, entering into the cold and white walled operating room with white garbed, masked creatures walking back and forth, and with the final experience of being anesthetized.

If it is impossible for a parent to stay with a child during hospitalization, then a daily visit should be arranged. And although one hears it repeated frequently, it is not true that children do better without these short visits. There may be tears when the father and mother leave at the close of visiting hours, but the satisfaction and reassurance gained by the child far outbalances any detrimental effect caused by the period of unhappiness following the visit.

And also in regard to the child's fear of separation, a tendency of many physicians should be mentioned. This is the tendency, when a child is crying vigorously, to tell the child, "Stop crying or I'll send your mommy out of the room." A threat such as this can only build up a fear and hatred of the physician.

The importance of certain activities which are related to specific age periods has already been noted. The tendency to finger suck during the first few years and the tendency to masturbate during the period of approximately three to six years are certainly most obvious. Somewhat more subtle is the intense interest in the anal region as well as in the excreta around the two year level.

During the periods just mentioned small children apparently derive great satisfaction from these activities. As they grow older these interests slacken and new interests arise in their place. But during periods of strain and stress and unhappiness children and even adults will frequently revert to the satisfying activities of earlier periods. Children of four and five years will frequently resort to finger sucking when unhappy, bored or sleepy. Children whose bodies have been shocked by accident, operation or severe emotional disturbance will also frequently revert. I remember very vividly a four year old boy who had been run down by a truck and severely injured. His skull was fractured, his ribs broken and one lung had collapsed. In spite of sedation he was crying and tossing about in the hospital bed until someone suggested giving him a pacifier. The child quieted immediately and sucked constantly on the pacifier during the weeks of his convalescence. Adults also frequently revert to this so called oral stage of childhood when under tension. The nervous business man chewing on a cigar stub, the worried college girl smoking one cigarette after another while studying for examinations are examples well known to all of us.

But the knowledge of these developmental activities is of special interest and importance to the physician in his understanding and handling of children. It is the physician who directs the parents in their handling of the child and it is his duty to see to it that the natural urges and impulses are not unduly thwarted. The results of such restrictions must be fully understood to grasp their importance.

FEEDING AND SUCKING

It has been said that a young infant wakes to eat and eats to sleep. The greater part of his waking period is devoted to eating and when he is completely satisfied, he relaxes and falls off to sleep. During these waking periods, while he is being fed, he gradually learns to know his mother or mother substitute and associates with her presence the satisfaction or unhappiness experienced during this waking period. He gains trust in his mother if she satisfies his most important needs during these waking periods—and these most important needs are the satisfaction of his desire for food and his desire for adequate lip stimulation, usually called oral stimulation. This latter need is entirely separate from the necessity of sucking as an adjunct to eating.

If we realize that the primary need of a young child is to feel that he is loved and wanted then we must realize that the basis for this understanding rests in the early months of infancy when the baby looks to his mother for the satisfaction of his needs. Since the average mother looks to the physician for direction, the role of the physician in effecting a desirable mother-child relationship assumes great importance.

The physician who insists that an infant be maintained on a rigid feeding schedule is not only frequently causing the child unhappiness but often preventing complete satisfaction from the feeding as well. At times the baby experiences hunger considerably before the scheduled moment, while at other times the feeding is given before the infant is really hungry. In both cases, the mother is associated, in the child's mind, with an unpleasant experience and an infant learns that it cannot expect to gain full satisfaction of its needs from its mother—the first important step in the formation of the desired relationship.

We have already discussed the sucking satisfaction of a child as an instinctual need, entirely separate from the sucking urge to satisfy hunger. It has been pointed out that this sucking need is most intense during the first two years of life. To deprive a child of this sucking satisfaction during the period of intense need will usually cause great frustration.

With this fact in mind, the child's physician will avoid weaning too early from a bottle to a glass, and will watch for evidence of lack of oral satisfaction throughout infancy. It has been demonstrated that many crying infants, classified as colic babies, may be relaxed and completely satisfied if given a pacifier on which to suck.[12] It has been shown, also, that infants who finish their bottles rapidly are prone to finger sucking. Many physicians have been successful in eliminating or diminishing the degree of finger sucking by fitting the infants' bottles with slow flowing nipples.

Along with the subject of sucking needs should be considered the question of breast feeding. It has frequently been stated that "breast feeding is the best feeding"—that it establishes a relationship between mother and child that cannot be otherwise obtained, and that the desire for oral satisfaction is more easily gratified. It may be that the desire for oral satisfaction is more easily gratified by breast feeding than by bottle feeding.

However, the decision as to the advisability of recommending breast feeding should depend on whether or not nursing will be of the greatest mutual satisfaction to the mother and infant.[13] A mother who desires to nurse should be given every opportunity and encouragement, but mothers who would rather not nurse due to certain specific fears, and mothers who dislike the very thought of nursing, should not breast feed their babies.

Mothers who cannot nurse because of economic circumstances should be reassured that their infants will not suffer physically or emotionally from receiving formula feedings. But whichever method a mother finally undertakes, there should be no sense of inadequacy or self-reproach and she should receive every encouragement from her physician.

TOILET TRAINING

Every physician who deals with small children has repeatedly experienced a situation where a child of approximately 18 months to three years of age has anxiously called to go to the bathroom for a movement the minute the physician arrives. And during this same age period are found the large majority of toilet training problems. Of frequent occurrence are the children who resist toilet training, some screaming and opposing violently any attempt to place them on the toilet seat or potty. Others offer very little, if any resistance, sitting quietly on the seat without functioning, and then defecating in their pants or on the floor as soon as they are taken off. Still others will resist the toilet or the pot and make a habit of having the bowel movement in a closet or other out of the way place where they feel unobserved. And there are also children who resist toilet training to such a degree that severe chronic constipation results, at times even producing a megacolon.

This is the same age period during which children so often handle and smear their feces and seem to show special interest in the excreta. These activities and attitudes demonstrate very vividly the extreme emphasis the average child of this developmental level places upon the functioning of his bowels.

The observations related are not by any means unusual, but are noted by all pediatricians and physicians dealing with large numbers of small children. Because of this apparent focus of interest this period has been termed the "Anal Period."

Of course it must be realized that this is the age area during which most parents are attempting to toilet train their children and naturally an unusual amount of attention is paid to the excretory area. It is not our purpose within the limits of this chapter to enter into argument as to whether this anal interest is instinctive or whether it is aroused almost entirely by parental attitudes.

However, the act of defecation is instinctive and difficulties arise when parents attempt to direct and regulate these instincts to conform to our culture. If handled poorly conflicts will undoubtedly occur which may undermine the parent-child relationship.

Apparently the mother of today has been so molded by her own upbringing and the impact of advertising that she develops considerable anxiety if any suggestion of constipation occurs and usually expresses her anxieties to the physician. In his advice as to toilet training, constipation and any digestive abnormality relating to the anus the physician can be of the greatest help—or may be extremely detrimental.

The formerly accepted policy of "habit time" for bowel movements can only aid in fostering resistance. The suggestion of using a daily suppository at a specified time is also detrimental for it not only causes considerable discomfort as well as resistance, but produces an abnormal sensation, prevents the bowels from functioning spontaneously and often establishes or starts a dependency on abnormal anal stimulation.

It should be the policy of every physician to reassure the mothers that a daily bowel movement is not a necessity and that a child might even have a normal two day cycle. If a child is in no distress, shows no abdominal symptoms and has no difficulty passing his movements there should be no concern even if the interval should extend as long as three or four days.

As a matter of fact it is of extreme importance that the mother be warned not only to guard against placing too much emphasis on the regularity of the movements but to refrain from showing any anxiety over the quality of the movement. I remember very vividly one three-year-old child who had been under treatment for celiac disease. The child had improved but the mother anxiously awaited each movement and ordered the child not to flush the toilet until she had made her observations. Finally the child resisted and developed a severe and chronic constipation with an evacuation every seven or eight days—after the use of strong catharsis, suppositories or enemas. And then the child was entered in nursery school which she enjoyed immensely—and every day at school had a normal movement without the slightest difficulty. No movement at home on Saturday and Sunday but complete regularity at school during the remainder of the week. After the mother became aware of the situation and showed no apparent interest in future evacuations at home the condition subsided entirely. This case serves as an example of one of the causes of chronic constipation.

However, the greatest cause of chronic constipation in children, from the pediatric point of view, is still the mother who forces the child in toilet training, who uses terms such as "filthy," "dirty," "nasty," when by chance a diaper is soiled. These are usually meticulous mothers and their constipated children are, as a rule, also meticulous—not only reacting against the parental pressure but attempting not to do anything which might be "filthy," "dirty," or "nasty." When such constipation is severe the children occasionally withhold to such a degree that a megacolon results. I would venture a guess that over 80 per cent of all megacolons are emotional in origin.

The treatment of this type of constipation is almost uniformly successful.

It involves reassuring the mother and relieving her concern about impaction, directing the mother to show no apparent interest in the time, number or consistency of stools, giving a pleasant tasting (often disguised) laxative to keep the stools soft, and letting the child and mother play with and wallow in finger paints and plasticene without any concern over the consequences of "getting dirty."

Before leaving the subject of constipation it should be noted that various objects for dilating the anus have been advertised to the physician as a means of gradually stretching the taut anal sphincter. These objects are of more harm than benefit and only tend to cause a child to tense the muscle further. The common statement of so many physicians that digital examination of the anus of the constipated child shows it to be extremely tight is undoubtedly true, but this tautness is only functional and related directly to the resistance of the child. It is rarely organic.

THE GENITAL PERIOD

By the time the average child has reached the age of three years he has usually passed the period when oral stimulation is of such extreme importance. Most children, at this age, have also passed through the stage of toilet training although there may still be problems relating to it such as constipation or, at times, even soiling. At some level between the age of three and six years another body area seems to assume primary importance—the genital area.[6]

It is true that many smaller children, even as early as nine months of age, will frequently finger their genitals when they are undressed. It is obvious also that infants and small children who rock on their hands and knees, or who arch their backs and rock, derive a definite pleasurable genital sensation.[14]

However, after approximately three years of age the child develops a real awareness of his sex organs. He not only asks a great many questions concerning them but learns that by handling them and rhythmically stimulating them he can gain a great deal of sensual pleasure. This masturbation is a normal activity during this period and is of no unusual significance unless it is practiced excessively to the exclusion of most other activities. It should be considered not only as a normal but a necessary activity in the psychosexual development of the human being—for in order to develop normal sexuality, both men and women need to have a sensation of pleasure developed in the genital region.[23]

But in spite of the fact that every modern textbook on pediatrics states that there is no harm in *masturbation*, many physicians still concur with the anxieties of parents and advise on means of preventing such activity and means of treating children for this "disgusting" action. Penis and clitoris are being examined for elongated or irritated foreskin, sedatives are being used, hands are being tied, circumcisions and even, at times, clitoridectomies are performed, and numerous are the threats in efforts to eliminate masturbation.

The dangers which result from the repressive and often painful measures are extreme, for the threats and punishments force a child to fear and repress these sexual feelings, and the anxiety not only becomes a barrier to normal development but may tend to frigidity and impotency in adult life.

It is important for the physician to avoid any unnecessary manipulation or operative procedure on the genitals during this period, such as circumcisions, catheterizations, and cystoscopic examinations, all three of which are performed far too frequently. Many, if not most of the boys of this age period, who have undergone these procedures, look upon them as castration activities and feel that they have not only been punished but damaged as well.

It should be noted that this is the age period when little boys on seeing nude girls feel that the latter have had their genitals taken from them, and little girls are envious of the external sex organs of boys and feel they have been deprived by their parents. Every little girl has tried to urinate like a boy. In many cases this envy of boys continues on into adult life.

FEARS AND RESPONSES OF THE PRESCHOOL CHILD

The child, between the age of approximately three and six years, is usually beset by many fears. These are partly due to the fact that during his upbringing he has been warned repeatedly not to touch fire, electric outlets, unfamiliar dogs and cats, broken glass, gas ranges, to stay on the sidewalks, to go slowly downstairs, to avoid deep water, etc., etc., etc. However, their greatest fear still remains that of separation from their parents as has been mentioned earlier.

A somewhat similar fear, although not as deep, is that of loss of their parents' affection and the symptoms of these fears are frequently a source of investigation by the physician. These are most frequently observed during the period following the arrival of a new infant in the home, at a time when the child fears that most of the affection of his father and mother have been shifted to the younger child.

Enuresis and even an actual reversion to soiling often arises, but at times the reaction is more subtle. Some children will try to follow the example of the sibling. I have seen two children, one of three years and one of four years, who started to have difficulty walking after having been very well co-ordinated. Both children had such extreme difficulty that neurologic disease was suspected. In one, a tentative diagnosis of cerebellar tumor was made. In both cases it was found that a younger child at home was learning to walk and stumbling frequently (and receiving special attention for the efforts).

Other children, instead of reverting to infantile activities, will complain of frequent and severe headaches or attacks of abdominal pain.

Also of interest and importance during this period is the child's reaction to *surgical and other traumatic experiences*. Of course a great deal depends upon the emotional stability of the child and on the preparation the child has had for the experience.

Most children have anxieties prior to a traumatic experience of which they have some previous knowledge and all children have anxieties as well as helplessness following the experience.

Some children will react to the trauma by reverting to an earlier infantile pattern such as finger sucking, bedwetting or incontinence. Others will react by repressing the whole memory of the painful experience and of the fears and anxieties associated with it. Later, although the memory of the experience may still remain repressed, the fear and anxiety which accompanied the incident may break through and come to the surface. Then the child develops what is known as an anxiety neurosis. A child with this condition will suffer from attacks of anxiety without understanding the reason for his fears.[5]

Fortunately, the tendency today is to shorten the period of convalescence as much as possible. The former method of complete rest in bed during convalescence with little opportunity for activity could not help but cause a regression of the child to a period of over-protection and complete dependence. An effort is also made at the present time to offer the convalescing child play activities which will occupy him during all his waking hours in order to relieve as much as possible the emotional tensions caused by the many factors associated with the illness. We have learned that rest with inactivity and leaving the child to his anxieties and regressions is usually of much less benefit than a regime of moderate activity. It is also important that the child's education be continued while he is hospitalized so that he is not handicapped in school.

THE GRADE SCHOOL YEARS

At approximately six to seven years of age the child enters another period of development. The changes that occur as children enter this stage are rather easily observed. There is no longer an intermingling of the sexes. Boys tend to go with boys, and girls with girls. They form groups, and clubs and even gangs—and each child not only makes an effort to be important as an individual in this unit but also desires to make for himself a place of importance as a member of the group.

This is a period of ego development and both the parents and physician should add their efforts in aiding the child to maneuver his way through this period successfully.

Every effort must be made to assure that the physical status of the child is in the optimum condition. Both mother and physician should refrain from speaking of the child's shortcomings in the presence of the child, and he should receive a great deal of reassurance.

The interest and direction of the physician may be of the greatest importance during this period. Defects of vision and hearing must be corrected. Anything that disfigures a child such as protuding ears or teeth should be also corrected.

Enuresis at this time is almost entirely emotional in origin.[10] It may be due to hostility to parents who are constantly naggy and scolding, it may be due to repressed masturbation, it may be due to certain fears associated with the genitals—there may be any number of causes depending on the experience of the individual child. The harmful effect of cystoscopic examinations in the study of enuresis has already been mentioned. It should be stated that nocturnal enuresis is never a urologic problem unless there are symptoms during the day as well.

Circumcisions also should be avoided during this period as well as during puberty unless urgently needed. There is sufficient evidence already reported of the severe emotional trauma to boys who have undergone this operation. In most boys circumcised at this late age there is a feeling of mutilation and even castration.

A few words must be said about *habit spasms* or *tics* which are not uncommonly seen by the physician.[18] These are most usually noted during the school age period and are evidence of some anxiety from which the child is suffering. As every physician knows it involves the repeated spasm of a particular group of muscles, and must be differentiated from chorea which is general and involves muscles throughout the body. The origin of these spasms may be physical. One child may have had an irritation of the eye at the outset, another a sore nose, a third may have noticed another person with the particular tic and becomes imitative. Whatever the particular source, the specific muscles become the focal point for an expression of an inner conflict and the tic may remain as such for months or even years. The old attempts at remedy, such as standing a child before a mirror so that he might observe himself, or the frequent remarks of parents and others concerning the tic, are of greater harm than benefit and only cause increased concentration on the activity as well as bringing to the child a certain amount of added attention, which may be somewhat satisfying.

The underlying causes for the habit spasms may be obscure and may be extremely difficult for the physician to determine without psychiatric aid. But at times the situation underlying the condition is superficial.

Among my patients was a girl of six who had twin brothers whom she would frequently push and even occasionally knock down as evidence of her sibling jealousy. One day one of the twins developed poliomyelitis and for a time had paralysis of his lower extremities. After he was hospitalized his sister developed a severe facial tic with blinking of eyes and wrinkling of nose. While her brother was still hospitalized her mother bought her a doll which she immediately named after the brother. The next day she asked if she could arrange a "big party" for her doll, and several days later had all her friends at the house doing honor to this namesake of her brother. Almost immediately after the party the tic disappeared and never again returned.

As children approach puberty many new problems arise which often call for the opinion of the physician. Probably the matter of greatest concern is the *inequality of growth* among children. In some girls there is considerable breast development at ten years of age while others anxiously await the development until 14 or 15 years. The appearance of axillary and pubic hair, and, in boys, the growth of the genitals and the change in voice—all these as well as the marked variations in height make this period one of great concern for those children who are slow in maturing. Boys and girls who were formerly outgoing and aggressive may temporarily withdraw and ask if there is any means of hastening their outward evidences of maturity. It is far from adequate to read them statements from authoritative sources explaining the normalcy of this variation in growth, and it probably increases an underlying hostility for parents at this stage to mention that the parents themselves were slow in developing and, therefore, the condition is one of normal hereditary sequence.

If a boy is greatly upset emotionally because of his lack of development at the age of 12½ or 13 years there is certainly some rationale in giving inoculations of testosterone or Antuitrin-S which will not only soon increase the size of his genitals but cause a gain in height as well. Usually the endocrine system of the body continues the development after the first artificial "push" has been discontinued.

In the case of girls the method of hastening puberty has not as yet been safely established, for any artificial pressure may upset the development of the normal menstrual cycle.

During the school age period and during pre-puberty, one finds a great many children who are obese due to overeating. Here, also, the vast majority are children who are unhappy and who compensate for this unhappiness by the pleasure they get from eating. These children certainly should not be sternly placed on a restricted diet and scolded if no loss in weight occurs. Much more may be accomplished if the physician attempts to gain some insight into the emotional environment of the child in order to realize, if possible, some of the factors involved.[3, 11] Often if the child feels the affection or warm interest of the physician, he will attempt to work with him in the effort to arrange a limited but satisfactory diet.

Pre-puberty and early puberty bring with them a great many emotional upsets which are especially pronounced in the case of girls.[4, 24] All children go through an upsetting period when they are neither child nor adult, and when they desire to break from the family ties and, at the same time, feel a need to remain with their parents.

Most physicians have observed these children and understand their reactions. They are highly emotional, laugh easily and cry easily. They may complain of headaches, nausea and feelings of fatigue. Girls have the added anxiety associated with menstruation. The impressions which have been built up during childhood years concerning menstruation will affect them greatly. Their degree of acceptance of the fact that they are girls and will be women is also extremely important.

Girls who have heard this function spoken of as the "curse" or "getting unwell" are certain to be upset and very complaining when menstruation sets in. So, also, are those girls who have been distressed through their early years because they were not boys, for menstruation only emphasizes to them over and over again, the fact that they are women.

Occasionally, in early adolescence, girls are seen who—in their fear of growing up into adulthood, with all its implications, sexual and otherwise— attempt subconsciously to commit suicide. These are the adolescents who develop a severe degree of anorexia and, in certain cases, even spit out all saliva, lest the swallowing help strengthen them. It is interesting to note that menses usually cease during this condition.

Such cases, as soon as recognized, should receive psychiatric help, but the close care of a physician is of the greatest necessity since they usually greatly diminish the protein reserves in the body.

Once in adolescence, the child usually responds to medical and surgical care very much as an adult does, although he is still upset sexually. Gynecologic and urologic examinations may produce much more severe emotional reactions than in an adult.

It should be remembered by all physicians dealing with children that they are not adults or even *little* adults. They are young human beings growing up through certain developmental processes and are reacting to the conflicts that must arise in the process of growing up.

BIBLIOGRAPHY

1. Bender, L.: Infants reared in institutions; permanently handicapped. Child Welfare League Bull. *24:* 1945
2. Bornstein, B.: A phobia in a two and a half year old child. Psychoanalytic Quart. *4:* 93, 1935.

3. Bruch, Hilde: Psychosomatic Approach to Childhood Disorder. Modern Trends in Child Psychiatry. New York, International Universities Press, 1945.

4. Deutsch, H.: Psychology of Women. New York, Grune & Stratton, 1944, vol. I.

5. English, O. H. and Pearson G. H.: Emotional Problems of Living. New York, Norton, 1945.

6. Freud, S.: Three contributions to the theory of sex. *In:* Basic Writings of Sigmund Freud. New York, Modern Library, 1938.

7. Freud, A. and Burlingham, D.: War and Children. New York, Medical War Books, 1943.

8. Gerard, Max: Psychogenic tic in ego development. *In:* The Psychoanalytic Study of the Child. *2:* 133, 1947.

9. Goldfarb, W.: Effects of psychological deprivation in infancy. Am. J. Psychiat. *102:* 1945.

10. Katan, A.: Experience with enuretics. *In:* The Psychoanalytic Study of the Child. *2:* 241, 1947.

11. Lehman, E.: Feeding problems of psychogenic origin. *In:* The Psychoanalytic Study of the Child. *3, 4:* 461, 1949.

12. Levine, M. I. and Bell, A. I.: Treatment of colic in infancy, by use of pacifiers. J. Pediat. *37:* 750, 1951.

13. ——: Modern concept of breast feeding. J. Pediat. *38:* 472, 1951.

14. ——: Pediatric observations on masturbation in children. *In:* The Psychoanalytic Study of the Child. *6:* 61, 1951.

15. Levy, D. M.: Fingersucking and accessory movements in early infancy. Am. J. Psychiat. *7:* 881, 1928.

16. ——: Experiments on sucking reflex and social behavior of dogs. Am. J. Orthopsychiat. *4:* 203, 1934.

17. Lowrey, L.: Personality distortion and early institutional care. Am. J. Orthopsychiat. *10:* 576, 1940.

18. Mahler, M.: Psychoanalytic evaluation of tics. *In:* The Psychoanalytic Study of the Child. *3, 4:* 279, 1949.

19. Pearson, G.: Emotional Disorders of Children. New York, Norton Co., 1949.

20. ——: The effect of operative procedure on the emotional life of the child. Am. J. Dis. Child. *62:* 716, 1941.

21. Ribble, M.: Rights of Infants. New York, Columbia University Press, 1943.

22. Spitz, R. A.: Hospitalism: An inquiry into the genesis of psychiatric conditions in early childhood. *In:* The Psychoanalytic Study of the Child. *5:* 53, 1945.

23. Tausk, V.: On Masturbation. *In:* The Psychoanalytic Study of the Child., *6:* 61, 1951.

24. Zachry, C.: Emotions and Conduct in Adolescence. New York, Appleton Century Crofts, 1940.

CHAPTER 13

Psychiatric Aspects of Dermatology

MORTON HECHT, M.D.

Dr. Hecht received his M.D. from the University of Maryland; received his graduate training in Syphilology and Dermatology at the New York Skin and Cancer Institute and further postgraduate training at the Post Graduate School of New York University—Bellevue Medical Center. He is a Diplomate of the American Board of Dermatology and Syphilology.

Dr. Hecht is now a staff member of the Dermatologic Staff of the University Hospital and the New York Skin and Cancer Institute, New York University—Bellevue Medical Center, as well as a number of other hospitals. He is a charter member of the Group for Study of Psychosomatic Problems in Dermatology, and has a private practice of Dermatology in New York City.

INTRODUCTION

PEOPLE ATTACH GREAT EMOTIONAL value to their skin. The extent can even be estimated somewhat quantitatively in terms of the billions of dollars spent on cosmetics, suntan lamps and vacation resorts where vacationers fry themselves to the particular shade which gives them the feeling of being healthy and good looking. At other times, and in other places, just as much effort was expended to keep the skin fashionably white and delicately pale when positive emotional value was attached to these characteristics.

The outstanding characteristic of the skin is that it can be seen and touched. It is a medium of communication from person to person. Thus, the skin serves on the one hand to *communicate emotion* (blushing with anger, shame, excitement), *arouse emotion* (a beautiful schoolgirl complexion, a pockmarked, grimy face), and serves as *recipient* of emotion (being stroked gently, pinched, or beaten), as well as a carrier of *emotional meaning* (one feels healthy and good looking or sallow, oily and dirty).

All of the material presented in the general introduction to this book, and in the chapter on the personality of the physician, is applicable, *mutatis mutandis*, in the field of dermatology, and should be considered on connection with this chapter. Evidently skin⇌emotion is a two way reaction, indicating that in the skin as in all other organs, one must consider possible effects of each upon the other. We shall refer to the two directions of this interaction as psychosomatic and somatopsychic, always remembering that the above equation represents a dynamic equilibrium, in which each side is constantly acting on the other so that this verbal separation is to some extent artificial.

Skin disorders generally give rise to less disturbance of physical function than do disorders of most other organs of the body. Dermatologists rarely have to hospitalize their patients or even see them at home. For the most part they are ambulant and functioning apparently at their usual level of responsibility. Despite this apparent lack of interference with physical function, it will be shown that there are good grounds for believing that emotional functions are widely and severely affected in dermatologic patients.

VISIBILITY

Skin lesions cannot be denied. All are evident to the patient himself; when on exposed areas, they are equally evident to those around him. It follows that all skin lesions affect the patient's concept of his body image in very much the same way that this concept is affected by disorders of the extremities in orthopedics. These effects are not obvious in preverbal infants whose body image concepts are not readily divined, but psychiatric investigation at later ages may indicate that such effects have been present even in early postnatal life. Certainly at later ages the effects of skin lesions on the patient's self esteem are devastating. Children and adults alike shy away from the person with evident skin lesions. Patient and friends tend to view skin lesions as something dirty, disgusting, bordering on—if not actually—venereal, and contagious.

The simplest case of an evident, if transitory, skin lesion is the common phenomenon of blushing. (It is, however, not so simple as it seems because the blush is usually emotional in cause as well as in effect.) In any case, the sufferer is always quite self-conscious of his blush and feels that he is thereby attracting attention to himself, about which his feelings are highly ambivalent; on some level he enjoys the exhibition, while on another it is painful to him. The blush is always allied to some form of guilt, usually with a marked sexual tinge.

Psychoanalysts actually speak of "erythrophobia," the fear of blushing, as a specific problem associated with exhibitionism: it is as though in some people, the face and neck may vicariously experience the blood engorgement which in others ordinarily occurs during sexual excitement (in the erectile tissue of the genitals). People afflicted by fear of blushing behave as though they want to communicate their sexual excitement to their environment (which, of course, may sometimes be true as in the case of the blushing maiden).

Excema, pustules, discolorations such as unusual birthmarks, and especially oozing lesions and markedly scaly ones such as psoriasis, often produce feelings of disgust in the afflicted and in those around him. Psychoanalytic investigations have shown that these reactions arise from an association of the skin lesions with dirt. Such dirtiness is perceived as though every oozing opening of the body were a cloaca, and the exuding material were fecal or urinary. Our social training sets up severe taboos against such things and the afflicted person may well feel beyond the pale of social acceptability.

The visibility of the lesions is the crux of the reaction pattern of people with *acne vulgaris*. This disease most commonly occurs on the face and causes little other subjective disturbance than the feeling arising from its obvious presence. Occurring usually in adolescents, the picture is complicated by interactions of parent and child. Parents, especially mothers, tend to aggravate the child's own guilt feelings about this disease by an almost universal incrimination of dirt in its origin and exacerbations. On a deeper level, the parent probably associates this dirt with sexuality. In any case, the adolescent with acne generally feels that his or her blemishes are retribution for forbidden sexual desires or acts and often links it directly with masturbation. It is not always erroneously said, "After you are married, it will all get better." An interesting sidelight on this is that mothers frequently think their child's acne affected by faulty eating habits, especially regarding sweets. Many physicians have helped to sustain this idea for which there is actually no objective evidence. Since the child often finds much pleasure in eating sweets, it may be that this represents a desire on the part of the physician and the parent to punish the erring one.

The guilt and disgust felt by people with almost any skin lesion would lead us to believe that skin disease is almost always experienced by the patient as some kind of justified punishment. In recent years, this often takes the form of some degree of cancerphobia which is present in increasing numbers of adults with skin disease. Of course, these people are influenced today by the growing propaganda on the subject of cancer prevention.

The "Leper" Complex

The above mentioned factors of visibility of skin lesions and the social reactions against them are some reasons why people with skin lesions feel ostracized. Another powerful factor in making them social outcasts of major or minor degree, is the imagined or real *contagiousness* of skin lesions.

We can speak of the sum total of these emotional reactions as the "leper" complex because leprosy is the best known of the diseases associated with these sentiments. Horrible to behold and dreaded because of their supposed contagiousness, lepers were driven from society to wither away in miserable degradation.

Leprosy, of course, plays but a small role in contemporary Occidental society. Venereal disease, with its skin manifestations, has inherited some of the stigma. Even though syphilis is today relatively rare, a surprising number of adolescents, particularly, watch with secret panic the development of a pimple after their first kiss. An unclear skin is often associated with loose living and/or with masturbation, as has already been mentioned. Shadows under the eyes are considered signs not only of general dissipation but also of sexual debauchery. Herpes simplex is frequently conceived of as something "caught" by kissing and (especially by medical students) is half jokingly considered a possible chancre.

Hirsutism. While excessive hairiness in women is admittedly somewhat disfiguring, even minimal hairiness causes extreme anguish as attested by the flourishing profession of electrolysis. For example, an occasional hair near the nipple or an excess on the arms and legs tends to make a woman feel masculine and devoid of feminine charm.

Baldness. When Delilah cut off Samson's locks, he was shorn of his power: thus does legend express the symbolic relationship between masculinity and hair. Prisoners often are shaven of the hair, and to cut off the scalplock of an Indian was to destroy him as a man. It is as though hair were associated with pubic hair and, thus, with sexual prowess.

Therefore, men may react to baldness with shamefacedness and embarrassment and try to cover it with toupés or artful brushing of remaining strands.

Related to this is the finding among psychiatrists that hair pulling in emotionally disturbed people may be an unconscious equivalent for pulling and manipulating the genitals and may be seen as some form of self mutilation.

ITCHING

In polite society it is not acceptable to scratch oneself publicly when one itches. Such scratching, particularly if it involves the ano-genital region, is treated as though it were a sexual gratification. In clinical psychoanalysis, it can be observed that when a patient becomes sexually stimulated in connection with some repressed thoughts, he may scratch himself, rub his eyes, etc. Scratching is seen to occur if the person feels a need for emotional warmth and desires soothing contact: they "itch for love" and gratify themselves by scratching (as once they were gratified by mother's soothing hand).

The Itch-Scratch Reflex. In the itch-scratch reflex we have an example of an intricate relationship of emotional causes and effects. The simple experiment of mentioning itching conditions, such as infestations, in a social gathering will show that the threshold of itch-scratch can be lowered in that psychogenic manner. In people without skin disease, the threshold soon returns to its equilibrium level before scratching really damages their skin, while many patients with chronic itching dermatoses seem able to stabilize themselves only after repeated vicious excoriations of their skin. Whether or not these crises are mainly psychogenic, as many appear to be, their psychic effects are undeniable.

1. The itching desire to scratch is accompanied by some kind of general feeling of tension which we may call the "inner itch." Questioning will reveal that the sensation is not confined to the skin, but is felt through and through.
2. The process of scratching is pleasurable and at the same time painful. When the itching crisis is relieved, the patient is left with pain in the area that had itched before.
3. At the same time that pain replaces the itch in the skin, the "inner itch" is completely relieved and replaced by a feeling of relaxation.
4. After the patient has excoriated his skin, his feeling of relief of itching is accompanied by a gnawing guilt over having further disfigured the lesions.

"*Squeezing Pimples.*" This wide-spread custom seems to hold a special fascination for its devotees. The pustules may actually become enlarged so that the explosive emptying of their contents may actually decrease the discomfort; but the true "squeezer" will manipulate his skin long before the lesions reach this state. To him emptying the pus is closely akin to the happy feeling obtained by a "good, cleansing" bowel movement or a genital orgasm. He has to "get it out of his system" and feels truly compelled to squeeze before he can relax.

Sweating. Body odor from sweating and other skin secretions has received much notoriety from advertisers of deodorants. The bad smell is—for many people—symbolic of anal odor. Curiously enough, the smell accompanying skin secretions may at the same time act as a sexual excitant; odor is an outstanding sexual stimulant in infrahuman species and—in modified form —in human beings (smelling a girl's hair, etc). Both the fecal connotations and the sexual excitatory ones are socially taboo, and account for the stigmas placed upon body odor and the fear of developing it.

Psychogenic Aspects of Skin Disease

Psychogenic mechanisms of skin disorders can be stated in terms that will be familiar to the most organically-minded physician. The skin is influenced by the autonomic nervous system and the autonomic nervous system is related to cerebration. The cortical-subcortical phenomenon of embarrassment can manifest itself via the autonomic nervous system as a dilation of blood vessels—as in blushing. Emotionally mediated alterations in vascularisation of the skin perhaps can influence its trophic status to an extent that may account for a variety of tissue changes. Furthermore, even in the presence of organic etiologic agents, emotions may act upon tissue barriers so as to produce variations of illness from sub-threshold states to the most acute and extensive flare up. Franz Alexander[1] distinguishes between conversion symptoms which symbolize repressed emotions, and vegetative neuroses which are physiologic correlatives of chronic emotional states. He thinks that both these mechanisms occur in psychogenic skin disturbances.

BACKGROUND FOR PSYCHOSOMATIC APPROACH TO DERMATOLOGY

The crucial problem in dermatology today is the question: does psychologic dysfunction really contribute significantly to the cause of many common dermatologic diseases?

Despite significant advances, large gaps remain in our knowledge from the classical frame of reference regarding the etiology of many skin diseases. A generation ago it was common to classify many inflammatory dermatoses under the name "eczema"—cause unknown. Out of this we have succeeded in defining, as a separate entity, *Contact Dermatitis*, in which it is possible to identify by means of patch tests, substances to which the skin reacts allergically, and whose withdrawal often leads to clearing of the eruption.

Atopic Dermatitis is a name that has been given to another type of eruption which is often seen in association with hay fever and asthma—the other atopic diseases—in the patient or his relatives. Here, inhalants or ingestants rather than externally contacted allergens, are thought to produce the eruption. These patients' skins usually react allergically to a number of inhalant and ingestant extracts experimentally introduced into the skin. These reactions do not mimic the original eruption as do patch tests in contact dermatitis, but rather cause urticarial wheals at the sites of introduction. It is even possible, by the Praussnitz-Küstner technique, to produce such wheals in the skin of a normal recipient, at sites where serum from the patient has previously been injected. Unfortunately, however, it is rarely— if ever—possible to discover by these means, specific allergens whose absence from the patient's environment regularly leads to clearing of the eruption. It seems likely that these altered reactions of the skin and serum of atopics, as well as the eruption itself, all may be related to some common underlying mechanism in which the psychogenesis may play a decisive part.

An important feature claimed in the definition of the atopic state is the so-called hereditary factor; the higher incidence of atopic disease in the families of atopics than in the families of other people. Aside from the possible confusion of hereditary and environmental influences, an analysis of published figures casts doubt upon the existence of any higher incidence at all. Incidence of atopic disease in the general population is stated as 10 per cent, and the incidence of atopic history in atopics' families is stated as about 50 per cent.[24] It is clear that the number of relatives investigated in a family will influence the number of families in which we shall find atopic history. If atopic disease occurs in random distribution among humans, the stated incidence of 50 per cent in atopics' families should be found if we consider five family members, if one person in ten has atopic disease. An effective hereditary factor should produce an incidence in atopics' families appreciably higher, to a degree dependent upon the effectiveness of the hereditary factor in manifesting the disease.

Among incriminated ingestants foods play the largest role. It has been popular in the allergic era to test for food sensitivities by means of wheal production by intradermal injection of aqueous food extracts. While atopic patients usually show several positive reactions to such tests, it is now widely accepted—even among allergists—that these tests do not identify causal allergens and that they contribute practically nothing to the management of atopic disease.

Recently there have been reports of success in treating certain eczemas by means of elimination diets in which causal foods are identified by exacerbations of the eruption on their ingestion with subsidence when they are not eaten. Efforts of the author and others to duplicate these results have met with almost complete failure. What can explain this difference in results when patients and technical method are presumably equivalent? The difference may lie in the approach of the doctor who administers the diet. Its nature may be guessed from the passage in Flood's report:[6] "It is necessary to sell the diet to the patient . . .." It seems clear that dietary injunctions can produce far-reaching emotional effects and that it is these which make the difference between successful and unsuccessful dietary treatment of atopic dermatitis. This argument should be equally valid regarding injections with positive reacting extracts as often carried out in treatment of atopic diseases. Certainly there can be no question of the psychogenic effects of injections upon the patient, although this factor has been neglected, with no attempt made to control it in most reported medical studies.

This brings up the interesting question of "unwitting psychotherapy." Unquestionably, this plays a role in almost all treatment by physicians who are unaware of their emotional effect upon their patients. It plays a major role in many forms of treatment, as evidenced by various forms of fads and quackery, and is responsible for the successes of healing cults. The author believes that it is just as important in the success of much of the injection treatments of allergies. Any physician who will take the trouble to substitute placebos for some of the specific substances recommended in such treatment, will be rewarded by the most glowing reports of their efficacy from his patients.

Dermatologists generally agree about certain correlations with neuropsychiatry. Thus, some neurologic lesions are associated with pathologic skin changes, e.g., tuberous sclerosis, and parkinsonism with greasy skin; herpes zoster of spinal ganglia with herpetiform vesicles in the corresponding skin; paralysies with dystrophic skin. Dermatologists agree that self-inflicted conditions, as in neurotic excoriations, trichotillomania, and delusions of parasitosis are psychogenic. There is no agreement (Sulzberger, 1946[20]) as to the role of psychogenesis in dermatoses other than these obviously psychogenic ones.

It has been aptly cautioned[22] that "the physician may easily delude himself that whatever disease he cannot speedily diagnose and remedy by other means, must be due to the mind and emotions."

Sulzberger and Baer[20] maintained that they have never seen emotional factors play more than a secondary role in any eczematous eruption. If we could prove that other factors are the primary etiologic agents in these dermatoses, the importance of the search for, and verification of psychosomatic etiologic vectors, would be greatly diminished. But this remains a most important problem for the simple reason that the primary causes of so many diseases of the skin, as of other organs, have heretofore defied our efforts at elucidation.

MULTIPLE CAUSATION

One's orientation in medicine is influenced by many factors. Interest and bias in favor of a psychological approach or an organic approach to some aspects of illness is predicated upon one's own personality and training. A special factor of great importance in influencing all of medicine today, and influencing it in the direction of organic medicine, is the pharmaceutical industry. In recent years, several of these concerns have grown tremendously in economic and, correspondingly, scientific importance. Through their free and elaborate medical journals they constantly remind us of the virtues of their products in the cure of disease and so act as a powerful though subtle influence against a psychosomatic orientation toward therapy. It should not be overlooked also that a large and growing fraction of clinical research is now financed by these institutions. There projects rarely fail to find a beneficial effect of drugs on the investigated disease. Perhaps, because of the large number of drugs as well as cosmetics that are applied to the skin, this propaganda exerts more influence on dermatologists than on some other specialists.

It cannot be emphasized often enough that there is no such entity as a psychic skin disorder. It is merely a question of how much psychic factors and how much somatic factors contribute to the etiology precipitation or prolongation of the dermatosis. Nevertheless, many clinicians vainly attempt to label various dermatoses as psychic or somatic in origin. However, the more the physician is desirous of understanding his patient, the more he can help by combining psychotherapy with dermatologic therapy.

It is desirable, of course, that a physician feel neither rigidly somatically nor psychogenically oriented: the integration and combination of both approaches is bound to be the most useful one.

REVIEW OF LITERATURE

There is clear evidence of a growing interest on the part of dermatologists in the psychosomatic question. A good index of this is the number of articles on the subject that have appeared in abstracts in the *Year Books of Dermatology and Syphilology*. In the decade 1931-1940, this publication listed only three titles concerning psychosomatic subjects while in the following decade, 1941-1950, 27 titles appeared under the same listing, thus representing an increase of 900 per cent.

The credit for the earliest and most prolific writing in this field in the United States goes to Dr. John H. Stokes, Professor of Dermatology at the University of Pennsylvania, who began in 1930 to publish a long series of papers on the effect of emotional states on the skin. Stokes has summarized his views in his textbook, *Fundamentals of Medical Dermatology*,[17] and more briefly in his chapter in MacKenna's, *Recent Trends in Dermatology*.[19] Stokes' views on psychogenic mechanisms in skin disease are expressed thus in his text: "The mental states responsible for cutaneous manifestations are usually factors, not sole causes. The tension frame of mind . . . in predisposed, usually vagotonic persons . . . is by far the commonest element." For correction of this mental state, Stokes recommends to the patient: "Ask yourself, a hundred years from now, what will this matter? Ask it again." We can see that his psychiatry is of a homespun, non-analytic texture. Stokes' and Beerman's[19] critical comment on psychosomatic investigation is worthy of note. "Its conclusions are valid for the eye and judgment of the investigator (we had almost said the votary) but they just do not make sense to the commonalty. The lack of objective mensuration, the paucity of experimental studies under anything like adequate controls, the fact—among others—to which we have called attention that there exists no adequate study of 'normals' for base-line comparative purposes, and that much of the pathologic material reported has too much of an 'I had a case' quality, all impede investigation and discredit conclusions. There is, too, the omnipresent ignorance on the part of the dermatologists and psychiatrists of the elements of each others' terrain. There seems to be also an exceptional distrust of the investigator's warp and prejudice in all things involving psychical appraisals. The very word 'psychic' carries dubious implications of charlatanism and art-magic, of which we must certainly rid ourselves if real progress is to be made."

Josef, Peck and Kaufman[10] have reported an interesting case in which the relief of a dermatosis by means of psychotherapy and hypnosis was accompanied by the outbreak of psychosis. It has been held that a skin disorder, especially when accompanied by scratching, may (as do many other psychosomatic illnesses) serve as an outlet for emotional tension, and that ill-timed interference with this channel of release may lead to serious intrapsychic manifestations.

It has been observed[2] that allergic manifestations have a significantly smaller incidence in psychotics than in normals with similar physical environments and that allergic manifestations may even alternate with psychotic interludes.

Spitz[15] has observed many cases of atopic dermatitis in emotionally starved infants, and speaks of it as an emotional deficiency disease.

In the flood of literature on psychosomatic dermatology that has appeared in recent years, it is disappointing to find almost all reports falling into Stokes' "I had a case" category. There have been several attempts at classification of dermatologic-psychogenic relationships (English,[5] Lewis,[11] Brandt[3]) which collectively have shed too little light on the basic problem of proving the part of psychogenesis in otherwise inadequately explained dermatoses, in a way that is objectively valid to more than the eye of the investigator.

Most of the articles have been descriptions or analyses of the character of one or a series of subjects with certain dermatoses, often with an attempt at correlation of exacerbations and remissions in the skin with emotional changes. There have been several attempts to correlate specific neurotic characteristics with certain skin diseases, e.g., urticaria,[7] and atopic dermatitis[15], and statements that this is impossible in some cases, as in psoriasis.[25] There have been reports (Lynch[12]) of association of certain skin diseases with presumably psychosomatic disease of other organs. There are a few reports of the use of hypnosis in experimental production and alteration of skin disease.[13]

URTICARIA

There are disappointingly few examples of attempts at experimental verification of psychosomatic effects upon the skin. Graham and Wolf[6] offer an exception with their experimental study of the effect of emotions in interview situations upon cutaneous vascular reactions. The authors claim that they produced urticaria in their subjects by creating—in the interview

—stressful situations in which the patients felt resentment over unjust treatment. This was associated with vascular dilation. Anxiety, they stated, was accompanied by an opposite change in the vessels. In as much as most, if not all, of their patients also had dermographism, it is possible that the wheals which these investigators observed were mediated by scratching and did not follow directly from the resentment. It has been pointed out[22] that various drugs which cause extreme vasodilatation do not produce whealing. Urticaria, a reaction that can be observed to develop over a short period of time, and which, in most cases, is not explainable on allergic hypotheses, should provide an ideal opportunity for such an experimental approach; it is to be hoped that other attempts will be made to verify these findings.

Grant, Pearson and Comeau, in 1936,[8] described a clinical variant of urticaria occurring only rarely which they called "cholinergic-urticaria." In persons susceptible to this syndrome, the authors found that they could reproduce the lesions, consisting of minute wheals, by the injection of acetyl choline. The same syndrome was described in a group of patients in this country in 1938 by Hopkins and Kesten.[9] Both British and American authors found that attacks of this disease were regularly precipitated by strong emotions of any character, without specificity. Attacks also are precipitated by exercise and exposure to heat. It is thought that the lesions in the skin are mediated through cholinergic autonomic nerves causing release of acetyl choline in the skin, to which these patients appear to be hypersensitive.

From the psychological point of view, Graham and Wolf[7] found that their patients developed urticaria only when resentment was a prominent part of their patients' emotions. Davis and Bick[4] were unable to observe changes in urticaria during stress-producing situations. English[5] states that urticaria results from intense longings for gratification, and Stokes maintains that urticaria is characterized psychologically by the "tension frame of mind."

STRESS REACTIONS

Selye[14] believes that stress—whether emotional or physical— produces somatic effects through the pituitary-adrenocortical system. Sternberg and Zimmerman[16] have attempted to find an exaggerated response to stress through this medium in patients with atopic dermatitis, using exposure to hot, humid air as a stress. They believe that atopic allergic symptoms are related to Selye's concept of "alarm reaction." It would be desirable to follow a similar experimental approach using emotional stresses of various kinds. If Selye's concepts apply here, it is possible to see how various types of emotional stress might lead to similar somatic responses. In the individual patient, it may be true—as Wittkower[25] says—that there is no short-cut to finding the importance of emotional factors in etiology other than a careful psychiatric examination.

SUMMARY

The skin and its disorders is of great emotional significance because of its visibility and its function as a carrier of emotion, as stimulus for sexual excitation and recipient of gratification. A number of disorders have specific meaning as representing undesirable dirtiness and arousing associations which are socially taboo.

The question of psychogenicity of dermatologic illness is one fraught with emotion for the dermatologist himself. The mechanism of psychogenesis can be conceived of in conventional medical terms. The clinical literature on possible psychogenesis of skin disease is large; the experimental verification of such postulates is nebulous. It is hoped that the future will bring progress in combined psychiatric and dermatologic research.

BIBLIOGRAPHY

1. Alexander, F.: Studies in Psychosomatic Medicine. New York, Ronald Press Co., 1948.
2. Bellak, L.: Manic-Depressive Psychosis and Allied Disorders. New York, Grune & Stratton, 1952.
3. Brandt, R.: Tentative Classification of Psychogenic Factors in Etiology of Skin Diseases. J. Invest. Dermat. *14:* 81, 1950.
4. Davis, D. B. and Bick, J. W., Jr.: Skin reactions observed under wartime stress. J. Nerv. & Ment. Dis. *103:* 503, 1946.
5. English, O. S.: Role of emotion in disorders of the skin. Arch. Dermat. & Syph. *60:* 1063, 1949.
6. Flood, J. M.: Personal communication.
7. Graham D. T. and Wolf, S.: Pathogenesis of urticaria: Experimental study of life situations, emotions and cutaneous vascular reactions. J.A.M.A. *143:* 1396, 1950.
8. Grant, R. T., Pearson, R. S. and Comeau, W. G.: Observations on urticaria provoked by emotions, by exercise, and by warming the body. Clin. Sci. *2:* 253, 1936.
9. Hopkins, J. G., Kesten, B. M. and Hazel, O. G.: Urticaria provoked by heat or by psychic stimuli. Arch. Dermat. & Syph. *38:* 679, 1938.
10. Josef, E. D., Peck, S. M. and Kaufman, M. R.: A psychological study of neurodermatitis with a case report. J. Mt. Sinai Hosp. *15:* 360, 1949.
11. Lewis G. M. and Cormia, F. E.: Office management of neurodermatoses. New York State J. Med. *47:* 1889, 1947.
12. Lynch, F. W.: Apparent association of lichen planus with vascular hypertension. J. Invest. Dermat. *13:* 43, 1949.
13. Seitz, P. F. D.: Experimental approach to psychocutaneous problems. J. Invest. Dermat. *13:* 43, 1949.
14. Selye, H.: Alarm reaction and the general adaptation syndrome. J. Clin. Endocrinol. *6:* 180, 1946.
15. Spitz R.: The psychogenic diseases in infancy: An attempt at their etiologic

classification. *In:* The Psychoanalytic Study of the Child, Vol. 6. New York, International Universities Press, 1951.

16. Sternberg, J. H. and Zimmerman, M. C.: Stress studies in the eczema-asthma-hayfever diathesis. Arch. Dermat. & Syph. *65:* 392, 1952.

17. Stokes, J. H.: Fundamentals of Medical Dermatology. Philadelphia, Department of Dermatology Book Fund, 1942.

18. Stokes, J. H. and Beerman, H.: Psychosomatic correlations in allergic conditions: Review of problems and literature. Psychosom. Med. *2:* 438, 1940.

19. —— and ——: The dermatology of yesterday, today, and tomorrow. *In:* MacKenna, R. M. B. (ed.): Modern Trends in Dermatology. New York, Paul B. Hoeber, 1948.

20. Sulzberger, M. B. and Baer, R. L. (eds.): Yearbook of Dermatology and Syphilology, 1945. Chicago, The Yearbook Publishers, 1946.

21. —— and —— (eds.): Yearbook of Dermatology and Syphilology, 1946. Chicago, The Yearbook Publishers, 1947.

22. —— and —— (eds.): Yearbook of Dermatology and Syphilology, 1950. Chicago, The Yearbook Publishers, 1951.

23. Sulzberger, M. B. and Zaidens, S. H.: Psychogenic factors in dermatologic disorders. Med. Clin. North America *32:* 669, 1948.

24. Walzer, M.: Atopic allergy: Reaginic sensitivity. Ann. New York Acad. Sci. *50:* 743, 1949.

25. Wittkower, E.: Psychological aspects of dermatology. *In:* MacKenna, R. M. B. (ed.). Modern Trends in Dermatology. New York, Paul B. Hoeber, 1948.

CHAPTER 14

Psychiatric Aspects of Dentistry

SOL J. EWEN, D.D.S.

Dr. Ewen received his D.D.S. from the Columbia University Dental School, interned at Montefiore Hospital, was Chief of the Dental Clinic at Bronx House and worked in the New York City Dental Clinics, exclusively with children, from 1938 to 1941.

He took postgraduate courses in Orthodontia at New York University, Post Graduate School of Dentistry. He also attended courses at the William A. White Institute of Psychiatry as well as a course on Psychoanalysis in Dentistry at the New York Psychoanalytic Institute.

From 1948 to 1950 he was Research Assistant in Psychosomatics at Columbia University Dental School. He is now a Lecturer in postgraduate Dentistry; he is a member of the National Honorary Dental Society (O.K.U.).

I——DENTIST-PATIENT RELATIONSHIP

EVERY PATIENT COMES TO THE DENTIST at a time when he needs help in solving a dental problem. He has chosen his dentist, possibly, because a friend has suggested him, or, perhaps, because he feels that this dentist is best equipped to handle his case. When the patient steps across the threshold of the dentist's office, however, he brings with him more than the desire for dental health. Inevitably, he carries with him his reaction to dental care, dental pain, and the dentist himself; his vague but powerful feelings of fear and anxiety; and his attitude toward figures in authority.

The mouth is an area to which most people attach great importance. Sometimes this results in fear of any instrumentation or alteration of the part; sometimes it leads to endless and fruitless search for the right dentist. In most instances, the anticipation of pain through dental treatment brings forth greater anxiety in the patient than he would feel at the prospect of pain through treatment of other body areas.

The patient approaches the dentist then with mixed feelings. On the one hand, the dentist is the authoritative figure who not only understands tissue breakdowns, but can heal them. He is endowed by the patient with almost mystical power to control or ward off dental ills. On the other hand, he is regarded with fear and hostility because of the nature of dental treatment. The patient, as a result of this conflict, develops feelings toward the dentist which are almost unique and may be compared only to the feelings he might have toward a surgeon.

The dental bur and stones, the injections, the sound of steel against tissue, all provoke a fear that harm may come from these ministrations. The patient feels that his teeth are decaying and foul, and he feels resentment that his mouth and teeth should betray him in this way. The resultant emotion-complex—the need for the dental attention mixed with these strong feelings about the mouth tissues—produce anxiety. Such an anxiety state may persist for months preceding dental care and prevent the patient from getting to the dentist, or it may erupt suddenly on visiting the dental office without any warning whatsoever. While anxiety is a universal reaction of dental patients, it varies in character and degree according to the emotional age development of the patient. Since, in any case, the patient is unable to avoid the treatment, having selected to appear there himself, (or having been brought by a parent), his outward response appears to be a willingness to undergo treatment. Underlying this willingness are feelings of resentment and hostility, together with a sense of panic which may cause sweating, shaking, pallor, rapid heart beat, etc. In some instances, the effort to escape may take the form of missing appointments or delaying treatment as long as the anxiety persists. The anxiety response is the key observable symptom-complex in the dental patient and it is this emotional configuration which must be dissolved by the dentist, wherever possible. Since sensations of threat vary with the individual in degree and form of expression, the dentist should study the personality structure of each patient to determine which modes of behavior and response the patient may use to express his reactions to dental treatment and the dentist.

There are two basic forms of the dentist-patient relationship. These require separate approaches in treatment: (1) reassurance applicable to all adults and (2) the uncovering of fears, applicable only to children.[11]

Before proceeding with these approaches, it is important to recognize *what the usual patient feels about his mouth,* in coming for treatment. The dental patient feels a deep fear of the interference with the tissues of the mouth. He has a feeling that part of his body is decaying or disintegrating. He has a feeling that his wholeness and completeness have been disturbed. He may be ashamed of the discoloration or irregularities of his teeth and of his mouth. He is concerned with the pain which occurs on the applications of heat, cold, and sweets, and is particularly distraught when he finds that his teeth are mobile. With any one or more of these feelings, his sense of security is weakened. A general retreat, which may be momentary during the actual dental treatment, or may persist at various times while the patient is under dental care, takes place. The patient at this time is only involved with himself and as such becomes over-dependent upon the dentist who is treating him. This state of dependency, of leaning, and of self involvement remake the patient into a child-like personality.

With the patient in this state of dependency, it still devolves upon the dentist to perform his professional task.[5-9] It is his job to relieve physical symptoms, increase chewing efficiency, make the mouth and teeth more attractive esthetically. In addition, in adult mouths, since there has been a certain amount of natural wear, it helps the patient to know what changes have taken place, and, therefore, what limitations of structure and function exist in the patient's mouth.

At the same time, the dentist feels it necessary to instruct in competent home care and mouth maintenance, thereby providing the patient with good health standards and a positive satisfaction in rebuilding his mouth tissues. In this way, the patient receives emotional impetus for improving his mouth tissues and a sense of well being in mastering a difficult personal situation. These various forms of treating the dental patient, reassure the patient, give him a sense of support and well-being, re-educate some of his attitudes toward himself and thereby help him to resolve the anxious state in which he originally found himself. There are, of course, technical procedures in the office which the dentist and his assistant may use or alter to make dental instrumentation and the dental environment more acceptable and less disturbing. In some instances adults feel reassured when other members of the family—a husband, a parent, or the like—are asked to be present at the initial appointment. They may even be called in at such times when prosthetic appliances, such as porcelain jackets, or dentures are being inserted. This method provides an avenue for the reacceptance of the patient by those close to him and in whose estimation the patient places great value.

The dentist may solidify his relationship with the patient most effectively during the original mouth examination. A clear statement that what is being done is routine and not unusual, explaining the use of instruments and the various tests, and giving a final diagnosis soon after the examination, serves to relieve heightened anxiety. Irrelevant data about other patients treated, the dentist's feelings about his work, his special position in the field of dentistry serve only to upset the patient and confuse the issue which brought the patient for treatment. The specific use of non-professional language and the frequent repetition of words of reassurance help to soften tension. There are instances in which drug therapy, that is, the use of seconal or nembutal preoperatively, serve to prepare the patient for dental care.

The Dental Interview. The most effective method for working with fears and anxieties is the knowing use of the guided interview procedure.[1,2]

What is the Guided Interview? Kinsey in his work on *Sexual Behavior of the Human Male*, defines the interview as a "planned conversation." To us then, the dental interview must become a planned conversation between the dentist and his patient (or others) which has a specific purpose, or purposes in mind.

Any situation in which one person calls upon another for the purpose of satisfying or fulfilling an existing need may be characterized as an *Interview Situation*. The interview is an effort to establish through planned professional conversation, a working relationship in order for two individuals to effectively communicate their feelings to one another; a patient who comes to the dental situation with pain, with fear, with doubts or questions; a dentist who has feelings as well as specific goals and procedures to carry out his work. Feelings of pain, discomfort, and the very prospect of talking to an unknown or little known individual (dentist) about physical discomforts, attitudes about the mouth and teeth, and even social and financial situations directly related, all are fundamentally disturbing to the patient. The dentist is concerned with making a good impression, saying the "right things" to the patient, putting the patient at ease, and striving to draw out pertinent information, and wondering what to do with the patient who "will not talk." With these factors as background, the prime goal of the dental interview is to establish a warm relationship between interviewer and interviewee so that essential factors which motivate the patient to seek help will be related to the dentist who in turn becomes more effective in helping his patient.

*How To Conduct an Interview.** Every interview has a beginning, a middle and an end. The first ten minutes of interviewing often prove to be the most important ones with the patient. At this time the new patient is more emotionally upset about his prospect of dentistry than he may ever be in the future with the dentist. Dr. Robert H. W. Strang† has made the observation that the patient observed without seeing the dentist may reveal important facts about himself. Concern and anxiety will show in wringing of the hands, frequent wiping of the brow, lip-biting, excessive smoking, moving around the waiting room haphazardly or even in direct expression of fear to the dental assistant who has welcomed him. Through direct observation or a momentary talk with the dental assistant, the dentist may get his first impression of the patient.

Most important in the beginning, is to obtain the "on top" feelings—how the patient feels about his teeth or pain, right then and there. The patient should be encouraged to talk first and freely, occupying most of the time of the interview. The main instrument at this point is "Active Listening."

---

* It must be pointed out that the interview must be adapted to the individual patient. Some will need more cautious handling, others less, possibly some hardly any. It must be kept clearly in mind that it is not our purpose to make psychiatrists out of dentists. While an understanding attitude to a patient is helpful in all cases, the patient will resent too much prying.

† Personal communication and lectures at Temple University.

Active Listening requires:

1. Permitting the patient to unload emotionally.
2. Finding out the patient's purpose in seeking help.
3. Noting how much the patient leaves out. (When last seen by a dentist, regularity of dental care, kinds of work done, number of dentists seen in last few years, exactly what the patient expects of the new dentist being seen).
4. Emphasize recent dental history to ascertain current feelings about dentists, doctors and professional men in general.

The kind of language which the patient uses very often is helpful in revealing individual personality traits. Most often the fears and doubts are not expressed directly. The patient may express his feelings in the way he talks, rather than through what he says. In any case, it is safe to assume that the patient is anxious and concerned.

If the first step in interviewing is handled well:

1. The patient is emotionally quieter.
2. The patient realizes that the dentist has given him time to understand clearly what is bothering him.
3. The patient is ready to be questioned further.

Continuing Interview. In the next phase of the interview, indicate how much time is left, and that there are certain things to know, so that the work will proceed smoothly and to the patient's advantage. Here the instrument used is "Questioning." There are no rules or regulations as to which questions should be asked first, second or last. Questions grow out cf the responses given by the patient. Questioning is done in a friendly tone, and without accusation at any time. Usually the patient is ashamed of having postponed treatment as long as he has. A question like. "You haven't been to a dentist in a long time, have you?" could be substituted by a positive statement such as, "Has your mouth been in good health over long periods of time?" An additional, "I don't quite understand, tell me a little more," lets the patient know that more facts are wanted.

A plaster model of a mouth or a picture may now be used, not for educational purposes so much as to help the patient give more data. A tooth model with a filling in it, or the like, will help the patient differentiate between what he thought he had received, and what he actually had obtained under previous dental treatment. Through interested questioning, the patient will feel that he and his teeth are the most important problem to the dentist. Technical language has no place in the dental interview, at any time. Comparisons with other individuals except possibly to indicate that these problems are familiar ones need not be made. The dentist ought not use the interview as an opportunity to talk about himself, his position in the profession, or his outside interests. During an interview the patient and his problem are the core of the discussion.

This section of the interview is the most interesting because it is during this period that the *rapport* or common understanding is first touched on through the questions and responses. The rapport between a patient and his dentist resides fundamentally in the willingness of the patient to go through uncomfortable procedures, accept the dentist as a figure of authority, accept his professional advice and finally pay for services rendered, recognizing within his capacities the good which has been accomplished. The rapport, started at this time, must last through time and work, and sometimes, for many years. If the dentist shows a real interest in the patient during the interview, has listened without expressing negative judgment against previous actions in earlier dental situations, has accepted the *patient as a person*, for whatever he is, and has expressed a desire to help during difficult periods as work progresses, all these will lead to a rapport between patient and dentist. Through cultural and social influences, the patient always idealizes the dentist and endows him with qualities which may or may not be part of the personality of the dentist. The patient does this in order to feel that he is in "good hands"; as a patient he can trust his dentist to do the right things.

At some point the patient will indicate his reactions to the dentist but rarely overtly. He may say, "Well, let's get on with the work," or "You seem to understand me," or "You are the first dentist I ever told this to," or "Tell me what you think I ought to do." These few words are an indication that the individual is *willing* to be an active patient. These phrases may also indicate to the dentist that the patient is not ready to be a patient. If the patient jumps ahead into the work before adequate data is given, it is wise for the dentist to hold back and control the interview. When the dentist feels ready to move ahead into the next steps of treatment, the patient will sense it. Patients prefer to be directed and led into treatment by a dentist who is in control and not floundering in the interview.

It is possible during or following the question period for the patient to feel or develop a set of negative feelings toward the dentist. These feelings may set in immediately, or they may not appear for some time after work has proceeded. It is important to catch these as they appear, and to handle them immediately. Sitting down and talking things over for a few moments, reviewing the original problem, suggestions made, and agreements arrived at, help considerably, even if it means that another "talking out" situation is necessary for the patient to "feel better and get it off his chest." The interview process actually is never over between dentist and patient. For practical purposes the formal interviewing is over once work in the chair has begun.

Before the dentist is ready to proceed to the chair, the routine of the office is carefully described. Models, x-rays and other diagnostic tests are demonstrated and carried out on the patient in the first session. The technic of going about the diagnostic examination and the time and money they will take are clearly presented. Regular appointments are made, and lateness discouraged so that work may proceed apace. The mutuality of responsibility in carrying out the work is enunciated. In a sentence or two, a description of what is going to be done each time for the patient is given to prepare the patient for the session to follow.

It is possible to prepare the patient for what he is to expect in most dental situations, the next time, the next hour, the next year. The patient remembers a great deal and will only misquote the dentist's statements when he has not understood clearly what the dentist had in mind. Once the patient is away from the office and re-called by card or telephone, the interview is on again, and the same patient-dentist relationship is reactivated. A definite appointment for recall may be made at the time of dismissal, giving the interview its final continuing quality. If the work for a patient has been difficult for a dentist, the patient deserves some praise for cooperation, regardless of age. Some patients require long appointments, others short ones. Times allotted should vary even with the same patient. Building up a patient to "take it" may be to the dentist's advantage, but a short one once in a while is deeply appreciated. Just as the first five minutes of the initial interview are important, so the last sentence or two of the patient are valuable to note. The dentist may catch some indication of how the patient feels about what has been going on in their minds throughout the session. Often the assistant who sees the patient out of the chair to make the next appoinment can with a simple, "Well, how do you feel today?" get some reactions to the work going on. The dentist himself may at dismissal time, without ever appearing to rush the patient out, say, "By the way, is there anything you would like to discuss with me as we go along?"

It should never appear while developing the working relationship with the patient that the dentist is too sympathetic or overly concerned about the patient. Too many patients take their roles as patients seriously enough to want to over-depend on the dentist for many things. It is possible to be understanding and sympathetic without letting the patient lean too much or demand too much of the dentist or doctor.

For each patient the mode of appeal is different. As the dentist learns to meet people of all ranks and levels, to establish rapport, to sympathetically comprehend the significances of things as other people view them, to accept their attitudes and activities without moral or social evaluation, to be interested in people as they are and not as someone else would have them, to see the *reasonable* basis of what at first glance appears to be most unreasonable behavior, to develop a capacity to like all kinds of people and thus to win their esteem and cooperation—he will successfully master the interview technic.

The use of the guided interview, together with the other facts to be covered by the dentist, constitute the reassurance form of dentist-patient relationship. The second or uncovering form is that which is valuable in understanding the motivations which underlie the anxiety shown by the patient—usually the child patient. In using this form of interview, the purpose is to ascertain what factors in the life of a child have provoked frustrations so that mouth gratification has been minimal and disturbed patterns of mouth use produced. In most instances the clarification necessary to eradicate finger and thumb sucking, tongue thrusting, facial tics and other disturbing habits may reside in the province of a consulting psychologist or psychiatrist. The underlying material, however, is important to the dentist and should be obtained so that he may help the child remove the destructive habit and thereby help the proper growth and development of the mouth and the dental arches. (See section IV and section V on thumbsucking.)

II—Psychological Meaning of the Oral Area

From earliest infancy the mouth is the first psychological stage through which the infant lives out his first physiologic needs and his first emotional gratifications. At birth, with normal neurologic development, the mouth is prepared through the integration of the 5th and 7th nerve to receive many sensations and stimuli and to produce the most coordinated of muscular actions; namely, the sucking reflex. "During the first three to six months of an infant's life, sucking is his most gratifying and all-absorbing activity. . . . The baby is not only filling his stomach; he is getting his first taste of the outside world. . . . His initial sense of security, of pleasure, satisfaction and success, is closely linked with his mouth activity. . . . Mouth activity relieves tension and establishes relationship with the mother in an important way. Thus, the budding emotional and social feeling, as well as early feeling of the self, are connected with oral activity."[12] Ribble describes three types of oral activity: (1) The nutritional, with tasting and chewing; (2) the emotional, with smiling, crying and kissing; and (3) the intellectual, with word making. Incidentally, as these three activities are employed, facial muscular development proceeds apace, and may determine adequate or poor dental arrangement in the future. Through the mouth, then, the infant is able to emphasize his first abilities and power. Through the mouth the infant learns to recognize the separateness of the breast from himself and may express his pleasure in its proximity or his frustration in its absence.

Through the mouth, then, which is fundamentally a pouch, or organ of touch, the infant is able to establish his identity as an individual and to set up his first social relationship—that with his mother. Through the mouth the infant develops intake and output roles which clarify his relationship with the outside world. The mouth can take in breath, foods, solid and liquid; objects whose shape can be determined and tasted. The mouth may produce noises, meaningful sounds, saliva, vomitus, coughs, whistles and gagging which express on a physical level the feelings of the infant toward the outside world. These various functions are particularly valuable in clarifying the problem of the relationship with the mother. "The problem of the mother is not only to satisfy food needs for a baby but to help him feel secure and to understand him as a human being who is loved."[12] An infant whose mother has disturbed feelings, particularly in relationship to the child, or who is constantly worried or fretting at nursing time may produce early difficulties in the feeding of the infant. An infant rejected by the mother as reflected through inadequate, hasty or careless feeding can produce an infant whose sucking needs are *not* fulfilled and who resorts soon to the indirect gratification of thumb or finger sucking. In those human beings where proper mouth gratification has fallen short, the mouth may remain through life an area which must be forever gratified by indirect means, and in whom the emotional investment in the oral area remains inordinately high. Such individuals reflect this never-ending dissatisfaction through whining, complaining, spitting, gagging, mouth tics and other habits which reflect feelings of displeasure, disgust and dissatisfaction. These people are only able to communicate negative attitudes and responses through the mouth and in character structure may be described as the oral dependents or oral aggressors who remain fixed emotionally at a mouth level. On an emotional level, then, these are the demanding, domineering, grasping people or the leaning, dependent, clinging, childish personalities.

As infancy is left behind and childhood approaches, most major goals are centered around the socially acceptable mores, outlined and dictated by *parents*. The approval expressed by parental figures as the child fulfills their requirements along lines of bowel habit, cleanliness, neatness and social behavior becomes the major goal sought by the growing child. If disapproval is the only response expressed by parents, the child is constantly threatened and he may look upon himself as despicable and useless, or look upon his habits or even his waste products as filthy and ugly. He may then without too much effort fall back on the earlier pleasantness of the oral area as an escape, by once again being "a baby." This regressive use of the mouth as a secondary or substitute gratification to compensate for his inability to carry out the socially acceptable standards demanded by his parents may be repeated endlessly and take the form of a character distortion. In frustrating situations, these may take the form of overeating and obesity, undereating and self deprivation, excessive smoking, gum and candy chewing and cigar and pipe sucking. On another level, these people may use their mouths as social weapons and appear to sublimate their needs by adopting the careers of lawyers, singers, speakers, or clergy with the fundamental motivation of satisfying an unfulfilled oral need.

In the dental patient where the mouth has so much emotional value, the thought of dental decay, of oral pathology, or the expectation of dental treatment may produce a panic or anxiety directly proportionate to the amount of emotional investment which has been made in that part.

(Case History): College Football Player presented for extraction of a tooth. Patient seemed to go through the procedure without any untoward reaction. Ten minutes later, while sitting in the waiting room, patient fainted. Questioning as to what disturbed him produced the following: the patient felt ashamed that his mouth was no longer perfect. He had always felt as if he were a perfect physical specimen and this procedure had shattered this image of himself. He was so overwhelmed with the thought of failure that he went into a faint (4).

In female patients whose emotional and sexual life has been limited, displacement of these feelings to the mouth may take the form of resenting the intrusion of dental instruments in the mouth and the conception of dentistry as a physical insult to themselves. Resentment and hostility against dental instrumentation may prevent them from having dental work done for many years. They may also be quite suspicious of any suggestion which has to do with the alteration of tooth structure. Such a patient may go the rounds of many dental offices, resent the fee required for his treatment, and inwardly may be unable to submit to the ministrations of a male dentist.

One might conclude that "the mouth, psychologically speaking, is either directly or symbolically related to the major human instincts and passions: to self-preservation, to cognition, to love and sexual mating, to hate and the desire to injure or kill."[13]

With a history of psychological disturbances, these normal instincts may take on exaggerated forms of expression often leading to dental breakdown.

III—Specific Dynamic Meaning of the Mouth for Various Patients

Since the mouth has great early significance to the developing personality, it retains and is used by the individual patient to express unsatisfied needs and serves through life as a barometer of personality well-being. The mouth is a nutritional organ which may taste foods and partially digest them. It is a biting, aggressive organ which can triturate and mash up foods and other objects and, of course, may be used against another individual for physical assault. The mouth is a pleasure giving organ which as part of the skin has an extremely high tactile sense and in kissing, feeling, sucking and biting may impart emotional gratification. While these basic reactions are felt by all people, the *specific* attitudes and expressions of the dental patient toward his mouth, may only be observed through interviewing and direct contact.

Case Histories of Varying Character Structures and Their Attitudes Toward the Mouth.[17-20]

Schizoid personality with hypochondriacal symptoms: male patient, unmarried; age 28; youngest of four boys; occupation—civil service clerk; childhood history replete with illnesses of respiratory tract and generally limited to the head and neck. Patient was completely dissatisfied with his social and occupational status. Very mixed feelings with regard to leaving his job and the unpredictable possibility of finding other work. Had none or very few friends both at his work and in his own social milieu. Lived at home with his mother, who dominated the entire family picture. Outwardly, the patient was a very quiet, withdrawn, soft-spoken individual who had very few interests and marriage was the last of these. On presentation, the patient complained that his mouth was ugly; that it made him socially unattractive; that it prevented him from getting married; that it hindered him from being physically attractive so that he might obtain another job. With these attitudes went much self-depreciation and self blame. At examination time, the patient expressed the thought that possibly he was deteriorating both physically and emotionally and placed great emphasis on the drifting of his teeth and the discoloration of his gums. In this instance, we have a very immature, insecure, young adult, who in a period of anxiety about his total emotional status focuses his dissatisfactions by symptom displacement on the mouth. Through correction of mouth ills, this patient hopes to correct all his personal limitations.

Oral dependent (passive) with acute gingival infection: Female, unmarried, aged 22, student at a school of social work. She had transferred from a midwestern town to a large city, this change representing her first critical separation from her family. This patient was one of two children, the older girl, and was outwardly very attractive and enthusiastic about her work. She had very mixed feelings about her capacity to complete her studies as a social worker and had received serious criticism from school authorities on her methods of handling her first few clients as a student. Simultaneously, the patient had made several efforts to have satisfactory relations with two or three men and in each instance, had great fears of any sexual experience as well as feelings of conflict as to whether these companions could measure up to the standards previously set by her mother. At the time of presentation, the patient's future status as a student was in jeopardy. She had been eating irregularly with no definite time or control of diet; had subsisted on binges of sweets and liquids and had been smoking a great deal. She felt that her mouth had a bad odor and that the smoking had burned her tissues and brought about the acute attack of bleeding and infection. This patient is a fairly normal post-adolescent. With separation from the home, as well as natural disturbance over the direction which she should take for her own career, she became anxious, the patient's *fear* that her mouth had odors and had been contaminated and infected reflected her own criticisms of her failure to grow up.

Oral Hostile Character: Female patient, age 35 unmarried, chronic periodonti-clasia. Thi patient was undei th dental care of a periodontist, a general dentist and one or twc othei dentist-friend simultaneously. Outwardly, the patien' appearec to be a very sweet, gentle, almost overly leaning type of person. At first examination, she expressed the thought that she was finally in the hands of the best dentist she could find. Soon after this first visit, the patient would call at frequent intervals denanding immediate appointments, interrupting the regular schedule and would complain of the slightest sensitivity to sweets or thermal changes. In a childish voice, she was at the same time grasping and demanding, wanting her work to be done very quickly and at the same time feeling quite disturbed when fees were mentioned. She felt that all her dentists in the past had always "pushed her around." She said "Fate has made my mouth abnormal and always painful. I can't eat a bite without pain. Why don't you fix it up so that I can forget it forever." There are many factors which cannot be included in a thumbnail sketch. However, the simultaneous expression of complaints, dissatisfactions, the whining and the groveling accompanied by the excessive demands characterized the oral, hostile character in the dental situation. This patient attacked all men, particularly the dentists whc treat her "sickest" part—her mouth.

Obsessive Compulsive Character: Male, 50 years of age, married, one child. The patient is a robust, high-keyed person whose work is building, contracting and carpentry. The patient brushes his mouth five to six times a day, chews gum incessantly to keep his mouth clean, and places great value on the attractiveness of his hair, his teeth and his general facial appearance. While the patient was quite young, his father, also a carpenter, deserted the family, leaving the patient to carry the responsibility of sustaining the family. The patient expresses great confidence in his ability as a skilled artisan and at the same time seems to have great difficulty in obtaining regular work. In all his occupational relationships he is constantly finding fault in the technical shortcomings of his co-workers. The patient has suffered with gastrointestinal upsets from late adolescence; places very great value on foods and has suffered with a gastric ulcer for 12 to 14 years. Under periods of stress the patient clenches and grinds his teeth and sets up inflammation in his gums, particularly when his temper is aggravated and his personal situation is going awry. The patient feels that his mouth is foul and must be scrubbed incessantly in order to keep it clean. At the same time, he neglects to maintain his mouth in good dental repair. This patient is an example of a perfection seeking character with tremendous personal failings in many areas. The mouth, again, is used as the focus of blame for unresolved conflict. While the patient can well afford private dental care he is willing to undergo treatment by dental students who are supervised by "expert" dentists, as he expressed it.

Potential Schizophrenic: Male patient, unmarried, was seen in a clinic after having visited 15 other physicians and other dentists. Patient was a chemist, engaged to be married. His chief complaint was that his mouth "stank" and that he had a smell of rotten eggs coming from his mouth. In describing his symptoms the patient started the description by going back to the first physicians he had seen when he was 15 years of age. In an effort to overcome this smell, the patient would chew gum incessantly and drink great amounts of orange juice. The entire character of his speech was very rapid, overbearing and without stop. Great detail over each symptom, each test and each finding were gone into and no interruption by the examining dentist seemed to be able to stop the flow of words. The patient appeared to be in extreme panic. All clinical tests made were negative and upon examination no unnatural odor was ever found to come from the mouth. This patient was found to be extremely disturbed and was referred for psychiatric supervision.

These case histories all indicate that in various degrees of emotional disturbance, the mouth may be or may become a prime center of concern and the dentist is often the first professional consultant to meet with the complex of physical breakdown and emotional upset which make up the clinical syndrome manifested. In all instances of loss of security and feelings of aloneness or apartness, the mouth may be the emotional stage through which the sense of inadequacy and lack of mastery are either verbally or physically demonstrated.

IV— Emotional Factors in Dental Disease

Anxiety is the key factor which directly or indirectly contributes to the production of dental disease. There are several forms of anxiety, with their concomitant defense mechanisms which ensue, one of these being a basic anxiety or actual fear of dental instruments, and dental pain.

Under this heading may be included those patients who consciously or unconsciously avoid going to the dentist and in this fashion aid in the initiation or perpetuation of their own dental ills. There are also those who, once in the dental office, cannot tolerate any discomfort, pain, or instrumentation, and thereby make the procedure so difficult that a proper standard of work cannot be accomplished. In the light of this last factor, the whole subject of pain thresholds which have been studied by Wolff[24] has yet to be thoroughly studied in relation to the mouth. Suffice it to say, that Ryan[39] at Tuft Dental School, in his study of periodontal disturbances, has pointed out that patients under anesthesia or analgesia, with the eradication of concomitant anxiety, are able to subject their teeth to greater pressures and pains than those patients under normal dental circumstances.

Another anxiety form includes those defense mechanisms resulting in disturbing thoughts or ideas, which may prevent the completion of dental work. In this group may be included the various character disturbances listed in Section III, personality constructs in which the main theme is hysteria, phobias, or masochism.

McCartney states:[10] "Hysterical systems or conversion systems are unique creations of the patient invented by his unconscious for the expression of his particular repressed psychological content."

Frustration of deep-seated needs may be converted into headache, tachycardia, gastritis, colitis; or the tissues around the mouth may be used as a means of such expression. Nail-biting, thumb-sucking, smoking, excessive gum-chewing and the like may be the hysterical expressions of unfulfilled needs.

In hysterical patients vague pains of a non-specific character may appear and radiate through the mouth along confused neurologic lines.

A male Negro, 46 years of age, unmarried, presented with a pain in an upper left first molar area. In general appearance he was very well dressed, extremely soft spoken and presented his symptoms in a monotonous, almost unemotional fashion. X-ray, thermal testing, percussion, mouth trans-illumination, and pulp-testing all proved negative. The diagnosis made was: hysterical manifestations of pain superimposed on an extremely oral dependent personality.

Hysterical pains are more frequent during adolescence and during the menopause. During the menopause, it is not infrequent to find women with a history of sexual frigidity turning up with acute flare-ups of burning tongue, or flashes of pain in the palate or cheeks. In those instances where these symptoms appear in males—while this is very infrequent— these histories usually include impotence.

Such female patients will exhibit fear of pain, will resist the attentions of the dentist and will reject care by identifying with a parent who has expressed such resistance to dental care. In addition, the resistances may take the form of masochistic demands for extractions with underlying hostility to the surgery.

Very often a fear of masturbation or rape will be the underlying thought sequences that awaken tension in the dental situation, and the dentist's fingers may stimulate erotic feelings through the mouth.

Other forms of hysterical expression are the paralyses, the vague spots in the throat, extremes of wetness or dryness in the mouth, (xerostomia), inability to swallow (globus hystericus) and hysterical closure. While there is no somatic breakdown visible in the oral area with these symptoms, the ultimate effect is the prevention of adequate dental care for the patient.

Anxiety related to phobic ideas is another anxiety form. These dental patients fear infection from dental instruments, demand that the dentist wash his hands frequently, check the freshness of the dental towel, wipe the armrests with their towels, and generally question the sterility of all instruments used. These patients also fear that they may be infected with organisms of previous patients. These patients are extremely difficult to treat, for they are usually very suspicious of every move that the dentist makes; at the same time, with this form of unilateral thinking the whole problem of fees becomes very difficult to discuss. Phobic symptoms are usually superimposed on a basically suspicious or paranoid personality structure. In periods of climacteric hormonal change, it is not unusual to find these patients pre-psychotic.

In situations of personal loss, or death of a dear one, the melancholia, or depression which follows may take the form of self starvation, limitation of foods to liquids, and general self deprivation. There is an admixture of guilt that something could have been done to avoid the incident producing the depression. Reactions to the depression may take the form of fear of cancer, fear of pains, fear of teeth removal, fear of cutting down teeth, fear of bad tastes similar to medicines, fear of blood in the mouth, fear of choking, fear of kissing or touching anything or anyone with the mouth, fear of saying the wrong things—which might reflect deep-seated aggression or hostility mixed with the love which had been felt toward the lost one. The end result in these protracted depressions is a breakdown of soft tissues in the mouth and a complete avoidance of dental care—with the subsequent loss of teeth because of pyhorrhea or dental decay.

Anxieties produce habits or forms of activity which through their constant use lead to a physical breakdown of the dental apparatus.

1. Thumb or finger-sucking. Lawes, and others, having made a thorough study of thumb-sucking, expresses the thought that finger-sucking is an instinctive need and at the same time a powerful organic pleasure. Should thumb-sucking persist beyond the age of four years in the human being, it usually represents an expression of lack of emotional warmth and attention by the mother during the early feeding periods. Any interference, however, with the thumb-sucking habit provides such a strong secondary attention to the restrictive forces that are placed so that, if anything, the act is over-valued in the mind of the child and the habit held onto out of all proportion. The thumb for such a child is a means of retreat into a world of fantasy, and is an escape from the unpleasant realities which in some way or another have been disturbing to the wellbeing of the child. As for its somatic effects, thumbsucking is probably not as harmful to the dental apparatus as has been frequently believed. The problem of treating thumb-sucking is based mainly on the following techniques:

(a) The child should be permitted talking-out periods during which his relationships with brothers, sisters and parents are clearly depicted.
(b) The child should always be well fed.
(c) The thumb may be replaced by mouth toys or pacifiers, if the child is very young, or rusks, toast crusts, or foods requiring heavy chewing, should be provided at those times when the habit is resorted to.
(d) More human company at more frequent intervals through the day, and no period of solitude permitted.

With older children over the age of four, the use of a mirror so that the child can see what he is doing, may be used. At this point, chewing gum may even be permitted. As the hand is removed from the mouth innumerable times during the day, very gently and with reassurance, toys, tools, slices of food, should be provided to make up for the thumb. At bedtime, the mother or a mother-substitute should always be present to make this period pleasant and without anxiety.

In still older children, it is possible to discuss the habit openly, and having established a sound interpersonal relationship with the child in which small gifts may have been exchanged, the child should be encouraged to ask for help. In a 4 to 6 months' period it is possible to remove the habit completely. Parent education is a vital factor in this re-educative process. It is important that they realize that thumb-sucking involves no moral issue and at no time should punishment be meted out for its performance.

2. Bruxism—clamping, champing and grinding of teeth.[35] Overstress or traumatic occlusion may break down the gingivae and produce bone resorption. These patients unconsciously traumatize their teeth and seemingly try to chew them right out of the sockets. This organ neurosis is traceable to earliest childhood in which extreme hostility and aggressiveness are repressed, usually in a family of very great moral restrictions. Should this habit persist over the years, the entire occlusion may be destroyed. At no time should reconstructive work be attempted until the basic factors producing this habit have been removed.

3. Excessive gum-chewing, candy and lozenge-sucking, and eating.

4. Exaggerated patterns of chewing, particularly mushing of food without mastication and the excessive intake of liquids and semi-solid foods.[39]

5. Cigar, cigarette and pipe smoking.

6. Excess or diminished flow of saliva.[10]

All the habits listed above, in persistent form, are expressions of the need for mouth gratifications.[33, 34]

Most of them are traceable to emotional difficulties originating early in life. These habits are indirect forms of satisfying emotional wants related to rejection by the mother in innumerable ways in infancy and early childhood. When habits are intermittent in character, so that they appear and disappear in cyclical fashion in the history of the patient, the exacerbation is traceable to a conflict situation in which rejection or loss of face was involved.

A 12½ year old boy examined for protrusion of the upper anterior teeth, in which the posterior occlusion was perfect, gave the following history: There being six and twelve years difference between him and his next siblings, at each birth the thumb was once again utilized a a form of self-reassurance, of seeking the attention of the parents, and of reassuming the baby state, all for the purpose of bringing about a sense of well-being in this patient. Suffice it to say that the malocclusion could not be corrected while the unpredictable habit was part of the behavior system.

Another anxiety form are those anxieties which stem from oral pathology

216   PSYCHOLOGY OF PHYSICAL ILLNESS

or disfiguring lesions.[41] In this group may be included patients suffering from hare lip and cleft palate, anodontia (agenetically missing teeth) buck teeth, rat bite, and other physical irregularities and discolorations of the teeth.

The social stigma which produced tremendous feelings of insecurity prevent adequate ego formation in these patients. If correction of these defects is possible at an early age, future emotional disturbances may be prevented or ameliorated. In this sub-heading may be included all orthodontic care. Very little investigation has been made to determine in which patients the wearing of orthodontic braces and bands in some instances alleviates tension and makes the patient feel socially acceptable. In other instances, the same appliances may give the patient a sense of social disapproval and may produce emotional upsets of lasting character. It is important for the orthodontist to obtain a complete personal history of each and every patient and to follow through carefully as the appliances are placed, to make sure of the patient's reaction to these changes.

Another form of anxiety are anxieties producing soft tissue breakdowns. [26, 28, 29, 31, 40] Under this heading are included acute Vincent's infection, intractable cases of periodontitis simplex and periodontitis complex, angio neurotic edema, etc. Studies carried out by Mellars and Herms, and many others, seem to indicate that pH. changes, salivary changes, vaso-constriction and vaso-dilatation, and other elements, in periods of anxiety produce bleeding gums, swelling, mouth odors, and tissue necrosis.

Anxiety, with its subsequent protective devices, may produce lesions and physical disturbances about the mouth which range from frank avoidance of dental treatment to the direct initiation of decay and of tissue lesions through destructive habits.

V—DENTISTRY FOR CHILDREN

Dental treatment is one of the realities which children have to face at some point early in their lives. Usually, each child brings to the dental situation any of the fears or anxieties which disturb him as an individual. The attitudes or reactions which a child has toward the dental treatment, or the dentist are the end-products of his own personal history, particularly toward those elements of his background which may have developed exaggerated or inappropriate responses to doctors, or any adult who might minister to his health needs.

Some children cry, scream, shout, kick, bite or run away from dentistry. Some children accept, work through and help out during the dental situation.

Children have these different reactions to dentistry because as individuals each one has his own personality—his own complex of feelings and attitudes about the world and the people in it which characterize him as a person. Young as they are, children, having no other resources to call on, are most efficient in using their emotions and feelings in letting those around them know their reactions to given situations. The dental patient is first seen after the first dentition has made its appearance in the mouth, at about the age of $3\frac{1}{2}$ years old.

At this age in dentistry, the child patient feels the fear of the unknown and the strange; the office, the dental instruments, the smells, the uniforms, the noises and sounds, all tend to awaken in the child the desire to protect himself from danger. At the same time, there are many demands being made on the child by his parents to fall into the social habits which they believe are to his advantage in growing into a mature individual. Every child likes to feel that he is doing what his parents think is good for him. He wishes to be loved by his parents and will go to the dentist quite willingly if that is one of the activities which they feel he should experience.

The basic problem, then, which every child faces in going to the dentist for the first few times is: I must have my mouth and teeth treated by the dentist even though I do not know or am afraid of what he may do to me, because my parents want me to do so. The effort to undergo the dental treatment with the attendant misgivings and doubts produces conflict or tension.

While such tension is present to a greater or lesser degree in any situation which the parent suggests to the child, dentistry in particular produces a much greater *anxiety* than most other experiences.

Dentistry treats the mouth and the teeth—and to a child these parts have a greater importance than many other parts of the body. At birth, the mouth is extremely sensitive, and has an "erectile itching,"[46] so that sucking and pleasurable sucking motions are present soon after birth. The gratification of the mouth needs, both hunger and sucking-pleasure are the keystones to the well-being of the new-born child.[12] In infancy, the mouth is the best coordinated, most powerful, and most pleasureable part of the infant's body. As such, the mouth takes on tremendous importance to the child. During this period, the first dentition makes its appearance, and the pain around the mouth is great.

The infant's reactions to the ineradicable gum pain is aggressive shrieking and crying in an effort to wipe out the pain. While these pains are forgotten, they are undoubtedly repressed into the mind of the child and in moments of pain in dentistry, they are recalled and produce the "fits" and "crying spells" which the dentist sees. It would be helpful for the dentist then to get information from the parent on the "teething history" to gain some insight into the child under care.

By the time a child patient is $3\frac{1}{2}$ years, he is inquisitive and curious about the world about him. Having already been prepared at home for some of the social graces and restrictions of society, he outwardly at least, is eager to learn through new experiences, even dental experiences. Children at this age like discipline and orderliness, or predictability in the people around them. If a child has accepted certain social standards as pleasure-giving or valuable to his emotional economy he will eagerly accept the dentist into his scheme of things. The dentist in turn can become a good friend of the child, can be understanding but firm, sympathetic but definite in his routine, specific in his use of language, and in his appointment keeping. Children at this age still retain a natural quality of feeling the reactions of people about them sharply and accurately.

A calm soft-toned, effective dentist is sensed as quickly as a nervous, erratic, hasty, easily-upset dentist. A warm speaking voice, a few words of encouragement and praise, and no rushing, leaving it to the child to indicate his readiness to go on or stop, make for a good beginning in a dentist-child-patient relationship.

Young children have a great deal of physical energy and any effort to restrain them or close them in, will produce aggressiveness and hostility. Their interest-span is short and their appointments have to be kept in tune. A sick child, a tired child, a child in the presence of an older brother or mother, or grandmother, all these circumstances make for unsuccessful dental care. No parent should be allowed in the treatment room to jeopardize the dentist-patient contact.

The Temper Tantrum. The tantrum may be defined as a period of uncontrolled hostility which may take the form of gasping for breath, crying, shrieking, kicking out, etc., which directly reflect an equal amount of anxiety or extreme fear. It may last a few moments, or several hours, leaving the child physically exhausted. An acute tantrum may be traced to illness, disturbing situation at home, deaths or illnesses in the home, or confusing conversations relating to dentistry which were overheard at home. All these situations may bring on a minor psychotic episode during which the child cannot relate to anyone around him and discards all contact with people by going into the tantrum. No dentistry should ever be attempted during such an episode.

A girl of five years was referred for treatment. She entered the office shrieking and crying. A short conversation with the mother revealed a history of an older brother who was very ill, and who had been scheduled for major surgery. For months this child had been hearing confusing and disturbing talk about the brother's future. No child can express the mixed feelings about the brother, and the impending surgery. The mother's terror had been adopted by this child through close identification with the situation. The dentistry became for her a tremendous threat, for her mother was arranging for surgery for the brother and for dentistry for her. Her conflicting feelings towards her mother brought on an unmanageable tantrum at the very door of the office.

In young children, few defenses exist, so that fear of the dentist may take the form of vomiting, spitting, crying, or any *physical* expression of fear. Not wishing to antagonize his mother he may appear in the dental office and still not be able to go through with it. This may lead to much rinsing, washing, asking lots of questions—in general trying to put off the evil moment.

On the other hand, a three year old is already aware of the world about him at home—and can be prepared for meeting with other adults or parent-like figures outside. Some children enjoy knowing their physicians or dentists because the visit represents an adventure or game participated in away from the home. The dental visit then takes on the significance of an educational and new life experience for the young child. His sense of security can be bolstered and developed to recognize other social standards from those set up in the home. A dentist who clearly outlines what goes on in the office and tells the child what kind of behaviour is expected in the chair, in the waiting room, where play is permitted and where quiet is necessary, provides the child with new social values—which may serve to interest the child and make of him a cooperative, interested patient.

It is important not to underestimate a child at any time. A three year old has many definite elements of a developing personality. He may be a passive, withdrawn, quiet, outwardly gentle child, with hidden fears and anxiety; he may be a biting, aggressive, overtly hostile child in new situations. Illness, social situations in the home, economic deprivation, deaths, etc., may distort a child so that he may be "old beyond his years" and possess many protective mechanisms for getting what he wants, or avoiding what he fears. Here a knowledge of the family, father, mother, and some general information regarding the family set-up helps to prepare the dentist for something usual or unusual in a given child. Young children can feel wanted, happy, warm towards others, or they can feel rejected, unwanted, ugly, bad. They have attitudes towards themselves which have been implanted at home. The dentist in his own way, and in his own professional world can serve to lighten the burden which so many children carry by accepting the child as an individual, by giving him an opportunity to find his own way of meeting the dental bur and chair. Giving him time and encouragement will make future work easier. The lollipop, the reward, the movie, the ice-cream cone, do *not fool* a child. Sitting down and talking to him at eye level, letting him feel the size of the instruments and their tex-

PSYCHOLOGY OF PHYSICAL ILLNESS

tures, giving him a chance to run the instruments, showing him pictures of
teeth, fillings, and letting him tell you his reactions to all these things is
the way to a good rapport with the young child.

BIBLIOGRAPHY

I—Dentist-Patient Relationship

1. Garrett, A.: Interviewing—Its Principles and Methods. New York, Family
   Service Association of America, 1942.
2. Kinsey, A. C., Pomeroy, W. B. and Martin, C. E.: Sexual Behavior in the Human
   Male. Philadelphia, W. B. Saunders Company, 1948.
3. Bell, D.: Office routines—psychological factors that bring about more pleasant
   patient-parent-doctor relationship. Am. J. Orthodont. *36:* 81–108, 1950.
4. Coriat, I. H.: Dental anxiety: Fear of going to the dentist. Psychoanalyt. Rev.
   33: 363–367, 1946.
5. Gillespie, R. D.: Psychology for dental surgeons. Guy's Hosp. Gaz. *54:* 32–39,
   1940.
6. Ament, Philip: Psychotherapy in patient relaxation. J. Dent. Med. *5:* 307, 1950.
7. Edwards, A. T.: Psychiatric implications in dentistry. D. J. Australia. *22:* 589–
   595, 1950.
8. Burstone, M. S.: Psychosomatic aspects of dental problems. J. Am. Dent. A.
   33: 862–871, 1946.
9. Gibbs, F. G.: Psychosomatic aspects of dentistry. Dent. Rec. *70:* 241–245, 1950.
10. McCartney, J. L.: Psychosomatics in dentistry. J. Canad. Dent. A. *17:* 3–12,
    1951.
11. Witmer, H. L. (Ed.): Teaching Psychotherapeutic Medicine. New York Com-
    monwealth Fund, 1947.

II—Psychological Meaning of the Oral Area

12. Ribble, Margaret, A.: The Rights of Infants. New York, Columbia University
    Press, 1943.
13. Binger, Carl: Psychosomatic implications of pain. Rev. of the Proceedings of
    the Association for Research in Nervous and Mental Disease. Psychosom.
    Med. *6:* 250–252, 1944.
14. McCartney, J. L.: Psychosomatics in Dentistry. J. Canad. Dent. A. *17:* 3–12,
    January 1951.
15. Weiss, E.: Psychosomatic aspects of dentistry. J. Am. Dent. A. *31:* 215–220,
    1944.
16. Frohman, B. S.: Application of psychotherapy to dental problems. Dental Cos-
    mos. *73:* 1117, 1951.

III—Specific Dynamic Meaning of the Mouth for Various Patients

17. Tarachow, Sidney: Relationship of the dentist to neurotic psychological types.
    J. California D. Association *26:* 1950.
18. Friend, David: Dentist and His Patient: A New Concept of Dental Practice,
    New York, Revere Publishing Co., 1944.
19. Schultz, L. W.: Therapeutical management of the hysterical patient. J. Am.
    Dental A. *34:* 828–830, 1947.
20. Shaw, S. I.: Psychological interpretation of patient behavior: Case report. Dent.
    Items of Interest. *73:* 677–692, 1951.

21. Stern, E. S.: Some psychosomatic aspects of dentistry. Dent. Pract. *1:* 245–250, 1950.

22. Swank, E. R.: Dental Practice and Management: Economics, Ethics and Psychology in Dentistry. Philadelphia, Lea & Febiger, 1947.

23. Wartenberg, R.: Dentist looks at patient; by a neurologist. Am. J. Ortho. *32:* 443–448, 1946.

24. Wolff, Harold G. and Goodell, H.: The relation of attitude and suggestion to the perception of and reaction to pain. The Proceedings of the Association for Research in Nervous and Mental Disease. Baltimore, Williams & Wilkins Co., 1943.

IV—Emotional Factors in Dental Disease

25. Sillman, J. H.: Finger-sucking: Serial dental study from birth to five years. New York State J. Med. *42:* 2024–2028, 1942.

26. Lawes, A. G. H.: Psychosomatic study into the nature, prevention and treatment of thumb-sucking and its relationship to dental deformity. D. J. Australia. *22:* 167–194, 211–236, 1950.

27. Foster, H. G.: Abnormal Mouth Habits. J. New Jersey Dent. Soc. *22:* 7–10, 1951.

28. Jones, H. S.: Emotional stress and gingivitis. Oral Hygiene. *41:* 657–661, 1951.

29. Mellars, N. W. and Herms F. W.: Neuropathologic manifestations of oral tissues. A. J. Orthodontist. *37:* 13–27, 1951.

30. Levy, David, M.: Thumb or finger-sucking from the psychiatric angle. Child Development. *8:* 99–101, 1937.

31. Campbell, D. G.: Psychosomatic mechanisms in oral diseases. Am. J. Orthodont. *32:* 459–466, 1946; Investigation of psychosomatic mechanisms in dental patients. Am. J. Orthodont. *32:* 459–466, 1946.

32. Carr, D. T.: Habits associated with dental anomalies. Am. J. Orthodont. *31:* 152–160, 1945.

33. Glaser, C. G.: Psychotherapy in orthodontics. Am. J. Orthodont. *32:* 340–354, 1946.

34. Johnson, L. R.: Habits and their relation to malocclusion. J. Am. Dent. A. *30:* 848–852, 1943.

35. Leof, M.: Clamping and grinding habits: Their relation to peridontal disease. J. Am. Dent. A. *31:* 184–194, 1944.

36. Massler, M. and Wood, A. W. S.: Thumb-sucking. J. Dent. Child. *16:* 1–9, 1949.

37. Mitchell, H.: Thumb-sucking: Practical appraisal from mental hygiene and orthodontic points of view. Canad. M. A. J. *44:* 612–617, 1941.

38. Pearson, G. H. J.: Psychology of finger-sucking, tongue-sucking, and other oral "habits." Am. J. Orthodont. *34:* 589–598, 1948.

39. Ryan, E. J.: Psychological Foundations of Dentistry. Springfield, Ill., Thomas, 1946.

40. Tishler, B.: Periodontia—some facts concerning occlusal habit neuroses. J. Am. Dent. A. *32:* 823–825, 1951.

41. Walker, M. B.: Psychological effects of malocclusion of teeth. Am. J. Orthodont. *27:* 599–604, 1941.

V—Dentistry for Children

42. Bell, Juliet, O.: Psychological Aspects of Dental Treatment of Children. Madison, Wisconsin, J. Exper. Education. 1943, 86pp.

43. Fulton, J. T.: Dentistry's greatest challenge: Emotional security of children. J. Dent. Child. *16:* 8–9, 1949.
44. McDonald, A. E.: Psychosomatics and Hypnotism in Dentistry. New Orleans, Author, 1949.
45. Sognnaes, R. F. and White, E. L.: Oral conditions of children in relation to state of health and habits of life. Am. J. Dis. Child. *60:* 283–303, 1940.
46. O. Spurgeon English and Pearson, Gerald: Neuroses of Children and Adults. New York, Norton, 1945.

CHAPTER 15

The Personality of the Physician as a Factor

LEON L. ALTMAN, M.D.

Dr. Altman received his M.D. from the Long Island College of Medicine and—after internship—was a Psychiatric Resident at Hudson River State Hospital in Poughkeepsie as well as resident at the New York State Psychiatric Institute.

Later, he was Assistant Physician at Stony Lodge in Ossining, New York and served from 1941 to 1946 in the Medical Corps of the United States Army in a variety of capacities including Assistant Chief, N. P. Service, Billings General Hospital and Chief N. P. Service, 110th General Hospital, ETOUSA.

Dr. Altman is a graduate of the New York Psychoanalytic Institute. He was Instructor in Psychiatry at the Vanderbilt Clinic, Columbia University and is now in private practice. Dr. Altman is a Diplomate of the American Board of Neurology and Psychiatry and an Associate member of the New York Psychoanalytic Society. He is a Fellow of the American Psychiatric Association.

W E STRIVE CONSTANTLY to improve our methods of understanding what is wrong with our patients. Insofar as the doctor's personality plays an important part in therapy and may be either a valuable asset or a liability, we may and should try to understand what may be accomplished by certain personalities. To know oneself is a distinct advantage in knowing and understanding others; we may never really assume a knowledge of what is wrong in others without an awareness of what is wrong in ourselves.

It is not a particularly new idea that the physician himself, with all those characteristics loosely subsumed under the heading of personality, exerts a truly potent influence upon his patients for their well-being or for their discomfort. Only more recently, however, a better scientific appreciation of the role of the physician in promoting health or disability has been expressed in the term "*iatrogenic.*" "Iatrogenic" conveys the meaning of a physician-induced factor in the status of patients, for better or worse. Whether it be through influence, suggestion, emphasis, attitude or form of treatment, this factor by itself is capable of producing effects of either an alleviating and curative nature or of creating dysfunction and disturbance. It is a provocative yet simple fact that the mere presence of a physician has often had the effect of producing a subsidence of symptoms in the hitherto ailing patient. The "King's Touch" was an example of the person of the healer himself constituting a sovereign remedy which sometimes accomplished wonders as great as the medical "miracles" wrought by religious veneration. On the other hand, it is just as conceivable that the same type of influence might be brought to bear in an opposite and less satisfactory direction, in promoting or aggravating or doing nothing to diminish suffering.

Patients themselves are very much aware of the personality of their physician and may indeed, in an intuitive if not a scientific way, express their appreciation of this factor not only in the way they feel about him personally but in their response to treatment as well.

It may be that in the future a systematized knowledge of personality interactions will be utilized in selecting a certain kind of person as physician and a certain kind of person as patient. Others may have had experiences in which they applied just this kind of principle in treating or referring patients; probably many doctors have considered the advisability of matching patient with doctor.

The patient may not directly attribute the success or failure of his treatment to the personality of the doctor but, at all events, it is something they are bound to pay as much attention to—whether they are aware of it or not—as the medicine he may prescribe. How much time did the doctor spend on them? What does his office look like? What does he look like? What does his voice convey? Whatever else he may get from the doctor, the patient will carry away with him impressions such as these and many others.

What the Doctor May Mean to the Patient

The doctor's personality is of particular importance since he plays a very important emotional role for the patient. The simplest aspect of this role is the fact that the patient is a "sufferer" and expects help from the doctor. This fact alone implies a certain dependency, a heavy emotional investment which, at best, is comparable to the expectations a child may originally have had towards the parents.

Thus, the doctor is seen as a parental figure, an authority who may be feared, respected, loved or hated, obeyed or made fun of, much as a particular person may have felt towards father and/or mother or an older sibling. In fact, most people first meet with a doctor as children and some of their relationship to the old family doctor will carry over to doctors in their later life.

The result of the fact that the physician may stand emotionally in *loco parentis* is that patients often behave irrationally towards their doctors. They may behave as though they were children. Thus, patients may want undue reassurance; a large proportion of night calls is related to the fact that people, from their childhood days on, are more afraid of the night and the terrors it seems to hold. All day long they may have managed their irrational or rational concerns over some ailment; but at night they may become unable to subdue their anxiety.

By the same token, patients may be jealous of other patients of their doctor's, just as they perceived siblings as rivals for the affection of their parents. They may at times suffer from imagined complaints simply because they feel neglected and want somebody to be interested in them, to worry and, in turn, to reassure them; the doctor fits these needs admirably. Thus, approval or disapproval, interest or the lack of it on the part of the doctor, are of special emotional importance.

The medical fee is such an embattled problem for the same emotional reasons. Since the patient really wants the doctor to love him like a parent and be interested in him solely for personal reasons, the fee is a jarring note. It is a reminder that the doctor has other motives aside from and above and beyond the affective and ethical tie. Therefore, if all other things are kept equal—it is probably true that the more immature a patient's relationship to the doctor, the less willing he is to pay the bill. The money becomes something the doctor is taking away from him rather than giving him. (By the same token, a doctor with a hostile attitude may make his fee an instrument of aggression while a very inhibited physician may feel obliged to charge such low fees that it constitutes a hardship for him and lowers him in the eyes of his patients).

For a large proportion of the population, the doctor is a person of higher cultural, socio-economic standing than is the patient himself. A sense of awe may carry over from the childhood days when mother would put on her best and straighten out the house before the doctor arrived. These factors combine to make the physician a very impressive figure—one whose every word may weigh heavier than anyone else's and, therefore, needs extra careful weighing by the doctor himself.

Of course, the doctor is often feared because some of his procedures may hurt, some of his judgments may mean tragedy, separation, a change in the entire life pattern.

The doctor often shares the most intimate secrets of the patient. It may make the doctor a confidant, father confessor, judge of morals and conduct. For children, the doctor is intimately connected with all secrets of life. His little black bag is often associated with the arrival of babies, loss of a parent, removal from home. To him one bares parts of the body which otherwise are shamefully covered.

Such considerations are, of course, not entirely unknown to the doctor who is alert to the effects of his treatment and the responses of his patient. Nevertheless, one usually takes oneself for granted and the busy doctor cannot always take the time to assess the results of his own personality upon his patients. In the midst of all his duties he is understandably more concerned with his patients and what he is doing for them rather than with himself. Still, it is not only what he does but *how* he does it that may have a profound and determining effect upon the perplexing problems that arise in the course of practice.

A common and frustrating experience for any doctor is the recognition that his treatment is not producing beneficial results. Despite his skill and good intentions, and despite the fact that the illness may be readily identifiable and treatment standard, he does not get results. The doctor's chagrin is justifiably more acute when the same patient with the same complaints is treated by another colleague with the same prescriptions or interventions, but with entirely different results. Assuming a reasonable degree of equality of all other factors, we are entitled to wonder what it is that makes a disease process exhibit a refractory quality with one physician and not with another. The effect of a doctor's personality on a patient may well be the major factor in success or failure.

A comprehensive study of personality problems in doctors would be beyond the scope of this chapter. To begin with, personality is not an easy thing to define briefly. It is frequently considered synonymous with character, attitude and all those attributes of a person that strike our attention through his appearance and actions, but there are many more complex factors to be considered. At any rate, loosely summed up in this admittedly unsophisticated and incomplete way, we continue to speak of "personality." The personality of the physician is at least as intriguingly complex and baffling in its particulars as any other.

What makes a particular person take up the study of medicine? Why is one doctor successful and contented whereas another is not? Such questions cannot be answered glibly. Neither is it possible to say with anything approaching assurance why a certain doctor succeeds with a certain kind of patient. Attempts are usually made to determine what kind of person is most suited to begin the study of medicine when the prospective doctor is considered by a medical school.

No individual can be delineated accurately and exhaustively in terms of a single or one-dimensional character trait. In any person there is always an intricate overlapping, fusion and blending of many elements as well as the determinants for them. For instance, although there is such a seemingly wide disparity between the manifestations of a person with inflexible convictions and one beset by vacillating doubt, there is a relationship between the two. Their kinship can be demonstrated when they appear in the same person. Consequently, the outlines suggested here can be no more than descriptive approximations.

Although we may not always know how to define personality or how to pin-point the quality of a person that may affect us powerfully, we can recognize the reactions that are produced by certain more or less easily recognizable traits without too much difficulty.

If we are going to discuss the effect of the physician's personality upon the patient, we do not wish to create the impression that the doctor should be the one person in the world who has no personal problems or deficiencies. We can hope that doctors will be relatively well adjusted people; where their own shortcomings cannot be otherwise diminished, we would like to ameliorate the effects, at least, by offering the doctor some awareness of his difficulties so that he can try to hold them at a minimum of interference with his work.

For the sake of this goal we wish to discuss a few outstanding personality syndromes and their possible effects upon doctor-patient relationships.

The Need To Be Appreciated

While we cannot consider all the intricate roots of the desire to be a doctor, it would probably be readily agreed that some form of altruism, some wish to be helpful to others, enters in very frequently. Directly related to this desire is, of course, the wish for recognition of one's services.

There is nothing wrong with wanting appreciation, affection and recognition of one's capacities. There is something wrong, however, if these needs are omnipresent motives in dealing with people. The doctor who has the excessive need to be loved by his patients may over-extend himself—probably unnecessarily—merely to reap affection. He may demand recognition from his patients in a way which causes them to be resentful. He may have the need to show off in dramatic procedures and highflown attitudes which the patient sooner or later perceives as fake. If he pictures himself as the savior who—in the last moment—prevents mortal peril, he will frighten his patients and they will eventually mistrust him. The doctor's wish to be liked by his patients must not stand in the way of his integrity. He can be effective only if he has the patient's respect. As Strauss[1] has pointed out, for instance, a physician who is in awe of his patient's social or financial position and lets this feeling enter into the interpersonal relationship, will lose the respect of the patient and will be misused.

Similarly, Strauss points out that a need to be considered omniscient may be a serious defect. Such a doctor will fail to ask for consultations in questionable circumstances, and thus harm the patient and himself.

An inherent flair for the dramatic may be a component of some doctors' approach. He may be a person of warm enthusiasms and profound antipathies, hot and cold in turn. His disposition to emotionalism may be in his style, his speech, in everything. Emotionalism in his patient arouses his own abundant emotionalism to a corresponding degree. He may even participate in his patient's joys and sorrows, joining in with them as though they were happening to him too. He will be truly "sympathetic" but not necessarily thereby more understanding. He will be particularly easily misled by the patient who has a capacity for passionate presentation and dramatic magnification (the kind of reaction most often met with in the hysteric). Demonstrativeness is his meat but if he eats what the patient feeds him he may never learn what lies beneath it. He is quite unable to be dispassionate. His ardor produces considerable heat but not much light and he may finish his days' work in a state of great exhaustion.

For instance, there is the example of the physician who treated several members of a large family in which he was interested as a personal friend. At the same time, he would counsel them in their personal affairs and relations in a compassionate way. Because of this kind of involvement he was, however, unable to discern the obvious manner in which the ailments for which they consulted him had a way of travelling through the family, each one taking turns at being disabled, suffering accidents, becoming exhausted, competing with each other to outdo the last sufferer. The doctor was too busy suffering with them to perceive the "me too" aspect of their illnesses which, in fact, had no other contagious or infectious character.

The patient is likely to interpret and feel this doctor's attitude as one of considerable kind interest in him and be gratified by it. Another type of patient, however, will view with alarm the intense interest or even devotion that the doctor shows, preferring him to remain steadfast, unmoved, uninvolved and dispassionate. The patient may even fervently hope that the doctor will see through his actions which are a source of discomfort to him but which he cannot by himself stop and even try to get the doctor to tell him to exert control. This can be likened to the way in which children are grateful for the restraining influence of parents when their own tempestuous feelings get out of control and can no longer be handled by themselves. Or else the patient may wonder why the doctor gets so involved, why he seems to take things so personally. He is disturbed to find the doctor reacting or being shaken. He wants him to remain firm and composed.

Impatience

Doctors naturally want to get results. It is as frustrating to the physician as it is to the patient not to see the expected change take place when much hard work has been invested. Some doctors have the type of personality that cannot bear frustration. They may feel tempted to behave as though they believed in magic; they engage in dramatic and heroic treatments, take chances and are not as careful and cautious as they might wish to be. They may feel called upon to promise more than they can safely be sure to give and the result will be a sense of failure shared by both patient and physician.

Some patients may admire a show of speed on the doctor's part and feel that he is a "go-getter," that there is "nothing slow" about him and that he is the sort of doctor who will get things over with quickly. He may then be disillusioned when the promise is not kept and all the haste is defeated by the natural timetable of biologic events. Most patients have the understandable need to know and to ask: "When will it be over?" and "When will I get well?" Most doctors err conscientiously on the conservative side knowing it is better to do so. They may not always be aware, however, of their own tendency to want to hurry things along.

Projecting

We speak of "projecting" when a person unwittingly ascribes to others undesirable feelings, fears, beliefs, etc., which he has himself (usually without being aware of them).

Many doctors project their own fears. Sometimes cardiac patients are prohibited marital relations when there are no real contraindications because the physicians' own notions about the dangers of sexuality interfere. Sex is probably the area of counsel where doctors most frequently are guided by their own prejudice and inclination.

Hypochondriasis on the part of a doctor may lead to overconcern and overprotectiveness in patients. A doctor who feels insecure may be inclined to suspect that his patients do not trust him and may behave defensively.

Hostility

The least desirable traits of one's own are the ones most likely to be ascribed to other people. Not to see the beam in one's own eye but the mote in the other's—expresses this fact.

Buried resentments and lingering angers seeking an outlet will find an available object all too readily in the patient. The doctor who has such feelings and disowns them, may impute them to the patient. He then feels that the patient is hostile and antagonistic. Under a mask of hostility, the patient may be trying to be friendly and the same will be true for the doctor similarly situated but they will never get together. In such a case, even the patient's symptoms may be interpreted as defiant acts, provocations and a source of embarrassment. Ultimately, the patient has got to be gotten rid of so the doctor may again feel at ease. It would have been simpler if the doctor had recognized his hostility and rid himself of it.

This is not the only way in which aggressive feelings on the part of the doctor may manifest themselves in his relation to the patient. Some doctors express their unconscious sadism by telling frightening stories about other patients or discussing all the possible dangers in the greatest detail. They may rationalize that the patient ought to be informed of all possibilities but overdo this reasonable tenet greatly. Such an attitude will produce fear in the patient as well as anger and fancied complaints.

The type of patient who turns the tables on the doctor probably never trusted any authority—starting with the parents; he is so skeptical because he still looks for an omniscient, omnipotent, all-loving parent and hides this need behind suspiciousness of everyone. If the doctor feels a need to pacify, the patient will only become more insistently inquisitive. If the doctor feels hurt in his dignity, he will offend the patient.

It is useful to remember that the patient has a right to know if he is dealing with a reputable physician but nothing can be gained by permitting oneself to be abused.

Cautiousness

Fear of upset is the guiding principle in this person's make-up and attitude. He has many fears himself and tries to deny them by refusing to acknowledge anything seriously wrong even in others. He is alarmed by pain, suffering, emotion or the disagreeable in general and consequently tends to deny these things, hastening to assure himself and others that it is not so. He will be unable to tell the patient something unpleasant. He might tell his patient, "This will not hurt," and then it does. He would not like to tell a patient that he has a serious problem. His evasion or silence or attempts at soothing only alarm and depress the patient further. Although there are patients who neither ask nor wish to be told the facts for fear of what they may find out, these patients are the very ones who react to the cautious doctor with the feeling, "No one is telling me the truth, therefore it must be awful and worse than what I already fear." The best antidote to this understandable anxiety in a patient is a realistic appraisal of all facts and possibilities without undue exaggeration.

Indignation

By "indignation" I mean the attitude which expresses itself in, "This is right and the other is wrong," particularly that the patient is wrong and *at fault.* Anyone can be wrong, including the doctor and the patient. I mean to distinguish this attitude from authoritativeness which I would conceive of as a quality derived from experience and understanding, in no way synonymous with "authoritarian" or dictatorial attitudes. Most patients appreciate and are helped by a definitive attitude. They do not feel better off for being allowed to get away with anything. They may even, as children will do, try to get the doctor to tell them they must stop an injurious course of action and may go so far as to provoke punishment. They want to be stopped. They want to be "told." And yet they do not want to be forbidden anything. The doctor who rises in fulsome wrath does not have authority. Indignation is still not understanding.

Officiousness

The physician can use his professional status and its prestige as a form of ostentation. His office and manner may be designed to impress and to convey importance. He may even assume a professional manner intended to command admiration and respect. Diplomas and testimonials may be displayed to good effect like badges of office before which the patient is expected to make proper obeisance.

Some patients will undoubtedly respond as this doctor wishes them to. They may have a need to feel abject. Others may feel that such interests interfere with the doctor's concern with themselves.

A 54 year old man, in the course of an annual physical examination and check-up, was informed that he was suffering from diabetes which was not severe but which, nevertheless, required some care and might be managed without insulin provided he obeyed a dietary regime to be prescribed. After several months of treatment and supervision, no control of the diabetes could be established because the patient refused to cooperate. The patient was a prominent, affluential, and imperious person accustomed to exerting leadership in a large corporation. The doctor treating him was an eminent internist with a wide reputation, recognized as outstanding for his experience and skill and was a commanding person with an impressive manner and address. The patient was subsequently successfully brought under diabetic control by another internist, not a more proficient clinician, but an unassuming, modest person without imposing manner. He was quite sincerely unaffected by the patient's towering economic and social status since he himself saw no need for it. The patient, however, was impressed by the doctor who remained unimpressed by him.

While shabbiness and lack of dignity are certainly no recommendations for the doctor, signs of conceit may make the patient feel, "He puts on an act, he isn't natural; dare I trust him?"

Flirtatiousness

In his relations with the patient, the doctor shares many problems with other professionals, such as lawyers, teachers and ministers. There are some aspects to his situation which are unique. There is the fact that, for the doctor, the taboos concerning physical modesty do not hold.

This factor alone often creates certain definite notions in the patient's mind—particularly as regards the female—in view of the fact that the majority of the doctors are still male. Such ideas may either create anxiety that will keep her from a much needed examination (see chapter on gynecology and obstetrics) or may, at times, bring frustrated patients to the office more often than is necessary. They will not recognize (in the large majority of cases) that they invent reasons for a visit because of some hidden gratification. Nevertheless, in their very manner they will exhibit a flirtatiousness which may be every bit as subtle as it is unconscious.

Such flirting need not be confined to the conventional methods of soulful come-hither looks. The doctor's office provides better means. The patient may present herself as appealingly helpless or gratefully adoring. She may just be a little too careless in her drapery or in the way she behaves during the physical examination and thus try to arouse some more personal interest in the doctor.

Sometimes the patient's wish to be found attractive may take really indirect and devious means of expressions—means which it may be difficult and sometimes impossible to anticipate. To illustrate the subtlety which such wishes of the patient can take we present the following illustration:

A family physician had been treating a young unmarried woman for many years. Following a consultation with him, in which she had requested his advice and help in obtaining a diaphragm and instruction in contraception, she returned for a follow-up visit, radically changed from a pleasant, appreciative patient to an embittered and antagonistic one. The doctor had referred her to a competent gynecologist for the purpose she had requested—preferring, with good reason—not to perform this service himself. The change in the patient's attitude was accounted for by her feeling that her doctor, in sending her elsewhere, had refused to acknowledge her as a woman and did not approve of her as such. These feelings were part of a general tendency to extensive day-dreaming with very erotic content. The whole episode became known only years later in the course of an investigation into the problem of her infertility. She expressed her reaction by saying, "I felt I wasn't good enough for him."

Of course the doctor had behaved entirely rationally and appropriately. The patient had invested her medical request with a sexual meaning and interpreted the doctor's referral as a rebuff (see section on consultation in chapter on General Practice). Frequently, patients may act more openly seductive.

Naturally, the ethical doctor will refrain from a manifest response to the patient's lure. Nevertheless, it is difficult for the unaware to avoid a psychological response. And that is where the real harm may be engendered. In the first place, the neurotically flirtatious patient is immature and has little real genital interest. (If a doctor were to permit himself a response, be it even with legal matrimony, he would very likely be deeply disappointed.) What she sees in the doctor is an authority figure by whom she wishes to be admired, whose loving care she wants, whose parental license she needs, and whom she likes to have fantasies about, rather than have realistic contact with.

It will be helpful for a doctor to remember that the feelings of the patient are the result of his specific function for her rather than of his individual person. The patient who feels particularly admiring and affectionate and gratefully loving towards him, would and probably did feel similarly towards other men in similar relationships to her. Such a patient is usually unduly attached to her father and finds a permissible substitute in the doctor. A doctor who is particularly affected by such emotions expressed for him, is probably an insecure person who needs adoration and the feeling of being superior to a woman.

If a doctor is flattered by such attention, the patient will establish a tyrannical, demanding relationship and will expect him to be at her beck and call. Once this state of affairs is arranged, even the slightest refusal will produce the severest hostility; now she will feel doubly rejected and betrayed and will visit whatever vengeance she can upon him. Probably a large percentage of all the accusations of seduction made against doctors by patients are based upon fantasies predicated upon flirtatiousness rather than actual events.

The least that is likely to happen if a doctor either accepts, encourages or promotes flirtatiousness with a patient is that the patient will become frightened at some point and leave his care. Furthermore, the necessary objective judgment of the doctor will be impaired in relation to a person to whom he is at all sexually responsive. He will be distressed, inclined to show off, and lose the necessary detached though friendly interest, marring the uncharged atmosphere in which he can best function.

Dogmatism

What doctor did not sometime in his own early history play childhood's doctor game, possibly inspired by the man who had the enormous power of telling those other powerful people, the parents themselves, what to do? *For of the most high cometh healing.* That is to say, that being a physician gives one an almost direct relationship with God from Whom such abilities are derived. Even the diploma secured by the person about to treat other persons calls witness to very special dispensations: the "Rights, Privileges, and Immunities Thereunto Appertaining." Here is implied a very great immunity notwithstanding the imposition of equally great and serious obligations. This combination of power and immunity, if it continues to have a strong appeal and personal value for the doctor, is surely manifested in many ways which do not escape the attention of those who come to him. For some patients, this attitude (manifest or latent, betrayed or concealed) reveals itself on the part of the doctor and has an extremely reassuring effect, satisfying the patient's need for pacification and infantilization. For other patients, it is, of course, antagonizing and irritating. In either case, the patient is not an ultimate beneficiary. No doctor is really omniscient. Therefore, a lordly manner—while it may be initially reassuring—will be its own undoing because it is unrealistic and contrived. Sooner or later the patient may be disillusioned and then confused should his disease progress in a way other than as foretold. (None of this means, on the other hand, that it is not possible for the physician to be sure of himself. Without any convictions he would be useless.)

A busy and successful young practitioner had earned the gratitude of a married woman who was trying to become pregnant by suggesting a course of thyroid and hormonal treatment, soon after which she became pregnant. Two years later she consulted him again for severe lower back pain with sciatic radiation down one lower extremity. He proposed and proceeded with caudal block which did not provide relief even after several weeks. When the patient commented on this, expressing apprehension about being disabled, the physician assured her he would succeed even if he had to immobilize her in a plaster cast. This was her last visit to him. She consulted another doctor with whom she remained in treatment even though the condition persisted over many months, finally subsiding without sequelae. No definite diganosis was ever established; all x-rays were negative and only slight neurologic signs, such as diminished deep reflexes in the extremity which returned later, were found. Considerable patience was demanded of both doctor and patient.

SUMMARY

There are certainly just as many factors operating in the interpersonal relationships of the doctor-patient setting as there are between any other two individuals who may come together for whatever purpose. No single motivation could possibly account for the many subtle exchanges of feeling and reaction mutually aroused in such situations. However, the doctor-patient relationship has special characteristics. It is usually and primarily a "group of two" with a distinctive and important ethical understanding written into the code of medical practice from antiquity. Each patient is, therefore, not merely scientifically unique but has the right to consider himself the sole interest of the physician.

For a patient, symptoms, organs and disease are not merely something interesting which do not differ from other similar conditions, but are something that really belong to him and are part of himself and his life. Thus, it is a deep humiliation, even though this may not be acknowledged, to be considered only the "carrier" of symptoms or of a disease or a diagnosis.

In one way or another, for any human being—patient and doctor included —disability, disease, suffering and injury carry with them deeply buried and strongly toned implications of life and death and danger to one's very existence. It would probably be said that problems of life and death are the daily preoccupation and concern of almost every practitioner of medicine and it would be assumed that he had acquired an appropriate attitude toward them—pragmatic, sympathetic, unfearful but not unconcerned; above all, rational. No one's attitudes are completely rational and in this matter, perhaps, they are least of all. To the extent to which the doctor has learned to meet this problem in himself will he be disposed to meet it in others even where it may be exhibited, attenuated, partial and diluted in the form of symptoms, organ dysfunction, injury and disease. It may be deeply imbedded in the nature of the physician that there is a cure for everything. Not only arrogance but fear may initiate this fallacy by which nobody is deceived anyway and which may introduce more suffering than it is designed to alleviate.

What the doctor does and the way he does it is determined not only by his scientific skill and knowledge but also by the way he is affected by patients, their symptoms, complaints and diseases. These may excite *reactive processes* in the doctor to which he has to remain insensitive. Many such reactions—the extremely human feelings of compassion, irritation, despair and what not—active in himself, reach the awareness of the doctor. Many others, perhaps the majority of feelings and reactions, may never be recognized. All the same, illness has implications and arouses them in the doctor as well as in the sufferer and those about him.

No doctor can afford to let his involvement with a patient progress to such a point where he must go through the same experience as his patient. It would not help matters much if he were to contract his patient's illness, have his symptoms or become infected by the same contagious process. Nevertheless, it is inevitable that he should be affected because, without such resonance or disallowing, he cannot perform his task properly. He is still a participant but a seasoned and self-disciplined one, therefore able to help and to guide.

Upon consulting a physician for the relief of symptoms, a patient is also invariably approaching him with certain expectations. As we have mentioned previously, these expectations are predicated upon the patient's previous experiences with the forerunner of such help and comfort—the parents and other custodians who administered relief when trouble arose. At the point of contact with the physician, such previous experiences are reactivated and the doctor now plays a role in a drama conceived of by the patient along very definite and special lines. The patient, according to his previous experience, has come to expect not only prescriptions or manipulations but to be treated in a certain way. He observes the physician for signs of approval or disapproval, he watches his manner and behavior.

The doctor, likewise conditioned by intimate and meaningful past personal experiences, has an expectation of his patients. He sees them not only as people with symptoms but as human beings with a way of behaving or presenting their complaints. He responds in one way or another to the patient's demeanor, sex, appearance, mood and other forms of expression, their compliance, docility, cooperativeness, antagonism, etc.

The problems a patient presents, together with the way in which he presents them, constitute a drama for the doctor as well as for the patient. While it is not necessary and is even harmful for the doctor to hold himself aloof from it, if drawn into it as a participant without his awareness that this is happening, he is probably unable to understand the significance of his patient's symptoms because his own investment is so great. This is at the root of the ancient proscription which warned against the treatment of members of one's own family. It was a sound intuition that detected the impossibility of impartiality under such circumstances.

Without an awareness and understanding of one's own feelings toward others it is impossible to work with them accurately or with ease and composure.

BIBLIOGRAPHY

1. Strauss, B. V.: The role of the physician's personality in medical practice (psycho-therapeutic medicine). New York State J. Med. *51*, 753–757, 1951.

NOTE: See also the bibliographies for Chapter 2 and Chapter 3.

Index